Guthrie's War

Guthrie's War

A Surgeon of the Peninsula and Waterloo

Michael Crumplin, FRCS

Foreword by Sir Bernard Ribeiro
Past-President of the Royal College of Surgeons of England

Pen & Sword
MILITARY

First published in Great Britain in 2010 by
Pen & Sword Military
an imprint of
Pen & Sword Books Ltd
47 Church Street
Barnsley
South Yorkshire
S70 2AS

ISBN 978 1 84884 245 8

A CIP catalogue record for this book is available from the British Library.

Printed and bound in the UK by
the MPG Books Group

Pen & Sword Books Ltd incorporates the Imprints of
Pen & Sword Aviation, Pen & Sword Maritime, Pen & Sword Military,
Wharncliffe Local History, Pen and Sword Select, Pen and Sword Military Classics,
Leo Cooper, Remember When, Seaforth Publishing and Frontline Publishing.

For a complete list of Pen & Sword titles please contact
PEN & SWORD BOOKS LIMITED
47 Church Street, Barnsley, South Yorkshire, S70 2AS, England
E-mail: enquiries@pen-and-sword.co.uk
Website: www.pen-and-sword.co.uk

Contents

List of Illustrations

Foreword

As a past President of the Royal College of Surgeons of England, with no experience of military service other than in the combined cadet force at school, I remain in awe of the achievements of the many members of council and college who have served their country in war during the 200 years of the college history. None more so than George James Guthrie, the youngest member ever to be admitted to the college by examination and the first to be elected President of the college on three occasions. Guthrie's expertise as a military surgeon in Canada, the Peninsula and Waterloo is brilliantly captured by Michael Crumplin in this remarkable book. Guthrie's contribution to civilian surgery is less well known and yet his influence on civil practice, drawn from the lessons of war, was to prove invaluable to a new generation of surgeons unfamiliar with close combat and who were later to participate in the Crimean campaigns and the American Civil War.

Guthrie, in many ways, shared the same ideas as Baron Dominique Larrey, Napoleon's surgeon and surgeon to the Imperial Guard. He was often referred to as the 'English Larrey'. The French, in defeat, erected a statue in memory of Baron Larrey at the Val-de-Grâce Military Hospital in Paris, in 1843. Sadly, in victory, no similar statue of Guthrie exists. He is often compared with Sir Charles Bell, and although Guthrie was critical of Bell's military experience, the two had much in common. Both of Scottish descent they held the Chair of Anatomy and Surgery at the English College of Surgeons and both were founding members of new medical schools. Regrettably neither school, the Westminster nor the Middlesex (from which our author qualified), survives today.

Seven members of council served in the Boer War and four future Presidents served in the First World War. Colonel Sir Berkeley Moynihan (later Lord Moynihan), sent to America by the British Government to prepare their surgeons for conflict, noted that of the 30,000 medical practitioners in England, 10,000 had joined the Royal Army Medical Corps. The Corps subsequently won a larger percentage of Victoria Crosses than any other branch of the services.

Throughout the Second World War and up to today's conflicts in Iraq and Afghanistan, the lessons learnt by Guthrie, through six gruelling years of continued conflict, have been learnt and relearnt by countless surgeons, some of whom rose to high office in the college. The control of bleeding remains a problem even today as better body armour has improved the chances of survival. Limbs however are left at risk of fragmentation injury from suicide bombers or improvised explosive devices. The dilemma facing Guthrie, of whether to amputate or preserve a limb, still remains to this day and only experience on the battlefield can provide the right answers. His preference for firm digital pressure over bleeding vessels, rather than the tourniquet, did not endear him to his peers, particularly those in civilian practice. To be considered a heretic by some, and yet to be emboldened by the weight of evidence and experience to pursue a line of treatment which saves lives, is a quality few possess.

Guthrie's exemplary conduct and his commitment to his patients, ensuring continuity of care, are lessons we would do well to remember, as we face the impact of the European Working Time Directive of a working week reduced to forty-eight hours. The ability to audit and publicly record our outcomes, as Guthrie did, will be a necessity, not only in the interest of our patients' safety, but to ensure that our trainees are competent to perform surgery, yet experienced enough to know when not to.

I recently witnessed the first Military Operational Surgical Training (MOST) course in the Eagle Skills Unit at the college, which provides service personnel with the facilities to practise their operative skills on cadavers and simulated patients in our mock operating theatre. Guthrie would surely have approved of such methods to prepare our modern military forces.

Michael Crumplin in his previous book *Men of Steel* demonstrated his encyclopedic knowledge of surgeons and the men who fought in the Napoleonic Wars. His role as curator and archivist at the Royal College of Surgeons has provided him with access to surgical instruments, historical data and other memorabilia which add authenticity to his writing.

As a college we are indebted to him for his selfless commitment and for his timely portrayal of a much-admired soldier, surgeon and servant of this college.

Sir Bernard Ribeiro CBE OV FRCS

Acknowledgements

I must express my deep gratitude to the President and Council of the Royal College of Surgeons of England for their cooperation and support for this account of one of the brightest stars of their royal institution. Several key persons within the college have also been most helpful; Sir Bernard Ribeiro, past President, Mr Simon Chaplin, Director of Museums and Special Collections, Thalia Knight, Senior Librarian – also her staff and Mr John Carr, College Photographer. Similar thanks are due to the Royal College of Surgeons of Edinburgh, especially Dawn Kemp, Director of the College's Heritage. Another highly relevant and helpful source of information, data and images is the Army Medical Services Museum, Ash Vale, near Aldershot. The Director and Senior Curator, Captain Peter Starling, and his staff have contributed significantly to the production of this book.

Several individuals have proved most kind in lending data or images, Raymond Hurt, a retired consultant thoracic surgeon, with a long-standing interest in George Guthrie's life and career, Miriam Walls, Information Management Specialist of Parks Canada – Mainland Nova Scotia Field Unit, Colonel Gerald Napier for the fascinating details of the medical details of his illustrious forebears. I am likewise indebted to Mr Sydney Smith for his generosity in allowing use of a sketch of Guthrie, retrieved from the Westminster Hospital, prior to its demise. Colonel John Lowles has also been most kind in providing information, records and images of persons and events connected to the Worcestershire Regiment.

For my Grandchildren

Introduction

After the Battle of Camperdown had been fought against the Dutch Navy in October 1797, a most distinguished and technically adroit Scots surgeon, Mr John Bell from Edinburgh, was working among the injured sailors at Great Yarmouth Hospital. He made a heartfelt plea for reform of medical services in the armed forces. He wrote:

> The situation of a military surgeon is more important than any other. While yet a young man he has the safety of thousands committed to him in the most perilous situations, in unhealthy climates, and in the midst of danger. He is to act alone and unassisted, in cases where decision and perfect knowledge are required; in wounds of the most desperate nature, more various than can be imagined, and to which all parts of the body are equally exposed; his duties difficult at all times, are often to be performed amidst the hurry, confusion, cries and horror of battle.[1]

Although this might seem a trifle exaggerated, his views reflected the impact of combat trauma and hinted at the low standard of care given by naval surgeons at these times. Bell expressed the difficulties of remaining calm, organized and able under the most ghastly working conditions in the field, or the cockpit of a warship, that anyone could possibly imagine.

Following the war, John Hennen, a distinguished military surgeon, reflected in similar vein on the essentially pragmatic and isolated responsibilities of an army surgeon,

> To enable the young army surgeon the more effectually to apply his professional talents to the relief of the suffering soldier, it will be necessary to direct his attention to some preliminary points, a knowledge of which can be derived from field practice alone; without a due observation of these, his best regulated plans, and most zealous endeavours to do good, will often end in severe, and sometimes fatal disappointment. Were he always under the eye of his more experienced seniors, it would be superfluous to dwell on these points; but the exigencies or the casualties of actual service will often throw him at a distance from all professional aid,

and leave him totally dependent on the resources of his own mind, and on the scanty supplies to which original deficiency or subsequent expenditure may frequently reduce him. In this point the military surgeon is far less favourably circumstanced than his naval brethren. Their hospitals, their medical stores, their provisions, and all their little comforts, are as perfectly in their reach, after the most protracted engagement, as if no such event had taken place; their patients suffer none of the heart-rending privations of a soldier, lying wounded on the field of battle, without bedding, food, or shelter; and when he is removed, torn from his comrades, and sent to distant hospitals by a precarious and uncomfortable conveyance over broken-up roads, or intricate mountain passes.[2]

The personal privations of staff surgeons' assistants, according to George Guthrie, left little enticement to become a junior non-regimental surgeon. He pointed out,

the miserable and desolate state in which the medical officers, not attached to regiments, are situated in a campaign; from which you will perceive how necessary it is that some amelioration should take place in their condition; not so much on their own account, as on that of the persons committed to their care. These poor creatures suffer in a manner it is quite deplorable to think of, and which, I must say, is a disgrace to the character of the country, and to every man and woman in it possessing one spark of the common feelings of humanity. If an unhappy wretch of a doctor has to travel two-thirds of a day, generally on foot, at the tail of a cart of any kind, shivering and wet to the skin, without food, with scarcely a dry change of clothing, with no one to help him in the common necessaries of life, how can he attend to his sick and wounded? It is impossible. Self-preservation is the first law of nature. He must ascertain where he is to eat and sleep, how his clothes are to be dried, to seek food for himself and his beast, if he has one, and to do everything, if he wishes to live himself, except attend to his professional duties. On his arrival at the halting-place, he ought to see his people [patients] housed, put to bed if possible, and give directions for their food, make up their medicines, see them administered, bleed them if necessary, or dress their wounds. A man worn with his day's labor [sic], or however tired under a burning sun, may do all this for two or three hours more, if he has a hope of a tolerably comfortable place to rest himself in, or of something to eat, but not otherwise. At night he should again visit his sick, and arrange for a move shortly after daylight next morning, when all these duties are then to be repeated before the march is begun. Under existing disabilities, no man, with the enduring strength even of a jackass of Malta, or of Old Castile, could do it, and the sick must be neglected, and they have been neglected whenever the doctor was unequal to the duties.[3]

This wasn't after all, the sort of 'comfortable' surgery that we perform today, with patients who feel little or no pain, where there are plenty of support staff, modern technology and sundry drugs to maintain bodily function and combat infection. If we pause for a moment and put ourselves as modern clinicians into the mindsets of these former surgeons, it is surprising how much was learnt, how much was eventually achieved and how incredibly stoic patients and their surgeons were. This is quite apart from the fact that the majority of today's surgeons would be less skilled and intolerant of these rough, rapid and simple pre-anaesthetic field techniques.

While we have all heard much of the innovations and advances of the medical services for the French Republic and Empire, it is to me inconceivable that a military surgeon of the calibre of George James Guthrie has until recently been largely ignored by students of military and medical history. Fortunately, as we approach the bicentennial commemorations of many European and British (Allied) military campaigns in Europe and the Iberian Peninsula, a biography of Guthrie has been written by Raymond Hurt FRCS,[4] which allows this memorable surgeon to take his honourable place in the history of British military medicine and Wellington's army.

Guthrie, aside from many other talents, was clearly an exceptionally gifted clinician and surgeon, robust enough to perform well under fire, work tirelessly during and after combat, be outspoken surgically and withstand justified criticism from colleagues. His forthright, outspoken and confident nature allowed common sense not only to progress his craft in the field, but also to challenge well-established and often inappropriate surgical tenets where necessary.

This well assured sense of progress of surgery appears in the preface to the sixth edition of his *Commentaries on the Surgery of the War*. He reflects on his campaign experiences,

> The precepts laid down are the result of the experience acquired in the war in the Peninsula, from the first battle of Roliça in 1808, to the last in Belgium, of Waterloo in 1815, which altered, nay overturned nearly all those which existed previously to that period, on all the points to which they relate. Points as essential in the Surgery of domestic as in military life. They have been the means of saving the lives, and of relieving, if not even of preventing, the miseries of thousands of our fellow-creatures throughout the civilised world.[5]

In other respects, conscious of his station, he was modest and sensitive in his ways, turning down civil honours yet no doubt being elated at his professional achievements. These included being elected at a very young age to the Council of the Royal College of Surgeons of London (later England), holding tenure of Vice President five times then thrice the post of President of the College. Most of all perhaps he felt greatly honoured at being elected an FRS.

Britain lost around 40,000–45,000 men (about 9,000 from battle injury) in the Peninsular campaigns (1808–14), which was a major British (Allied) effort, in liaison with the Spanish and Portuguese forces, to overthrow Bonaparte's armies.[6] There were around 760 medical officers (principally surgeons, not including the 100 or so on half pay) in 1806, serving regular units, militia, garrisons and Foreign Corps.[7] By 1810 and 1815 around 1,200.[8]

Whilst some justified criticism has been meted out against the poor training, low quality of examination and inefficient or inappropriate behaviour exhibited by some of these practitioners, we really have few data on the ability of most field surgeons. We must therefore be cautious in our judgements of the abilities of these men. The beginning of the war made impossible demands on a largely volunteer medical staff. Metropolitan teaching hospitals could not adequately prepare a surgeon for combat surgery. So along with other war zones, the battlefields of the Peninsular War became the largest post-graduate surgical training schools in the British Army. Not only was there frequent opportunity for diagnosis and surgery, but also good teaching and attendances at dissections (post-mortems) and major surgical cases. Surgeons who did not perform well were just not going to last the course. Administrators of the capacity of Sir James McGrigor (who arrived in the Peninsula in January 1812) and his staff and network of staff (hospital) and battalion surgeons would soon become aware of shortfalls in performance. Whilst there were enormous teething problems in the first three and a half years of the war (1808–11), the last half of the war saw an impressive improvement in morale and results of the Army Medical Department. George Guthrie was a guiding light and by setting a great example in the Portuguese and Spanish campaigns, he was said to have been involved in the treatment of around 20,000 sick or wounded men between 1808 and 1814.[9] Not only a soldier's surgeon and very much a hands-on doctor, he also set a precedent by keeping records of cases and simple statistics of surgical cases and their outcomes.

When returned to civilian status after the war, he greatly regretted the failure of England to shoulder the responsibility of establishing a school and chair of military surgery. This was in stark contrast to the efforts of the University of Edinburgh (supported by testimonials from Guthrie),[10] which had set up a Regius Chair of Military Surgery running from 1806 to 1855. His efforts to allay this problem, by giving courses of lectures gratis on his experience of war and its surgery, underpin his significant sincerity with this issue. His writings on the war in the Peninsula formed the basis of instruction for military surgeons in the forthcoming Crimean War.[11]

As to lessons Guthrie tried so hard to teach, some would nonetheless be forgotten forty years later – one of them, for example, on the abuse of the tourniquet and inappropriate delay in surgery:

> At the Battle of Inkermann [sic] a young officer, the son of a friend of mine, was wounded in the leg by a musket ball, which caused much loss of blood. A tourniquet was applied, instead of the required operation being performed, and he was sent on board a transport from Balaclava. The leg mortified, as a matter of course, and was amputated. He died an eternal disgrace to British surgery, or rather to the Nation which will not pay sufficiently able men, and therefore employs ignorant ones – the best they can get for the money.[12]

I felt that to understand Guthrie's surgical efforts, it would prove interesting to both military and medical historians to trace and expand his progress through his early military life, but particularly to the Peninsular campaigns, whose bicentenary commemorations began in 2008. The majority of the text and references relate to his war experience. These bring another crucial dimension to the hard-fought Iberian battles and the contributions of this redoubtable man. Post-war activities continued to reflect his tough, outspoken, generous and committed personality.

Nicknamed the 'English Larrey', George James Guthrie deserves every bit as large an accolade as his renowned French counterpart.

1

A Flying Start

George Guthrie was destined to go far. He was born in London on the first day of May 1785. Of Scots origin with an Irish father, his ancestors were educated men – bishops, authors and soldiers. We know nothing of his mother but George's father succeeded his brother in a medical supply business. Guthrie's uncle had been a surgeon in the Royal Navy and had manufactured surgical plasters (Emplastrum Lythargyri – lead pla(i)sters which were used for their sedative and astringent properties) and other medical items, which were required by the armed services. There is scant knowledge about the paternal/son relationship, but since little of material came George's way, we might assume this was not a particularly memorable one.

George was educated in a private institution and there, at the age of 9, he met an educated French émigré cleric, the Abbé Noël, who by force of circumstances had been reduced to serving as an usher at this school. George had a good education – around six years with this tutor – who taught him, amongst other subjects, science and French. He spoke French so well that, in 1814, at the city of Toulouse, he was taken for a native. He was later to learn both Spanish and Portuguese. Apparently, Monsieur Noël had more to teach his eager pupil. George learnt much more of the physical world – taking measurements and also learning the elements of dead reckoning. His nautical sense and knowledge were later to save two ships. At 13, George 'a tall stout lad' had some sort of accident, during the course of which he came to be treated by Mr John Rush, who had been recently appointed (on 15 February 1798) as Inspector of Regimental Hospitals, to the Army Medical Board, serving with the Surgeon General Mr Thomas Keate and Physician General Sir Lucas Pepys. Mr Rush whilst caring for him after his injury thought him a likely lad. With considerable foresight he predicted that George might fare well as a military surgeon and so encouraged his family with this advice.[1]

Younger than usual, George became an indentured apprentice to Mr Phillips of Pall Mall, a surgeon, and to Dr Hooper, a physician of the Marylebone Dispensary and Infirmary. Mr Phillips was a surgeon practising in central London. In fact he was Surgeon Extraordinary to the Prince of Wales and his Household.[2] He took Guthrie on as an apprentice on 27 April 1798. This cost Guthrie's family £42.[3] Dr Hooper, a talented physician ('One of the ablest physician/pathologists in London'), produced a new medical dictionary and glossary of obsolete terms in

1802 and in 1815, a fascinating small 'crib book', to aid young candidates sitting their college exams for entry into military, naval or East India Company service.[4] This book provides some valuable research data and helps to unravel to some extent the quality of medical education and assessment by examination. It gives specimen questions and answers for the benefit of those students working for their service or civilian diplomas. Young George was clearly very attached to Hooper. In later years, he was to diagnose Hooper's frequency of urination, not as prostatism, but diabetes. Hooper expressed a wish that, should bladder surgery (for stone) be necessary, Guthrie should perform this for him and no one else!

Whilst apprenticed, Guthrie attended lectures at the Windmill Street School of Anatomy. During his apprenticeship in June 1800, it was suggested to George by Rush that he should act (unqualified) as a hospital assistant at the York Hospital, Chelsea. This was a military infirmary, originally near Eaton Square, on the site of the old Star and Garter tavern. Guthrie worked particularly for Staff Surgeon Joseph Constantine Carpue (commissioned as such in 1799) and was appointed 'deputy grinder' to him, that is to say, an assistant in the teaching of anatomy and surgery. Clearly this was not an easy arrangement, since Rush apparently had to reinstate his pupil on several occasions – no doubt there was some jealousy amongst other young surgeons working there. Our aspiring young surgeon, possessing no qualifications, was just not considered as academically up to the job as others around him. He was involved in the management of soldiers sick or hurt after the evacuation of the Helder in late November 1799. Guthrie slaved away all through the winter of 1800, but in early February 1801 Surgeon General Keate issued a directive that all hospital assistants should be removed from their post if they had not been properly examined. Of the four unqualified men in a similar position, three promptly resigned. Guthrie, however, reckoning that he knew as much if not more than those that he was 'grinding', applied to take the diploma on the day of the edict and took the exam on 5 February 1801. At just under 16 years old, he was the youngest candidate to take and pass this test in the history of the English College of Surgeons. He was quizzed during his examination by Mr Keate and a Mr Howard. Guthrie was fortunate to be able to compete at this time, for around 1800 a minimum age limit of 22 years had been recommended for candidates proposing to take the diploma examination.[5]

There are few data on the material nature of the examinations taken at this time. If we consider Dr Robert Hooper's revision book printed in 1815 for candidates about to sit the Diploma for Membership of the College, there is a focus principally on anatomy, surgery, materia medica and biochemistry. We thus gain some small insight into the barrage of questions that Guthrie was asked. In anatomy, for example, question 80, 'What are the muscles the subclavian artery [the main artery to the arm as it traverses the neck] passes between, in going over the first rib?' Answer, 'The subclavian artery, as it passes over the first rib, goes between the anterior and middle scalenus muscles.' A surgical question, number 315, 'In taking up the brachial artery, what nerve are you to avoid including in the ligature?' Answer, 'The median nerve which accompanies the brachial artery.' This was a query highly relevant to Horatio Lord Nelson's arm amputation, necessary after his wounding and failed assault on the mole at Santa Cruz, Tenerife, in July 1797. Nelson's median nerve was damaged during ligation of the brachial artery.

A materia medica/chemistry question 722, 'How is the liquor acetates plumbi [solution of lead acetate] made?' Answer, 'By boiling acetic acid and vitrified [crystalline] oxyde [sic] of lead together, to a certain extent; then setting the solution by that the feculencies [scummy deposit] may subside.'

While there is a massive dearth of basic physiology in these questions, what strikes us is the intensely practical nature of the conundrums. Most of the finer functions of the human body were yet to be discovered, so where there lay a significant deficiency in understanding of the physiological response to injury or the true nature of infection, for example, a plethora of simple empirics and procedures had to be learnt. A great knowledge of physiology and organ-specific disease would eventually direct therapy for the sick and injured, but this was yet to come. All that there was to guide the aspiring surgeon was an understanding of sound basic anatomy and chemistry and simple principles of evolving surgical practice.

Full of pride after his exam success, young George now had to find a place for himself in the army. Here was a youth who wished for adventure and longed for surgical experience. He must have soon thrilled at the exploits of the British expeditionary force, sent to Egypt under Sir Ralph Abercrombie and the sanguinary Battle of Copenhagen fought by Vice Admiral Horatio Nelson and Admiral Sir Hyde Parker against the unfortunate Danes.

As a rule, newly qualified surgeons would serve as a hospital assistant or mate. This would give the trainee some insight into complex management problems of contagion and major trauma, a far cry nonetheless from the turmoil of warfare on Foreign Service. Although George had performed some of these military medical duties already at the York Hospital, neither this experience nor that of others at similar posts could prepare any young man for the mangling injuries and devastating epidemics that would weaken Wellington's forces in the forthcoming Iberian campaigns.

The next appointment for our young man would be to serve as a battalion assistant surgeon. One of John Rush's last kindnesses – for he died on Boxing Day 1801 – was to recommend his protégé to Lord Frederick Montagu, senior Lieutenant Colonel to the 29th Regiment (Worcestershire) of Foot. Montagu passed him on to his more junior field commander, Lieutenant Colonel Byng (later Lord Strafford). Byng was 22 years old and the assistant surgeon of the battalion just 16.

There seemed to be great contentment in the unit, which felt well served by its youthful commanding officer and junior assistant surgeon. The battalion was on home duty between March 1801 and June 1802, when the 29th embarked for Halifax. The transient Peace of Amiens had been signed on the 27 March 1802. The battalion was shipped in five transports, the *Camilla, Hilberts, Queen, Matthew* and *Thomas*. Prior to sailing, a Major-General England published an order from Plymouth dock that expressed his thanks to the 29th for 'the regular, sober and soldier-like manner'.[6] In Halifax, Nova Scotia, there was, during Guthrie's service there, no war, contagion or civil unrest.[7] By all accounts the battalion was once again well behaved and at ease with the populace. The men were quartered at the North Barracks and it was noted that the 29th received several volunteers from the 66th Regiment and the Loyal Surrey Rangers, stationed there.

By coincidence in 1749, the 29th, then known as Thomas Farrington's Regiment, had been involved in the ground clearing and marking out of the settlement of the later town of Halifax. Following the founding of the city in 1749, the military garrison had swollen to around 1,500 men. With its large harbour, Halifax remained an impressive and valuable sentinel in the Atlantic, where the North Atlantic squadron of the Royal Navy was based.

The 29th remained in Halifax until 1807 and we know little of Surgeon Guthrie's adventures. The usual work performed by army and naval surgeons was humdrum day-to-day diagnosis and management of seasonal disorders, such as diarrhoea, influenza, pneumonia, scabies and other various infectious afflictions. Venereal disorders – syphilis and gonorrhoea – and minor injuries, fractures, head injuries, etc. would hardly have stretched Guthrie's skills to the extreme.[8] His pay was 5 shillings a day at this time. Socially, the sojourn in Canada was of importance to him, since he there met his dear wife-to-be. This was Margaret Gordon, an apothecary's widow and daughter of Walter Patterson, the Governor General of Prince Edward Island. They were married in July 1806. Guthrie had to pay the extortionate fee of £100 (equivalent today to £6,890.24!) for the licence to wed.

Regimental records noted that the men's queues (hair wrapped around a sliver of whalebone) were shortened to 9 inches around this time. Then the commanding officer, Lieutenant Colonel Byng, was transferred to the 3rd Foot Guards and, before departure, he was highly complimentary about the battalion, particularly the NCOs and privates. During the year of Trafalgar and Austerlitz, the regiment supplied a detachment to Melville Island consisting of three officers and seventy-five NCOs and men. Other smaller parties garrisoned Forts Charlotte, Clarence and Sackville, Point Pleasant, York Redoubt, Dartmouth, Cape Breton, Camperdown and the Light House. Guthrie undertook visits to these outposts and had to set up a regimental infirmary in Halifax, where the citadel housed the main garrison hospital. In the battalion hospital he would have a sergeant orderly and also employ women or convalescent patients as nurses and assistants.

In the midst of a global war, Halifax must have seemed a relative haven for Guthrie and the regiment. In his reminiscences and lectures, occasional cases of interest occurred, many of them related to accident, dispute or drunkenness.

> An officer was struck on the head in Halifax, Nova Scotia, by a drunken workman with a tomahawk, or small Indian hatchet, which made a perpendicular cut into his left parietal bone [at the side of the skull], and knocked him down. As he soon recovered from the blow, and suffered nothing but the ordinary symptoms of a common wound of the head with fracture, it was considered to be a favourable case, and was treated simply, although with sufficient precaution. He sat up, and shaved himself until the fourteenth day, when he observed that the corner of his mouth on the opposite side to that on which he had been wounded was fixed, and the other drawn aside [i.e. was moving normally]; and that he had not the free use of the right arm so as to enable him to shave. He was bled largely, but the symptoms increased until he lost the use of the right side, became comatose and died. On examination [post-mortem] the inner table [of the skull bone] was found broken, separated from the diplöe, and driven through the membranes of the brain, which was at that part soft, yellow, and in a state of suppuration.[9]

The skull consists of two thin sheets of bone, the outer table tougher than the inner, sandwiching a thin layer of marrow known as the diplöe between them. Our surgeon makes the point here that, whilst the outer layer can be cut neatly, fragments from the shattered inner table may be driven into the brain. In the above example the bacterial infection introduced by the blade of the axe and the patient's hair decided this man's fate.

Guthrie relates the tale of another officer of the 29th in Halifax, who had a self-inflicted injury during a 'drunken frolic', his own long sword blade making a similar wound to the previous case. The management included bleeding the patient 1500mls for five days and seemed to our surgeon to be successful! Invalided home, his ship was captured and the unfortunate officer was sent to Verdun as a prisoner of war. After rejoining the battalion for service in North America, he became totally disorientated after very little wine, even wandering into enemy lines. Guthrie rued the missed opportunity to trephine and explore his wound, being certain that he would have found and removed fragments of the inner table of the man's skull from the brain.

Before embarkation for Canada, Guthrie had accompanied his battalion at exercise on Berry Head, at the south end of Tor Bay, feasibly awaiting a favourable wind, en route to Halifax. Several men caught pneumonia and Guthrie bled the men 16, 14, then 12oz successively. This was followed by the administration of tartar emetic, calomel (a mercury compound), an antimony salt and opium. Disappointingly, all his patients died. The practice for treating pneumonia he adopted in Nova Scotia was more draconian. He bled his patients to fainting (ad deliquium) and repeated this four-hourly until the patient's pulse and heartbeat was so weakened as to be a threat to life! He commented that 'under this improved practice all recovered'(!). More likely, the infection was different, or the organism less aggressive. He recalls that, in British North America, the men were as healthy, the winds were sharper and colder, the vicissitudes of all kinds greater. Rum was cheaper, newer and stronger than the gin of Torbay. It wasn't only the surgeons who were impressed with the efficacy of venesection, so imbued into medical men and civilians at this time. Guthrie had a 6' 3" grenadier of his battalion, who apparently consumed a gallon of rum in an afternoon! Not surprisingly, he narrowly escaped death and only when Guthrie had abstracted, 'nearly as much blood [i.e. as rum consumed] in a few hours [probably 5–6 pints!]. His first bleeding was into the washhand-basin, until he fainted, lying on his back, and the bleedings were repeated as soon as he began to feel pain, and whenever he felt a return of the pain he used to put his arm out of bed to have the vein re-opened, for Jack Martin was a very gallant fellow.' Although Guthrie cites this as an extreme case, it underpins the large volumes of blood removed particularly in wounds and diseases of the head and chest.

In Nova Scotia, the regimental return of 2 April 1807 reported some data on the nationalities and physical status of those that made up Guthrie's battalion of 744 bayonets: 64 per cent were Englishmen, 21 per cent Irish, 13 per cent Scots and 2 per cent 'Foreign'; 67 per cent of men were between 5' 6" and 5' 9"; forty men were under 5' 5" and thirty-one, 6' and over.

On the 19 June 1807, after five years' garrison duty, the regiment was ordered to return to Britain. Prior to embarkation the senior garrison officer, Major-General Hunter, was impressed with the conduct and discipline of the battalion. Not only was their general content with the regiment's demeanour, but also the inhabitants of Halifax, who obviously felt in debt to the 29th. They presented a splendid silver chalice to the battalion, with a letter to General Gordon Forbes, Colonel of the regiment. In this missive, the citizens of the town praised the courtesy of the officers and the behaviour of the NCOs and rank and file over the five years' garrison.

Thirty-eight officers/staff and 744 NCOs, drummers and privates boarded five transports (the *Amphitrite*, *Crisis*, *Dominica*, *Sceptre* and *Zephyr*). A company under a Captain Thomas Egerton, with a lieutenant, three sergeants, a drummer and sixty-five privates performed duties as marines during the homeward journey aboard the naval escort, HMS *Mermaid*.

In Guthrie's formative years, we have noted that he had gained some valuable maritime instruction from his former tutor, Monsieur Noël. This enabled him to prevent his transport from foundering on its return. Having sailed safely to the Lizard, the 'Start-Point' for the night, an uneventful run was interrupted by a fog bank at 8am, when sail was shortened. The master reckoned they were at least fifteen miles from the Isle of Wight. Our knowledgeable surgeon caused much amused derision from the crew by announcing that they were only two miles offshore and just off St Catherine's Bay! Guthrie's opinion was soon vindicated when they peered forward through the lifting fog. There was land dead ahead. The ship wore and was soon out of danger. As the mist dispersed, they were hailed by a close-hauled fisherman, 'St Catherine's Bay! And if you had not gone about, you would have been ashore in five minutes.' The now nervous master, wishing a pilot, was reassured on the rest of the sail to their mooring, as Guthrie had spotted the appropriate buoys to guide them in.

Towards the end of July 1807, the regiment, after fair passage arrived at Deal, where the 50th (West Kent) Regiment was garrisoned, anticipating that it was to be included in the proposed combined operation and expedition to Copenhagen, to wrest the valuable Danish navy from the clutches of Bonaparte. In the event, the powers that be in Horse Guards considered the 29th must be unfit for foreign duties, after a prolonged service overseas. An officer of the 50th remarked, however, on the fineness and training of the 29th and commented on their band 'and their corps of black drummers cut a fierce and remarkable appearance while hammering away on their brass drums'. The regiment had been quietly posted for the last five years, in a most healthy state. Guthrie's camp duties at Deal continued with the same sort of peacetime practice, although more women and children would now have joined the regiment, adding more obstetric and paediatric cases to his duties.

The battalion was ordered to Foreign Service in the Mediterranean and marched to Brabourne Lees. After three weeks' accommodation in wooden barracks, it moved on to Petersfield, where the officers, including Guthrie, were well dined by the Colonel of the Regiment. Forbes informed his guests that they were to be embarked for a clandestine venture from Portsmouth. At Cosham, Colonel the Hon. George Lake, serving on half pay for the previous three years, took command of the battalion. Lake, the son of Wellesley's Indian veteran commander, General Lord Lake, had served under his father against the Mahrattas. Having breakfasted, the officers and men marched on to Portsmouth, where a series of flat-bottomed boats took the men in an orderly fashion out to the transports. The embarkation was cheered by a great crowd and accompanied by music, spoiled only by the crying of the women and children who had drawn a 'not to go' ticket at the embarkation point. Six women for each company, having drawn their tickets 'to go' by ballot, were perhaps more fortunate and despite the rigours of campaign and limited rations, would at least be with their men.

The 29th along with the 32nd (Cornwall), 50th, 82nd (Prince of Wales'

Volunteers), four battalions of the King's German Legion and two brigades of artillery, were placed in command of Major-General Sir Brent Spencer. Setting sail with sealed orders, the battalion did not get under weigh until 20 December. The convoy was shortly after becalmed and boats were lowered to allow exchange visits to other ships. Most likely Guthrie went over to see medical problems and mingle with colleagues on other vessels. Foul weather in the Bay of Biscay on 25 December forced most of the fleet to turn back to Falmouth. Sail was shortened and, on board, the men of the 29th could only share a small amount of meat cooked during the storm, seated on sailcloth on the decks with cross legs 'seated like Turks'! The hurricane had made a destined rendezvous off Lisbon impossible, so all except one of the transports bore up back to Falmouth. The *Neriod* with one company of the 29th managed to sail on for Gibraltar. The main force weighed again for Lisbon on 23 February, and approached the Portuguese capital, where they learnt that Marshal Androche Junot had now occupied Lisbon and the Tagus. The convoy diverted to Gibraltar, anchoring at the New Mole on 12 March 1808.

Guthrie's well-honed senses and basic nautical education once again saved his ship – the headquarters transport *Dominica* – with 400 men aboard. Anchored in the Bay of Gibraltar, off a bank, Guthrie dozing in his cot was aware that the motion of the ship was not that of a vessel moored by the bow and swinging to the wind on its anchor cable. He related:

> One of the transports having a detachment of the 29th on board, anchored on the bank in the Bay, and being in harbour, all had turned in, except the watch and mate. Being a bad sleeper on board ship, and knowing the carelessness of the sailors, I went on deck in the middle of the night, and to my astonishment, found the ship was drifting. The mate, on being awakened from his nap, would not believe it, until I showed him the cable, nearly right up and down. Well, we turned up all hands, got sail on the ship, and the moment we tacked, the battery at Algeçiras opened fire upon us [the Spaniards were not yet allies], and after some trials, they sent one shot through the accommodation box on the poop. We got half-a-dozen more shots from Cabrito Point, on passing, and then beat our way back to the astonishment of the fleet and the garrison, who could not understand what we had been after.[10]

On 14 March the regiment partly disembarked. They were somewhat surprised on 8 May, since the Spanish batteries at Algeçiras fired a salute, acknowledging the rising of the Spanish against French in Madrid. During the time at Gibraltar, Guthrie must have visited the Rock's garrison hospital and senior purveyor's offices to top up his stores for the ensuing campaigns in Portugal. More drugs, rollers, splints, candles, close-stools and other equipment.

A visit to Britain by representatives of the Junta of Asturias had resulted, in addition to Dalrymple's overtures with the Spanish General Castaños, assistance for the Spanish and Portuguese war efforts. Britain was bound to support her old ally Portugal. Thus with help from Britain assured, the force under Brent Spencer was destined for Spain. His force sailed on 12 June for southwest Spain and eventually landed at Puerto de Santa Maria, at the head of the Bay of Cadiz.[11] Wellesley's force meanwhile, would sail from Cork on the 20 July. He himself had embarked on the sixth rate HMS *Crocodile*.

Guthrie now had a reasonable chance to acquire new language skills and busied himself with studying Spanish. Such an opportunity was not to be missed, since dealing directly in diverse ways with the native population, suppliers and local doctors would have great advantages in the management of his patients. Spencer's force sailed from Cadiz and joined Sir Arthur Wellesley's group, which had anchored, near Figueira, off the mouth of the Mondego River on 29 July. Admiral Cotton, commanding the naval force, agreed with Wellesley to land here. They had learnt that militia, composed of students from the University of Coimbra, had captured an adjacent and potentially threatening fort from the French. Over 1–6 August, the men were put off in boats braving the bar with a strike force of around 8,743 officers and men. Spencer's detachment (4,993) started landing in the surf five days later.

Spencer's division being the last to land, Guthrie found that all local draught animals had been purchased. All officers of the 29th, Guthrie included, had to carry essentials in their haversacks and sling a cloak or watchcoat and a canteen of rum over their shoulders. Guthrie had his full complement of assistants. They were two in number. There was Edward Curby, who later got onto the staff in November 1812 after serving with the 29th since late March 1806 and who died in Portugal in 1813. There was also Lewis Evans, who had been with the 29th from November 1807 and who also went onto the staff in 1811.[12]

As the Allied force assembled on the beach, local people realized that here were protectors of the Portuguese. Local men in broad-brimmed hats helped carry the soldiers bodily ashore and the young women in white headscarves and their aprons laden with oranges, figs and grapes greeted one and all, crying *Veavo, vaevo, Englees*.[13] No arrangements had been made for the sick and wounded. Like other battalion surgeons, Guthrie would have had a horse but all his equipment and baggage required transportation. During these campaigns, it was always hard to procure carts or mules and Guthrie was ordered by Colonel Lake to obtain a large Spanish mule, on which were to be loaded the surgical stores and 'physic'.

He carried not merely medication and surgical instruments, but pewter urinals, candles, kettles, roller bandages and so forth. A canteen of regimental hospital utensils provided for 250 patients.[14] Usually two regimental panniers, large pitch-covered waterproof wicker baskets, were provided, but all Guthrie had on this occasion for a container was merely a 'biscuit bag, which I begged from the Master of the transport, there being nothing else to be had'.[15] There were many cases of heat exhaustion.[16] Marching on hot deep sand, the 71st lost four men of 'thirst' (heatstroke).[17] Rifleman Harris recalled the same problems on the march.[18]

A battalion surgeon's NCO orderly was responsible for packing up equipment, setting up an aid post, marquee, assisting at surgery, sharpening and keeping capital knives (large knives for amputation) keen and bright and other instruments oiled and wrapped in brown paper. Guthrie had no such person, but what he did have was two one-handed men, both of whom had had their hands removed by him for trauma during the sojourn in Halifax. These 'fellows', quotes he, 'could saddle a horse or mule nearly as quickly and as well as if their hands had not been amputated'.[19]

In Ireland, Wellesley had stridently fought for as many wagons and drivers as possible, but all he had managed to commandeer were two small wagon companies from the Irish establishment. So he had few enough draught animals, cavalry mounts and wagons – 47 vehicles and 564 horses – whereas the force that he now commanded apparently required to muster around 600 vehicles and 4,000 horses! After his experiences in India, he had clearly anticipated the transport difficulties in Iberia. He actually had only four wagons above those required for guns, ammunition, camp equipment and the forge carts. This paucity of vehicles and beasts certainly affected Guthrie and others like him, as a shortage of vehicles and draught animals was to plague the Army Medical Department right through the war. On 7 August, Wellesley reorganized his force into six new small brigades. Guthrie and the 29th were in Brigadier-General Nightingall's Brigade, with the 82nd Foot. That night, the exhausted 29th reached the main force and settled down to a paltry meal of ship's biscuit and rum. Guthrie's war had begun.

2

Actions and Sojourn in Portugal

Wellesley's command was to be later frustrated by two senior officers above him – Sir Hew Dalrymple and Sir Harry Burrard, and later, Sir John Moore. Castlereagh decided to reinforce Wellesley's contingent with Brigadier Acland and Anstruther's brigades, which later sailed from Harwich and Ramsgate. A force under Sir John Moore of around 11,000 men was sent on from the Baltic.

What of the allocation of surgeons to line battalions? By 1804 there were two surgical mates per battalion, who were shortly to be redesignated assistant surgeons, these young trainee surgeons would help their senior colleague with blood letting, taping and suturing, splinting fractures, purging and dolling out medications for ailing or damaged soldiers. When we consider that, not infrequently during the Peninsular War, some 20–30 per cent of Wellesley's army was to be incapacitated by disease, contagion or wounding, the Army Medical Department had a great deal to learn and put into good practice. Many committed young surgeons were soon to gain valuable experience and would become able to operate independently. Later in the war, with the agreement of the Commander-in-Chief, it would gradually become a sine qua non to promote acclimatized and experienced men rather than those sent out fresh from Britain.

The French Army had been fighting continental wars since 1792 and so their Service de Santé, over the previous sixteen years, had much experience from which to draw. They had conscripted many able surgeons and were better rehearsed than their British counterparts, although Britain had learnt harsh lessons earlier in the Low Counties, West Indies, Egypt and India. However, it should be remembered that, although the reputation of great French surgeons such as Larrey, Percy, Yvan and Girardot preceded them, the skills of these men were not universally available to the French soldiers. The Allies had a great deal to learn and so these early days of this war from 1808 to 1811 were a tough time for the surgeons and their patients. Much criticism of the medical staff was founded on attitude problems, poor training and ignorance. Frequently there was no medical man to fill an urgent vacancy. The pleasure in studying the experiences of George Guthrie is that he was totally committed, an active teacher and technically able, spending much time thinking about lessons previously taught that required revision and devising new techniques for preserving life and preventing deformity.

The day Wellesley landed, a French force under General Henri-François

Delaborde numbering around 4,000 bayonets and 250 sabres, with five guns, had been despatched from the south of Portugal by Marshal Junot. Our Commander-in-Chief had landed around 13,500 men – including Spencer's force, so outnumbering the French by at least 3:1. There were eight senior medical staff (a deputy inspector, four staff surgeons, two physicians and an apothecary), eleven hospital mates and a deputy purveyor, under the supervision of a physician, Dr John Warren.[1] At 38 years old, he was an experienced army doctor, who had served as an assistant or full surgeon in the infantry and cavalry for around two years, a staff surgeon for ten years and had been promoted Deputy Inspector of Hospitals four years prior to landing at Mondego Bay. There were also around eighteen battalion surgeons and twenty to thirty mates (assistants) accompanying Wellesley's infantry, cavalry and ordnance.

The senior medical staff directed arrangements in a brigade or division, provided care for senior officers and the headquarters staff, also assisted battalion surgeons at field or temporary hospitals. They were in charge of their various departments in the fixed, larger or general hospitals. These senior surgeons also performed dissections (post-mortems), taught, examined candidates for promotion and wrote up reports on their cases and occasionally discussed with Deputy Inspectors the abilities of trainees. By contrast battalion surgeons saw to the day-to-day routine medical chores and provided front-line support.

On 8 August in the early hours, Wellesley put the army under arms and on 10 August broke camp and advanced on Lisbon, via Lavos, Leyria, Alcobaço and Obidos. He had struggled with an inexperienced commissariat, stating that he required 130 mules each to carry 224lb of bread biscuit and also two carts for medical provision. En route, the soldiers noticed the rough treatment of the villages by the French. They had stolen what little food there was, destroyed the rest and burned various buildings.[2] Sensibly, the Commander had chosen the westerly coastal route south to maintain close contact with the Royal Navy and his supplies. This allowed the men to leave their Trotter knapsacks on board His Majesty's vessels and to carry just a watchcoat, in which were rolled up spare shoes and shirt. This concession would concede some reduction in effort (the men being not in the best condition after almost a month at sea) and allow four days' biscuit to be carried.

On the night before the Battle of Roliça, the 29th remained 'tranquil', apart from two privates being caught drinking in town. They were tried by drumhead court-martial and punished on the day of the battle. Guthrie, as one of his less pleasant duties, had to witness the flogging to ensure the victim was fit enough to stand the ordeal. Colonel Lake wished the dishonour of not participating in the combat to be part of the miscreants' penalty. The two men declared to Guthrie that they would have gone up in the first assault wave had the Colonel allowed it. One of these two men, a kindly soul called Private Needham, was an inveterate drinker.

Guthrie reckoned that this man had received around 15,000 lashes for drunkenness during his service. Needham broke free from the hospital sergeant and fought most gallantly on the heights. Perhaps, Guthrie mused, the gentle Needham could be regarded as the 'beau ideal' of a grenadier.[3] Needham was a strong swimmer and was later washed overboard from the forecastle of a transport in the Bay of Biscay. In a heavy sea, no effort was made to recover him.

Guthrie's rather more lenient views on corporal punishment probably reflected those of many of his colleagues:

> Indeed, I have seen many scores of thousands of lashes given, without being aware of any benefit being derived from them. It is of little consequence whether a man receives 100 or 300 lashes; my own opinion is, that he should receive neither: a brand is not affixed to a felon, and it should not be to a soldier. Nevertheless the British army must be occasionally flogged: it is mercy to the soldier to do it, and no discipline could be maintained before the enemy without it. In Great Britain, soldiers should be treated like wayward children, and no man, in my humble opinion, should receive more than two dozen lashes, and that on his bum, in the way of schoolboys of 16 sometimes get it; and then, with their coats turned, they may be made to do their duty the same day, the derision of all the children of the town. An old culprit cares nothing whether he gets one hundred or five hundred lashes[!]. I remember one of these gentlemen (Mr Dennis Reardon by name), who, for some misdemeanor [sic] was sentenced to receive 500 lashes. This the general commanding was pleased to commute for fourteen days' garrison black strap; that is, to work (or rather idle) fourteen days at the King's works, without 7d a day: but Mr Dennis declined the favour, and took the 500 lashes.[4]

So Guthrie's Peninsular War started with the Battle of Roliça on 17 August 1808. General Delaborde's force had advanced to Obidos and awaited reinforcement by the tough, one-armed General Loison, who commanded a force of around 9,000 and was at Abrantes, to the east. Although not a large engagement, Roliça was the first significant combat of the war, for which a clasp to the much-belated General Service Medal was finally approved, issued in 1848 (although wrongly spelled by the War Department as 'Roleia' on the bar). Redcoats had faced the French before – in Flanders with the Duke of York in the 1790s, under John Moore and Sir Ralph Abercrombie on the slopes of Morne Fortuné on St Lucia in 1796, Egypt under Sir Ralph Abercrombie in 1801, and under Sir John Stuart at Maida in 1806 – but this engagement heralded the beginning of Britain's long and protracted series of land battles in Iberia. These were not just a long tussle for the Allied soldiers, but for the Army Medical Department too. In terms of accruing medical experience, there was just no substitute for outbreaks of foul contagion or floods of freshly wounded men for the medical staff to prioritize, isolate, treat and salvage as best they might.

There was some spirited but somewhat rash skirmishing with the French at Brilos and Obidos, and Delaborde, having retired from his first position on a rocky eminence near the village of Roliça, made a further retrograde onto a ridge less than a mile long, above the village of Columbeira. After a sweltering four-mile march from Obidos to Columbeira, the 29th pushed on and stood to arms around the middle of the base of the ridge, which the French had taken up their second position. The British women and baggage were moved to the rear.

The advance had begun around 7am on 17 August and when George Guthrie and his two assistants finally gazed up onto the heights above Columbeira, they must surely have wondered what the day would bring them. Guthrie might have been an astute student and trainee but he now had time to reflect with some trepidation on the ensuing combat and on the collection of terrified and agonized men that would soon rely on that small chance of survival his skills might offer them. He brought his assistants and regimental baggage up to the village. His task was to set up an aid post for the battalion and help arrange a regimental or brigade field hospital.

The battle commenced with skirmishing in the plain before the ridge, with skirmishing French light troops being driven up the slopes. As Guthrie passed through this area, dotted with olive trees, he must have noticed the vineyards, onion fields and gardens filled with pumpkins and melons. The Commander-in-Chief had organized two flanking movements – westwards by Lieutenant-Colonel Nicholas Trant an Irish officer in the Portuguese service, and eastwards by Major-General Ronald Ferguson's men, with a delayed central assault to be mounted up four gullies to his front.

Units of the 60th and 95th were forward on the left of the line and were soon hotly disputing the base of the French position. The 29th came up with their band playing a country-dance. Immaculately dressed, the Hon. Colonel George Lake was addressed by a fellow officer that he and his battalion were dressed as if 'to be received by the King'. Lake prophetically replied, 'Egad, sir, if I am killed today, I mean to die like a gentleman.'[5] The smart and traditional battalion, standing ready to advance to their front, still wore queues, had powdered hair and had been carrying animal skin packs. Lake turned to his men and said, 'Soldiers I shall remain in front of you and remember that the bayonet is the only weapon of the British soldier.' When the light company under Captain Creagh was ordered to the front, some of the old grenadiers grumbled that they could do this duty just as well. The Colonel turned to them and said, 'Never mind my lads, let the Light Bobs lather them first, we will shave them afterwards.'

Arthur Wellesley's first action in Iberia did not go completely to plan.

Apparently Colonel Lake, on his seventeen-hand steed, in a burst of enthusiasm or being mistaken that the main assault had begun, led his men prematurely forward and ordered the heavy regimental colours to be displayed. He boldly scrambled up a rocky gully to the French positions, his battalion alone and unsupported. This was not Wellesley's intention – he had waited for a coordinated frontal assault up several gullies, having given some time for the flanking units to move round.

The situation for a battalion line surgeon at this particular combat was interesting. As became the habit, one of the two assistants (should there be two present fit and well!) would be sent forward to administer first aid and to direct casualties to the regimental aid post, where the principal surgeon and the second mate or other line surgeons would congregate to receive the surviving wounded. The rocky, and at that time, pine-tree studded, lightly shrubbed cleft, up which Guthrie's battalion had to move in to attack the French (70th Ligne and 2nd and 4th Léger], was fairly steep and our surgeon's dilemma was whether to stay back with one of his assistants and receive casualties at the village below the ridge or assume that the inferior French force would, as previously, from their first position, be shifted off the crest and back down to the village of Zambugeira around three-quarters of a mile behind the ridge on a gentle slope down and beyond. It was not the wisest move to send the senior surgeon forwards in an assault, but in fact Lake ordered him to advance seven paces to the rear of the colours and Guthrie commented adversely on this old-fashioned concept. It was in fact an ill-conceived notion, since although a wounded man was always certain of where the medical officer was to be found, the colours were like bees to a honey pot, and thus often the epicentre for the close attentions of the enemy. As an example, Lieutenant Dawson of the 45th was mortally shot carrying the colours at this action. Initially some wounded were brought down to the base of the ridge. It is clear, however, that Guthrie was soon up the defile with the casualties. We know that he was well forward, as he was onto the spot with the advanced casualties. He took some basic equipment – water, bandages and pocket instruments – also one of his two assistants, up the hill and no doubt, would soon be in league with a colleague or two from the 9th Foot (East Norfolk), which had shortly after come up the ridge.

Before leaving the village of Columbeira, Guthrie clearly recalled his first memories of the combat:

> to ascend the heights of Roliça, a soldier was shot in the leg: he jumped up three or four feet; and made a considerable outcry. A second was struck at the same time by a ball on the shoulder, which did not penetrate, but gave him great pain. A third received a ball on his buff-leather belt, on the right breast. I saw this man fall, and supposed he was killed: the ball however had only gone through his belt and made a mark on his chest, over the cartilage of the fourth rib, the hardness and elasticity of which had prevented

further mischief. He recovered in a short time, spat a little blood in the night, and after a large bleeding was enabled to accompany me on the 20th to Vimiera [sic], ready for the fight next morning.[6]

Half way up the gully, in an olive grove, the men dropped packs, watchcoats and bread sacks in the brushwood and briars, and the four line and grenadier companies moved on.[7] The single battalion sweating their way up a gully meant that enemy sharp shooting and volley fire would be concentrated on that unit and, although there was much rock and tree cover, the Worcestershire Regiment was hard hit, being so far in front. Lake and his grenadiers were soon face to face with companies of the French 70th Ligne and refused a demand to surrender. Lake, after losing one horse and remounted, called out 'Don't fire men; don't fire; wait a little, we shall soon charge!'[8] After this order he was mortally hit and four officers, their colours and thirty men were taken prisoner. Lake was shot at seven times by a certain Sous-officier Bellegarde, who grazed Lake's neck with one shot and killed him with his seventh round. The fatal shot killed Lake instantaneously, the musket ball passing from the upper part of his left chest through to the right side. A Sergeant-Major Richards stood over the dead colonel and received fatal injuries – thirteen ball, sword and bayonet wounds. As Guthrie gave the gallant Richards water in the last few minutes of his life he 'had coughed up a little blood, and died gasping, as if suffocated, the chest labouring on each side to do its work in vain'. One sword wound had pierced both sides of his chest. He uttered his last words, 'I should have died happy, if our gallant colonel had been spared', a sentiment shared by the rest of the casualties. Impetuous and erroneous, Lake's gallant but premature sacrifice had been costly to himself and his men.

The 29th's right wing was overwhelmed and the French started bayoneting the decimated unit, despite an intention to surrender. This despicable behaviour was fortunately soon checked by General Antoine François Brennier, who was in a few days destined himself to become a casualty. At one stage, four companies of a Swiss unit (4th Swiss Regiment), facing the newly arrived panting redcoats, advanced to surrender, but this was aborted by a French advance to take the colours.

The Allied assault gathered pace and after a few spirited and renewed assaults, the French began to fall back. Rifleman Harris commented on wounds received during retaliatory and energetic French rear-guard manoeuvres, when men resting and quaffing much-needed water, were decapitated or hit in the head and hands.[9]

There was much for Guthrie to do. There were no appointed staff surgeons in the vicinity and he was the most experienced surgeon available. A few injuries were unfortunately caused by friendly fire, from the 9th Foot, who had mistaken some of the 29th to their front as enemy. Had they been confused by the Swiss troops?

Wellesley's losses were four officers and sixty-six men killed, but there were twenty officers and 315 wounded (four officers and seventy-eight men missing). A bayonet charge[10] by the 9th prompted a renewed company assault by the remnants of the 29th, who pushed the French back, recovering their captured colours and in turn releasing some prisoners. Delaborde's men were skilfully handled in retreat but the general himself had been wounded. At four to five o'clock the ridge fell silent, camp was formed and the wounded collected and the burial parties set to work. Lake was buried where he fell and there is an extant and now restored memorial on the ridge (paid for by the battalion) and a plaque in Westminster Abbey. Both bear witness to his brave sacrifice. He was the first field officer to die during combat in the Peninsular War

Most of Guthrie's wounded comrades lay in a rough sort of row on the ridge and this being his first severe exposure to combat, he painfully recalled, 'They were all known to me name as by person: the conflict was soon over, and the difference in expression in begging for assistance, or expressing their sense of suffering, will never be obliterated from my memory.'

What nearby units could assist with medical support? The 9th Foot were the closest. They had been nicknamed the 'Holy Boys', since the Britannia figure on their hard leather shakos was apparently mistaken for the Virgin Mary. Hence the battalion was a favourite with some of the Iberian population, for here seemed to be a faithful band of men amongst Wellesley's heretic army! This regiment was about one quarter of a mile to Guthrie's right, struggling up a steeper gully than the 29th. Their surgeon, Mr Andrew Browne – an experienced fellow, who had served as a surgeon for eleven years, including a spell in the West Indies – was soon up with Guthrie. Together they pronounced that Colonel Stewart, commanding officer of the 9th, had a mortal belly wound. The wounded colonel begged the two surgeons to go to their work and expired that evening. Of the four assistant surgeons to the 9th, on the army list of June 1808, Thomas Forster, Thomas Bulkeley, George Gray and William Mylne, only two (Forster and Bulkeley) may have been there. Forster was later appointed battalion surgeon to one of the battalions of the 9th on 26 July 1810. Whilst Forster and Bulkeley went on with the 9th, Mylne died a year or so after the regiment had landed and does not appear to have been given credit for his Peninsular service. He may well have been sick. Likewise, Gray was not credited with Peninsular service and died in the early months of 1811.

The casualties suffered by the 29th were predictably considerable. There were 193 killed, wounded and missing (prisoners), which was a fair proportion of the unit (24 per cent). The 9th suffered seventy-two casualties in the action. Aside from the 9th and 29th, other battalions had received a total of 222 killed, wounded or missing. The French losses are difficult to calculate since many hurt men were removed by Delaborde's withdrawal. Warre recalls a rough figure of 1,000, when writing home from Peniche on 19 August.[11] Probably a figure of 600–700 is realistic.[12]

Arriving during the French withdrawal back down the track to Zambugeira, Guthrie focused his care on those around the ridge, and then advanced to look after the casualties in the village, where many French and British wounded had struggled for refuge. So rather than drag the casualties back down the gully, Guthrie set up a small field hospital in Zambugeira. Rifleman Harris noted that two or three surgeons were working away in the houses of this village and that much wine, escaping from perforated wine butts, was running away, mingled with the blood of the wounded![13] Guthrie recalled later having to correct a staff surgeon's serious surgical error,

> Corporal Carter, of the pioneers of the 29th Regiment, was wounded at the battle of Roliça, in August 1809, by a musket-ball, which passed through the anterior [front] and upper part of the fore-arm, fracturing the ulna. Shortly afterwards a profuse haemorrhage took place, and the staff surgeon in charge tied the brachial artery [i.e. only upstream of the wound in the artery]. That night the haemorrhage recurred and the man almost bled to death. The arm was amputated, when the ulnar artery was found in an open and sloughing state.[14]

This case emphasized to Guthrie that there had been enough blood flow down the other artery of the arm – the radial – to cause continued blood loss from the wound in the artery below the upstream ligature.

Whilst a temporary hospital might have been set up back in Obidos, Wellesley's forward movements with a stronger force would have soon closed this facility. Some staff surgeons would eventually arrive to assist the regimental doctors, a few were back at Obidos or remained on board the *Enterprise*, a nearby hospital ship to which the severely wounded men from Roliça were transferred. The medical management of such hospital ships was given over to a physician.

It was said that Guthrie and Browne actually operated on the majority of the casualties that day, as the bullock-carts and hospital staff were a long way to the rear. 'They came up, however, at night, worked with us on the 18th, and relieved me on the morning of the 19th, when I started for the army at Vimiera [sic], with the two carts, and stores in question.'

Up on the ridge meanwhile, the wounded required water and redressing of their injuries. Bandaging with linen rollers was a most important and reassuring first aid measure. Guthrie advised however that simple gunshot wounds of the soft tissues required only the laying on of a piece of wet lint or linen retained by a strip of adhesive plaster. He was critical of the application of linen roller bandages as usually practised. He commented that, 'A roller as a surgical application [i.e. straight onto the wound] is useless if not injurious. At the first and second battles in Portugal [i.e. Roliça and Vimeiro], every wound had a roller applied over it; it soon became stiff, bloody, and dirty. They did no good, were for the most part cut off with scissors, and thus rendered useless. When really wanted, at a later period, they were not forthcoming.'[15] What he is implying is that small damp dressings initially sufficed, saving the precious linen rollers for later definitive surgery or more serious wounds.

When casualties required more than a dressing, they were moved to shelter and sutures were inserted, fingers and probes were used to determine the site of buried missiles and a few limbs would require amputation.

One of Guthrie's foremost interests in these campaigns was the management of wounded arteries. Control of haemorrhage has always been a critical issue and various types of tourniquet,[16] digital pressure, packing and compression devices had all played a role. Having sufficient well-trained support personnel to direct temporary and life-saving control of bleeding was a very real problem then, so much so that self-help or that from colleagues was often the only salvation. A surgeon, through well-directed anatomical knowledge, would have to be familiar with approaches to every major artery in the body.

Guthrie had to control much serious haemorrhage at Roliça and he was often too late to save patients with bleeding injuries. We know this since, following Roliça and after Albuera, in 1811, he sent home some preserved specimens of such damaged blood vessels, following death or amputation, to his former mentor in London, Dr Hooper.

He learnt a lifelong surgical lesson at Roliça. During one amputation, his canvas-strapped screw tourniquet failed. Either the strap broke or the clasp loosened. Severe haemorrhage was swiftly prevented by Guthrie, who had the presence of mind to rapidly press with a finger or thumb accurately over the arterial pulse in the soldier's groin, thus immediately compressing the femoral artery, the principal blood vessel in the thigh. Often the victim was severely shocked and, with consequent low blood pressure, there would be little bleeding from other vessels – medium-sized arteries and veins. So Guthrie learnt that, with simple accurately maintained digital pressure over the principal artery, bleeding could be efficiently controlled at least as well as by the tight crushing pressure of the screw tourniquet.

He wrote about this simple control of haemorrhage with great conviction:

> There is always more blood lost, and particularly in secondary
> amputations, when a tourniquet is used than when the principal artery is
> compressed by one assistant, and two others are ready to press on the
> outside of the flaps, or upon the divided vessels, with the ends of their
> fingers; the force necessary the passage of blood through the common
> femoral, or the axillary artery [the two principal arteries of the leg and arm,
> respectively], being merely that of the finger and thumb, applied in a very

gentle manner, or even the end of the fore-finger of a competent person. I have rarely applied a tourniquet since 1812, and few persons have done more formidable operations under more difficult circumstances.[17]

Guthrie began to sort out the casualties. The dead, among them Lake and his sergeant, were interred where they fell. Lightly wounded men were sent off after being dressed to join their comrades. Potentially serious wounds required immediate attention.

> A soldier of the 9th Regiment was wounded at Roliça, in 1808, by the point of a sword in the left side; it penetrated the chest, making a wound somewhat more than an inch long, through which air passed readily, accompanied by a very little frothy blood, which was also spit [sic] up on any effort being made to cough; leaving no doubt of the lung having been injured, that viscus [organ, i.e. the lung] appearing to be retained against the wall of the chest. As the edges of the wound could not be accurately kept in apposition by adhesive plaster, two sutures were applied through the skin, and the man was desired to lie on the injured side, with the hope that adhesion might take place [i.e. between the lung and chest wall], as there appeared to be no effusion of blood into the cavity [of the chest]. He was freely bled on each of the two days following the receipt of the wound, and gradually recovered.[18]

A few more seriously damaged men rode on the scant carts available, their equipment being carried by comrades. The eight officers and NCOs and men of the 29th taken prisoner were hurried off with Delaborde's men to the Tagus and put on the transport *Vasco de Gama* lying up there.[19]

Injuries of the male genitalia were relatively uncommon. One such case occurred in a married soldier of the 29th, who was unfortunate enough to have a musket ball pass through the shaft of the penis from side to side. Guthrie comments, 'The man suffered very little inconvenience[!], and the wounds healed very well. He seemed to consider the injury as of no importance to himself, but had some idea there might be a difference of opinion in another party.'[20] The problems with wounds in this area were infection and deformity of the penis with scarring. Damage to the testes might result in infertility.

Although Guthrie's transport situation improved shortly, he regretted the improper supply of draught animals.

> By his Grace's [Wellesley's] dispatches, I see that two bullock-carts were demanded and granted for the medical stores of the army, which, his Grace further specifies, were to carry 25 bearers [stretchers], one case of utensils,

principally, I believe, tin kettles, spitting pots, and chamber pots, and one medicine chest; which specification I know to be critically correct, as the two carts with the above contents, came into my hands at Roliça to be taken on be me to Vimiera [sic]. I have no doubt there were plenty of stores on board-ship, but it is the arrangement, and the utter ignorance of the subject, which is ludicrous. Each surgeon should have a pair of wicker panniers covered with bull-hide, and duly filled, of a good form and size, slung, and fitted to a proper pack-saddle; and there should have been a horse-transport or two, to carry a horse for the field surgical stores of each regiment, and from half a dozen to a dozen spare ones, similarly accoutred, for extra stores, with a man from each regiment who understood the care of a beast.[21]

Four days later there was to be another and more severe conflict, further south at the town of Vimeiro, a little way in from the coast, east of the estuary of the Maceira River. Here there was less employment for Guthrie and he himself was wounded. He could not have continued to manage the more serious casualties from Roliça, since many would require prolonged convalescence elsewhere. In fact he had worked tirelessly for three days before moving on.[22] Those surviving their injuries from 17 August were removed from the field hospital buildings and moved back to Obidos, Oporto or the *Enterprise*.

Guthrie moved away slowly with his wagons to join his battalion,

I wished the carts at the devil in the first instance, on account of the delay they occasioned; but very soon took a particular fancy to them; for we found the French cavalry patrolling between Lourina and Vimiera [sic], to the great alarm of both the natives and ourselves. They counted on their fingers two patrols of an officer, and twenty men each, one being before the other on one side of us, and told us they would cut us to pieces if they caught us. I had some twenty old soldiers with me, all of whom I knew well, and two or three subaltern officers of other corps, who were taking advantage of the convoy, and whose duty it was to fight. I tied the heads of my second bullocks to the tail of the cart, which preceded them, and thus continued our march across the country, which was open, although hilly, and soon satisfied my old soldiers that, with their backs against the bullock-carts, they were not to be thrashed by a patrol of cavalry. The pots and pans arrived safe, ready for the battle of Vimiera [sic] on the 21st. The 20th was a beautiful day, and I spent it happily with three officers, my messmates, who are all since dead.

One died at Talavera, another at Albuera and the other in his bed.

At eleven o'clock that night, there was a false alarm and after settling, the battalion was under arms an hour before daybreak. For Guthrie, 'The morning of the 21st dawned upon us in all its brilliancy; distant clouds of dust announced the approaching contest; our breakfast of biscuit and water, with a bunch of grapes was soon dispatched; and we at last moved to the high ground on the left of the British position. The fight had begun before we got there, and the French advance was, as usual, valiant.'

Three days after the combat at Roliça, Wellesley had covered the landing of Brigadier-General Acland and Anstruther's Brigades at Maceira bay and now, with around 17,000 bayonets and about 1,500 Portuguese auxiliaries, he was ready to face Marshal Androche Junot's 13,000 men at Vimeiro. With the two fresh-landed brigades came a third physician, two further staff surgeons and six hospital mates, so increasing the senior staff to eleven and the battalion surgeons to around twenty-three. The battle was fought around the village, with Wellesley's men finally dispersed along two ridges either side of Vimeiro, most units were on a southwesterly ridge, to the south of which was a small hill with a plateau.

As the combat of the day evolved, Wellesley moved several battalions, including the 29th, away from that ridge to a northeasterly one. The battle on the 21 August was punctuated by a series of determined frontal and flank assaults by columns of French infantry and a spirited but ineffectual advance by the British 20th Light Dragoons.

After breakfast that day, Wellesley's men saw the dust of an approaching French force from the northeast – Junot was to try and turn his left. Three British brigades, including the 29th in Brigadier-General Miles Nightingall's 1,520 men, moved to the eastern ridge. There, the 29th left their knapsacks with the quarter guard and after helping haul some cannon up a slope, formed line. Meanwhile Brigadier Jean Thomière's brigade, two columns 400 yards apart and each thirty men wide, attacked the hill where Brigadier-General Henry Fane and Anstruther's brigades were posted. The 50th fired in a two-line deep formation, devastating the advancing French columns, which broke and ran. Likewise, the second column under Brigadier-General Charlot was met by the rolling fire of the 2/97th and then enveloped by the 2/52nd and 2/9th, thus breaking the next French column. Two further assaults by columns of General François-Etienne Kellerman's grenadiers were launched on the environs of the village and hill. These were both repulsed with the capture of some ordnance. There was some bitter fighting in the village between French grenadiers and the 2/43rd. An abortive charge by the 20th Light Dragoons and some Portuguese cavalry failed to achieve much. It was now around 11am and Guthrie with his assistants had yet to receive casualties.

After the French retreat and four failed assaults, many wounded of both sides had been collected into Vimeiro town. Guthrie was not there, remaining posted on the eastern ridge above the village of Ventosa, the next target for Junot's forces.

From the southeast, General Solignac had pushed his sweating columns, around 3,000 men, up the ridge towards the 1/71st, 1/40th, 1/36th and 1/82nd facing the French columns. Around 3,000 men delivering half-company volleys broke up the enemy assault yet again. Guthrie's battalion along with the 1/82nd soon reinforced by the 1/71st, was threatened by Brigadier-General Brennier's manœuvres. He had attacked with four battalion columns up the northern face of the eastern ridge, moving his men along the crest towards the rapidly reforming British 1/71st and 1/82nd battalions. These units were caught unformed, so the 29th, with Guthrie, doubled round to face the French right flank, once again halting the French columns. With the battalion finally formed four deep against a possible cavalry assault and their light company, with that of the 82nd, firing on the last unsuccessful French advance of the day, the action was finished. A meritorious casualty of these latter engagements was Piper George Clarke of the 71st, who continued his playing whilst shot through both legs.

Brennier was wounded and taken prisoner; Guthrie was also hurt, being hit fairly superficially, most likely by a spent ball in both legs, scuffing one and bruising the other. Luckily for Guthrie, the 29th had only fourteen casualties – two killed and twelve wounded: Brigade-Major Creagh of the light company, a sergeant and ten rank and file. Guthrie's wounds were dressed and he was soon helping his assistants with the treatment and dispersal of his battalion and French casualties, who were moved to Vimeiro. Dr Adam Neale, a hospital staff physician, watched from a farm used as a brigade dressing station and found himself frustrated at the scores of hurt men. Not a practising surgeon, he nevertheless comforted, dressed wounds, prescribed a little opium and, with a soldier's wife, made up some gruel for the injured. It was he who noticed a wooden bowl of amputated hands and a pile of limbs outside the church at Vimeiro, which was used as the principal operating station for Allied and French casualties alike. He was given charge of moving the wounded away to a newly opened hospital at Oporto in forty procured bullock-carts.[23]

There had been 720 British casualties – the French lost around 2,000 men and thirteen guns. Lieutenant-General Sir Harry Burrard, although supporting the action, had refused Wellesley the pursuit that might have bought near-complete destruction of the French force. Guthrie saw Sir H Burrard during the action and failed to be impressed, commenting that 'one sight of him quite convinced me he was unfit to command an army in the field'.[24] The only man perhaps pleased to remain static after the action would have been Guthrie. With relatively few casualties in his battalion and himself injured, he had time to recover and assist as best he might. He was involved with cases from other battalions. After Solignac and Brennier's assaults above Ventosa, he examined an officer of the 40th, from Sir Ronald Fergusson's brigade, who had a musket-ball injury of the thigh. After noting that the officer had no exit wound, Guthrie pulled on a long piece of shirt, lying at the mouth of the wound, wrapped round a ball three inches deeper! While he was doing this, 'he got a crack from a spent ball on his hind quarter, which made him jump, and we thought it advisable to retire into a water-course, which allowed our heads to be under cover'. It was a generally accepted point that if a missile could not be felt by the exploring finger it was going to be hard to extract by any means. This ball would have lain at the extreme depth for digital extraction. More important than the ball itself causing mischief was the piece of bacteria-laden clothing, carried into the thigh muscles in front of the missile.

Guthrie made a further and unusual point in one of his first lectures: that a missile need not be always retained and might fall out of the entry wound. In an unknown action, he comments on a 'Major Lightfoot' who

> was struck by a musket ball on the left breast; it went through his clothes, the integuments [skin/fat] and the outer part of the greater pectoral muscle, and slanted inwards for three inches towards the sternum [breast-bone], to which its track could be followed. It was evident that the ball had neither lodged nor penetrated, for no serious symptoms ensued. In all probability it had been ejected the way it went in by the elasticity of the cartilages of the ribs near the sternum.[25]

Having now emphasized that a wounded artery must be tied above and below the injury site to stop bleeding and recalling the case of Corporal Carter at Roliça, he treated a soldier who had received a wound of the arm, 'the brachial artery bled forthwith, the haemorrhage being stopped by the tourniquet. Warned by the preceding case, I cut down on the artery, carefully avoiding the nerve, which had been [mistakenly] tied in the former instance, and found the artery more than half divided. It was secured by a ligature above and below the wound: the bleeding did not afterwards return, and the man recovered.'[26] One of several French casualties treated by Guthrie at Vimeiro was an artillery driver who had been knocked off his horse by a musket ball, which hit the right side of his head during Brennier's assault.

> I took him under my care, thinking from his freedom from bad symptoms, and the slightness of the [skull] fracture, that he would probably do well. The next morning I found him apparently dying. A portion of bone being removed (he had not been trephined), a thick coagulum [clot] of blood appeared beneath, apparently extending in every direction. Three more pieces of bone were taken away, and the coagulum, which appeared to be an inch in thickness, was removed with difficulty with the help of a feather. The brain did not, however, regain its level, and the man shortly after died. The middle meningeal artery [an artery firmly attached to the inside of the

skull] which was torn across on the outside of the dura mater [the outer tough membrane covering the brain]; the wound did not pass through to the inside, and there was no blood beneath the dura mater. The convolutions of the brain were depressed and flattened by the pressure.[27]

Guthrie had correctly decompressed the brain and gently removed the clot of blood causing this mischief. Why did the man not live? Here, I think he left the removal of bone fragments and blood clot too late and the brain had been pushed down onto the base of the skull, so causing an irretrievable crushing of the vital centres in the mid brain.

A French soldier was brought to Guthrie in the village after the action. He had been wounded in the right side of the chest by a sword thrust. He had bled a good deal, was shocked and spitting up blood. Guthrie removed the handkerchief and a 'gaping wound presented itself, an inch and a half long, through which the cavity of the chest could be seen, the lung having receded [collapsed]'. Guthrie tried to close the wound with adhesive plasters, but these were not strong enough to keep the wound edges together: 'they were sewn together, and after the application of a compress he was much relieved'. He became feverish and unwell, then recovered and was shipped home from Lisbon with the French forces. Guthrie was to gain much experience in the management of chest injuries. Although he advocated prompt closure of open thorax wounds, this would not always prove the correct management. The accumulation of blood or air could fatally compress the heart and great vessels in the chest and, in such cases, Guthrie emphasized the need to drain the chest and open the wound up again. For immediate care on the battlefield, however, closure was often the correct manœuvre since then air and debris would not be sucked into the chest cavity by the negative pressure resulting from inspiration.

One injured prisoner of war was to benefit from Guthrie's linguistic skills. A French officer, hit in the face and bleeding from the wound, came under Guthrie's care. When Guthrie had treated him, the officer entrusted Guthrie with his account book, purse and watch. He was wise, for even though Guthrie could have absconded with the valuables, the Frenchman trusted him and was delighted when they were returned!

After the notorious Convention of Sintra (which Guthrie heartily opposed) was signed on 30 August, the 29th remained in Portugal and Spain. Three companies of the 29th were ordered to move to the naval arsenal and to cover the French evacuation. Guthrie and the 29th were posted out of town to Monte Santa, towards the end of the month. On 6 October, Sir John Moore was in command at Lisbon, where there seemed to be much confusion. The army was indolent and not in a particularly robust state, many reporting sick as there had been 'much intemperance'. Moore had brought substantial medical support with his force – ten medical staff with one deputy purveyor and twelve hospital mates, in addition to the battalion surgeons, etc. The two most senior medical men were Dr James Franck, Inspector of Hospitals, who was in overall charge until Dr James McGrigor arrived in January 1812, and Dr William Fergusson, Deputy Inspector of Hospitals, who was to take over the supervision of medical care for the Portuguese forces in November 1809. Three weeks later Moore set out towards Salamanca with about 20,000 men in four columns to join up with Sir David Baird's force of approximately 15,000 infantry, cavalry, wagon train and artillery advancing from Corunna. Baird was supported by Dr William Hogg (DIH), two physicians, two staff surgeons, an apothecary, a deputy purveyor, twelve mates and general hospital stores.

In early October the 29th moved from Monte Santa back into Lisbon, where they were billeted in the convent of St Domingo. Around 10,000 ill-equipped soldiers, invalids and malingerers were left behind in Lisbon, under the command of Sir John Cradock, who, with a Mr Villiers, regulated military and political control respectively. Now, around half the army was sick[28] and there was widespread unrest, insurrection and violence.[29] There was a lack of clothing, shoes and draught animals. The Portuguese capital was crowded with women and children. Guthrie had his work cut out dealing with seasonal afflictions, fight victims, alcohol excess and obstetric and childhood illnesses. The battered 29th was considered an unfit unit to make its way north with Sir John and had meanwhile sailed south for the Bay of Cadiz, where it landed on the 5 February. Our surgeon must have been considered highly competent, as he was placed in charge of the medical support for all the troops under Major-General MacKenzie. In Cadiz, Guthrie worked on his Spanish and Portuguese, in which latter he was now considered fluent. He returned to Lisbon on 12 March, the battalion having been recalled from the transient sortie to Cadiz. He apparently accompanied two battalions in an abortive march to Almeida, which was designed to support Sir John Moore's expedition. Guthrie, in one of his lectures, related rather strangely an 'animal magnetism' between the French and the British forces during this expedition. Presumably he inferred a form of telepathy. The force, recalled by General Cradock, returned to Abrantes. Guthrie then received those convalescents likely to return to duty, sick stragglers from Moore's army (Moore had sent around 1,500 ill men back to Lisbon) and prepared himself for the ensuing developments. New recruits for the 29th were being joined with the battalion to make up strength.

Following Moore's death and successful evacuation of the British army from Vigo and Corunna, Soult was on the Minho River and threatened Oporto. Cradock was unhappy to push his small, sickly and untried force too far from Lisbon. Help would be needed.

3

Striking Out

After the abortive mission to Cadiz in early February the 29th, along with reinforcements sent from Britain, joined with Beresford's Portuguese, since Cradock had now decided to advance northwards against Marshal Soult. On 29 March, Soult, commanding around 20,000 men, had occupied Oporto, spearheading a second invasion of Portugal. Apparently around 7,000–8,000 combatants and civilians perished in the sacking of the town. Guthrie's battalion marched to Buçellas and left there on 11 February, going on to Leira and then the 29th marched to Pombal, Condeixa and on 1 May into the university town of Coimbra. On 22 April 1809, Lieutenant-General Sir Arthur Wellesley landed at Lisbon. Within thirty-six hours of taking over command, Wellesley had decided to throw the French out of Oporto. Guthrie and the 29th made up the 6th brigade under Brigadier-General Richard Stewart with the 1/16th Portuguese and the 1st provisional battalion of detachments – part of Lieutenant-General Edward Paget's division.

Whilst discussing this campaign, at a place named San Antonio de Trojal, Guthrie had an unusual 'circumstance', which he thought interesting to relate to his students.

A soldier had suffered from bleeding for several days, in considerable quantity, from the mouth, which was perpetual; some was spit out with a little cough, some was swallowed, and neither medicine nor treatment seemed to have any effect upon. He became greatly emaciated, and his death appeared to be inevitably at hand, although I could not discover any particular disease about him. On visiting the hospital early in the morning, I enquired if he was dead, and was astonished at being told he had been quite well for two hours, and intended to live, for that he had coughed up a leech, which there could be no doubt was the cause of the bleeding, inasmuch as it had ceased from that moment. The man rapidly recovered. I was quite aware that in warm countries, in which leeches prevail, they are readily taken up by men and horses in drinking out of puddles, as thirsty animals, whether bipeds or quadripeds, will constantly do. They are usually what are called horse-leeches; or of that kind which hold on and suck at one end and discharge the blood at the other; but they commonly stick about the lips, mouth and throat, both in men and horses, from whence they are readily removed by the fingers or forceps, When they get above or behind the palate, they are still usually discovered with a little trouble; and when they could not, I never before or afterwards found much difficulty in dislodging them with strong salt and water injected through the nose, which by its own virtue, and that of vomiting had the desired effect. Whether this leech was in that place or not I do not know, but it certainly did all but kill the man.

Dr Robb [John Robb, served in the Peninsula 1811–14, previously surgeon in the 55th and 95th, then staff surgeon in June 1809, DIH in 1812] gave me the particulars of a case, which afterwards confirmed by Mr Maling [surgeon to 52nd Foot, who had examined the mortally wounded Sir John Moore en route back to Corunna town], who said he saw it, which occurred in the Light Division, and nearly killed a man, who had been drinking out of a puddle, or out of a canteen filled from one, in a more extraordinary manner. The man declared he felt something move in his stomach the instant he had drunk, and from that moment his torment were unceasing, both from pain and from the alarm he felt at distinctly perceiving something trotting up and down his stomach. The man became pale, wan, and miserable, and would have died, in spite of all the means employed for his relief, if he had not one day, at the end of about three weeks, vomited up a living animal, the cause of all his misery. The case is so well attested by the medical officers, who saw the animal before it died, that it cannot be disputed. They say in had four feet and a tail, and called it a salamander, I presume for no medicine (or digestive gastric juices!) having had any effect on it, rather from it deserving that name. It was so large that it nearly choked the man in coming up, so that he was quite satisfied it had grown considerably after he had swallowed it, and it was admitted to all who saw it that if it had not, it could not have been swallowed without as much difficulty as was experienced in bringing it up.[1]

Guthrie went on with the battalion, when it pushed the French out of Oliveira, south of Oporto, and then discovered a strongly held French position on the heights above Grijo. Some rifles of the 95th and the flank companies of the 29th, 43rd and 52nd pushed up against the French. Sir Arthur, lingering behind the colours of the 29th, was heard to say, 'If they don't move soon, I must let the old 29th loose upon them!'[2] The enemy's left flank was turned and the 29th moved into the village where they were 'indebted to their foes for shelter and food'. Some cattle having been recently slaughtered were left lying about. Guthrie had six wounded to care for.

The next morning the battalion moved into a suburb of Oporto, Villa Nova. Guthrie was irritated by an order from his general of division to remove all baggage animals to the rear, to assist with the element of surprise. Guthrie had need for his two mules – one for physic and surgical gear and the other for entrenching tools. The general was intensely upset and demanded the reason for the surgeon's challenge. On Guthrie's sarcastic response that surgical assistance and burial parties might be required, the general relented and allowed the mules to be returned. Guthrie angrily forced the general's ADC to go and bring them back to him![3]

Meanwhile, the 3rd Foot, having crossed the river, had commenced an assault on the convent of St Augustina da Serra. On Major-General John Murray deploying to Soult's left, the enemy began to withdraw, leaving the town in a state of confusion. All boats that could be used for a river crossing had been moored on the right (French) side of the Douro. Seeing the French confusion and being beckoned by the British, the boatmen brought over some craft from further down. The 29th were taken over and the grenadier company commenced firing at the retiring French troops.

Guthrie using his Portuguese communication skills had crossed the river earlier with his horse and noticed the shambles in the town. Abandoned military equipment littered the streets. The locals were not happy to loot this and begged the British to seize all the horses and draught animals. Guthrie having found that he was the only mounted officer around the streets considered it was not officer-like to deal in abandoned baggage, so he rode around looking for riding horses. In doing this our surgeon became separated from his unit that clearly had had no casualties and he

was overtaken by Sir J Milley Doyle at the head of the 16th Portuguese, also looking for them [the 29th]. I offered to show him the way, as they were only a little before us, and placed myself by his side at the head of his regiment. On turning a corner I showed him the 29th Grenadiers drawn up in a line on the rising ground at the end of the road. They soon perceived us and after a minute or two I saw Sir John Sherbrooke [Lieutenant-General Sherbrooke, who led the Guards and 29th, along with the 14th Light Dragoons] himself face the Grenadier company towards us, and to my astonishment they very quietly 'made ready' as if on parade.

Sir John [Doyle] and the Portuguese called out it was all over with them, and I thought so myself, for, knowing the old Grenadiers very well, I took it for granted that we were as good as dead. We were too far off to be heard on time, yet close enough to be shot, and it was quite plain they took us for French. I bethought me I had a red round jacket on, under my blue undress coat, and as little time was to be lost, I stood up in my stirrups and opened the blue coat as wide as possible, so that none of the red one should be lost. The Grenadiers at this moment came to the 'present;' I thought we were gone: when in an instant I saw them irregularly changing to the 'recover:' they knew me, and called out 'the doctor and the Portuguese.' I never was so delighted in my life, and galloped up to them forthwith.

Sir J Sherbrooke saluted me with, 'By God, Sir, if you had not shown that red jacket, I would have sent you all in a second more to the devil!' I knew Sir John very well, and said I hoped at all events he would have sent us elsewhere, but he would not hear of it. 'No, sir,' said he, 'I would have sent you all to the devil: you should have gone there and nowhere else!' and as it was well that Sir John would always do what he said as far as depended upon him, there was nothing to be done but submit. From that day the Portuguese never went into action, that I saw, without a white band round the left arm.[4]

A sight digression concerning Sir John is worth relating and underpins the not-infrequent incursions of British soldiery into convent life and the softer side of a gruff commander. Guthrie recalled: 'Sir John Sherbrooke was a good-hearted man, although rather irascible, and was always willing to do a kind action. If the severity of the physic and surgery would admit of a little descriptive episode.' There was a 'good kitchen' at the convent of Alcobaça, where

live fish did swim about in troughs, placed from one end to the other on the middle of the table, through which the river water constantly flowed; and the gardens were beautiful in the extreme. The padre gardien [sic] and the monks were always hospitable. They were obliged in those days by their charter to give a dinner and lodging to every traveller who passed and asked it, and about three half-pence [3–5 shillings or 15–25 pence in modern terms] on parting in the morning, and they received us with open arms on all occasions. The dinner was most joyous, the monarch and people of the respective nations were drunk with enthusiasm. I think I now see the jolly old fellows answering to our three times three with a thousand vivas; but they were not all old and the younger ones liked wine. On one occasion, when Sir John Sherbrooke dined with them, one of the younger ones was also successful in making love; for the English ladies who accompanied the soldiers were not fastidious, and one of them could not resist the solicitations of the handsome monk. He was caught by the soldiers in a situation unhappily for him *pas douteuse*. They immediately placed him on one shutter and the lady on another, and marched them joyously round the cloisters to the great amusement of the populace assembled at the convent to see the British. The next morning he had disappeared; his trial and punishment were summary; he had been sentenced to a slow death on bread and water, in a small stone cell, from which he was never to be drawn alive. The entreaties of Sir John Sherbrooke prevailed not. The superior honestly admitted, that he would have forgiven the offence at the pressing entreaty of the English general, if it had not been so publicly manifested; but that the character of the order was at stake, and it must be as publicly known that the punishment had been exemplary. Sir John kept up correspondence with the old padre and after the battle of Talavera, was congratulated by the old prelate. When Sir John replied in gratitude, he begged once again, as a great favour, for the release of the young monk.

Guthrie goes on,

> Sir John Sherbrooke, when he told me this story, declared that he had felt that day to be one of the happiest of his life, when he received a letter from the superior, enclosing one from the young man, thanking him for his life, and stating the horrible imprisonment he had undergone, and the utter destitution of hope in which he lay, when Sir John's interference when his pardon were announced to him.[5]

Returning to Guthrie's eventful day in Oporto, he continued,

> Shortly after this I accompanied the light troops to the front, and had a little skirmish with the French runaways, who were making their escape from the end of every street. Some of them brought up a gun, but on seeing us, and also that the road was occupied, as it turned in front of us, dismounted and left the gun with the four mules that drew it. These I seized, but what to do with a gun and four mules I did not know, more particularly after my failure in horse-stealing; so I settled the matter by taking possession of the best mule, which I carried off, and it served me very faithfully through the Talavera campaign.

Guthrie recorded but few details of casualties after this action round Oporto. One interesting case consisted of a young soldier, who had received a French ball in his head. Rather than fracturing the cranium, the missile had forcibly prised open the suture line of the cranium – the gap between two plates of skull – which had not yet united in young recruits. Guthrie commented that this injury was dangerous (apart from the risk of infection, blood vessels might be torn) and he subsequently saw other cases at Albuera, Salamanca and Orthez.[6] It was during this action that Sir Edward Paget parted company with his right arm but there is no evidence that Guthrie was his surgeon.

Their pursuit was halted and in the evening, they were ordered to march back to the town, where they were given a street in which to find billets. Sherbrooke's men were complimented on their actions. The number of casualties for Guthrie's attentions is not recorded. Apparently none of the 29th was killed.

On 17 May, Sir Arthur Wellesley, having ascertained that Soult had destroyed his artillery and stores and had crossed the border, decided that to pursue the French was not advisable. Stewart's brigade moved to cantonments at Povo de Lanhoso. A general hospital was set up at Oporto on 24 May. Guthrie does not mention the large number of French wounded captured in the town.

On learning that Marshal Victor had taken Alcantara and was threatening Portugal by way of Castello Branco, Wellesley was forced to react. The 29th was at Coimbra by 1 June and by 8 June was at Abrantes. Here it learnt that Marshal Victor had retired to Talavera de la Reyna, whilst the Spanish General Don Gregorio Cuesta, who had recently suffered a reverse at the Medellin, was on the Tagus, watching the French. On 12 June, Guthrie's brigade crossed the river and took up position on its left bank. The return of the 29th battalion on 15 June showed thirty-three officers and staff, thirty-six sergeants, fifteen drummers and 600 rank and file fit for duty. At Plasencia, around 140 kilometres from Talavera de la Reyna, where the battalion was on 9 July, a (brigade) hospital depôt was established under the military command of a Captain Patison of the 29th, who was later taken prisoner (along with around 400 patients and assistant surgeon Curby) on 31 July by Marshal Edouard Mortier. The brigade consisted of the battalion of detachments, the 48th and the 29th Foot. Guthrie and the brigade moved off on 16 July. It arrived on 21 July and bivouacked in olive groves to the left of the town of Talavera. The next day the enemy's forward troops were driven back. An Allied advance on 24 July found that the force under Marshal Victor had fallen back to link with reinforcements under King Joseph Bonaparte. Wellesley halted, but General Cuesta's men rushed on and on the morning of 26 July, it was learnt that Cuesta had suffered a severe check. Over that night and the following morning, the Spanish, along with their baggage, cattle, sick and wounded streamed to the rear in some disorder. This hindered British efforts to form up around Talavera since an imminent French assault was announced.

The battle lines at Talavera ran a little in front of the town and then north of it for four to five kilometres. The dried up bed of a small stream – the Portina – lay more or less between the armies running north to south. About half way along the Allied front the ground rose to around 115 metres, forming the slope of the Medellin hillside, up to what was called the Northern Plain; the Portina cut a ravine across which the French would have to attack. The physical effort for the French troops was considerable on 27 and 28 July, particularly as the heat was severe as they struggled over rocky terrain and bone-dry grass, wheat and barley. They had no decent town base to shelter and recover their injured or sick men. The Allied wounded had some earth walls and olive groves to shelter in before they could be moved to their right behind the lines, transported over a kilometre or two to a field hospital around half way down from the Medellin to Talavera and from there to the shelter and cooler buildings of Talavera.

The 29th had bivouacked about a quarter of a mile outside the town on the Madrid road. Charles Leslie an officer of the 29th commented, 'Wounded men from our advanced guard [from a forward position at the Casa de Salinas] began to come in.'[7] Dinner was cooked in haste, tents and baggage were packed and the drums beat to arms. Richard Stewart's brigade was to move to the left of the Spanish troops and artillery, who had replaced Hill's 2nd Division nearest to the town. Passing through the Spanish lines, the 29th witnessed cries of *Rompez los Franceses*. The 29th marching behind the 48th reached the lower slopes of the hill and rested a few hundred metres behind the front. Towards evening the battalion was exposed to artillery and infantry fire and was ordered to lie down. The firing died away. Perceiving a potential weakness in the disposition of the thinly deployed British troops (Colonel Donkin's brigade) at the Medellin eminence on Wellesley's left flank, Marshal Victor ordered General Ruffin's division (9th Léger, 24th and 96th Ligne) to attack and intense firing was heard at around 9pm. General Hill led the 29th up at speed. Only the volleys and random flashes of musketry displayed the opposing formations. Wheeling from column of companies into lines the 29th were engaged in a vehement contest, particularly with the 9th Léger.

The enemy was driven off the hill and soldiers of Guthrie's battalion lay down amongst the dead and dying, exhausted, 'the furred shako of a dead French soldier forming in many cases a pillow for the night'.[8] They probably occupied dead ground here, which would do nothing but encourage Victor for the next day's onslaught.[9] During the night, sleep was disturbed by the perpetual rumbling of gun carriages as Sir Arthur brought up ordnance ready for the morrow. Guthrie set up his battalion aid post/forward dressing station. There was known to be a small house used for this purpose behind the centre of the lines.[10] Although not recorded he would have likely sent forward his most experienced assistant surgeon to help with the dressing and removal of battalion casualties. He and the other junior surgeon would have gathered with other regimental surgeons to receive casualties and direct survivors south to the shelter and relative cool of the town.

The 29th was now formed up on the left of the 48th Regiment. At daybreak on 28 July, a strong French column was seen to be advancing. The French artillery fired up the hill on Wellesley's left so late in the French advance as to put its own infantry at risk. The 29th lay for a while on the rocky ground to escape French fire, whilst Ruffin's men perceived that the ground was thinly defended. As they surmounted high ground, General Stewart shouted, 'Now 29th! Now is your time!' Engaged for a while in a fire-fight, Sir Arthur ordered a charge and the 48th and right wing of the 29th launched forth. The French assault was driven back, with the capture of 'two silk standards', apparently on poles to which had been screwed the eagles.

After a further French attack, the soldiers assembled in the ravine and retired in order to their own lines. Leslie was hit by a musket round at around 7am.

> I received a ball in the side of my thigh, about three inches above the right knee ... at length my friend, Andrew Leith Hay perceived me. He raised me up, and then, taking the musket out of the hand of Corporal Sharp of my company, he directed him to conduct me out of action, and to find the surgeons ... In quitting the field, I passed near Sir Arthur Wellesley, the Commander-in-Chief. He looked at me, seeing the blood streaming down my white trousers, but he said nothing.[11]

There was a time for retrieving and assisting the wounded of both sides. Soldiers mixed with the enemy wounded, giving desperately needed water to them. Casualties were recovered and carted to the field hospital or city and the dead buried in the stifling heat and parched soil. Thirst was always an immense problem[12] and Private Hewitt recounted as he gave water to the wounded, 'many a poor wounded fellow did I that day receive a blessing from, when I held to his parched lips the anticipated cup'.[13] Whatever else, there was more severe conflict to come and the surgeons' work was far from done. Around 2pm, French batteries opened fire again. British battalions, despite lying down for cover, received some terrible mutilations and their corpses were dragged off before the bearers returned to their seemingly calm prostrate ranks. The inevitable fresh dogged infantry assaults by war-hardened French veterans followed – men under Generals Leval, Lapisse and Sebastiani advancing on the Allied lines in temperatures above 100 degrees Fahrenheit. Overenthusiastic forward movements of the Guards and a pounding of the King's German legion caused high casualty rates. Around 500 guardsmen were lost in around twenty minutes. Major-General MacKenzie and his brigade were hard hit. Of 2,200 bayonets, fifteen officers (including MacKenzie) and 600 men became corpses or casualties. The four German battalions (the 1st, 2nd, 5th and 7th) were the greatest sufferers as a group, receiving 51 per cent casualties.

One wounded man was spotted wandering around apparently not complaining. His head had been struck by a round shot which had driven in bone and squeezed out some brain tissue. Guthrie made the point that some severe cranial strikes had surprisingly little constitutional upset and frequently the adrenalin surge and fear of action hid the serious nature of injury. The soldier later died. Another casualty had an unfortunate outcome after one of the French attacks:

> A soldier of the 29th Regiment was struck on the right parietal bone in a similar manner [by a musket ball], shortly after daylight, at the battle of Talavera, during the first attack on the hill, the key of the British position.

He walked to me soon afterwards, to the place where the wounded of the evening before had been collected in the rear [i.e. the field dressing station]. Being otherwise employed, I heard his story, but could not attend to him at the moment, and found him sometime afterwards insensible, with a slow, intermitting pulse, breathing loudly, and supposed to be dying. The fractured parts were sufficiently broken to admit to the introduction of two elevators [steel levers], by means of which they [fragments of bone] were gradually removed, together with a large coagulum of blood, which had depressed [squashed] the brain. When this had been done, the brain regained its level, [i.e. returned to its former shape after the compression] the man opened his eyes, looked around, knew and thanked me. The pulse and breathing became regular; he said he suffered only a little pain in the part, and should soon get well. He died however on the third day.[14]

Had he recollected the blood clot, which again on this occasion fatally compressed his brain, or was his death as a result of early sepsis? How often such cases must have been a disappointment to the surgeon.

Wounds of less critical areas could prove just as mortal. Colonel Donellan of the 48th having been struck on his knee by a musket ball, was observed on the field by Guthrie. This was a painful, serious and potentially fatal injury most often demanding amputation. The wound

gave him so little uneasiness, that he could scarcely be persuaded to proceed to the rear. At a little distance from the fire of the enemy, we talked over the affairs of the moment, when, tossing his leg about on his saddle, he declared he felt no inconvenience from the wound, and would go back, as he saw his corps was very much exposed. After he had stayed with me a couple of hours [presumably Guthrie had dressed his injury, extracted a ball and administered water], I persuaded him to go into the town. This injury, although at first to all appearance so trifling, proceeded so rapidly as to prevent any relief at last being obtained from amputation, and caused his death in a few [four] days.[15]

His demise was probably as a result of joint infection and septicaemia.

Naturally many of Guthrie's cases were simpler. One of these was seen out on the hillside:

A soldier was struck, on the hill of Talavera, on the breast-plate [brass cross-belt plate] by a ball, which, as he believed, had gone through his body. He was white as a sheet, and desperately frightened. On opening his coat, I found the ball had indented the breast-plate, and made a round mark on the skin, without going deeper. I did not see him again for several days, until after crossing the bridge of Arzobispo, on the retreat to Truxillo. He was then engaged in disembowelling a fine fat wild hog, amongst a herd of which we had, unluckily for them, just fallen. He recognised me at once; said that as I told him, he had been more frightened than hurt; that he had been bled largely and well physicked and after two or three days had thought no more of it. I am bound to add, that in gratitude, he offered me a leg of the pig, which having nothing to eat, I could not but accept. It supplied a dinner for three others who are now no more.[16]

It was at the time of this latter case on the battlefield that Sir Arthur Wellesley was struck and bruised near the left clavicle (collar bone) by a spent ball.[17]

Many wounded men at Talavera were beyond the help of a surgeon. Lieutenant Close of the 1/48th on Wellesley's left centre, had earlier been advancing against French columns crossing the ravine, lay down, taking cover from artillery fire.

When Ensign Van der Meulen was wounded, I went to take the colour from the sergeant who held it. When I arrived at the centre a shell fell. We lay down until it had burst. My head was between the legs of a soldier, and a soldier was on my right and left side close against me. The shell burst; the man whose legs my head was protected by had half his head carried off; the other two were dreadfully mangled: the body of one was laid bare from his loins to his breast, and both legs of the other were carried off near the knee.[18]

Many were injured by the French artillery firing ricochet shot and common shell – the rolling or air-burst shells causing mayhem.

Guthrie's colleagues received several of the wounded of the 23rd Light Dragoons and 1st KGL Hussar casualties after the debacle against the French 27th Ligne and Merlin's cavalry. Apart from the usual combat injuries, there were broken heads and bones to bandage and set after many tumbles for mount and trooper in a dried up ramblas.

One soldier on Wellesley's left was later brought to Guthrie. This man was fortunate, to have survived a through-and-through chest wound. The ball had gone in, striking the left sixth rib and

had passed out four inches nearer the back. As the point of the finger indicated the presence of broken bone [note the exploration of the wound by the surgeon's finger], I enlarged the anterior [front] wound, and then found that the ball had driven some spiculae [splinters] of bone into the surface of the lung, which appeared to have been previously attached [i.e.

stuck] to the pleura costalis [the internal lining of the chest cavity] at that part. These having been removed, together with a piece of coat which had been carried in with the ball, a small clean wound was left, which gradually healed up, the man accompanying me on the retreat over the bridge of Arzobispo.[19]

Marshal Victor was intensely frustrated at not being allowed yet a further assault on Wellesley's line and was reluctant to follow the French withdrawal. Around 10pm, the firing ceased.

Around 1,500 corpses, hundreds of horses and 13,000 wounded lay out on the field – 4,000 of them Allied combatants. There were around 9,000 French casualties and 3,000 Spanish. At the end of this second day, as the wounded streamed into Talavera, Guthrie and his fellow battalion surgeons were overwhelmed. The thousands of wounded took over two days to get in. The French in their retreat had apparently collected some of their most injured men in seventy to eighty bullock-carts. Another ghastly problem awaited the injured. The tinder-dry crops and grass had been burning since around six o'clock, set alight by hot wadding and shell bursts. A history of the 24th recorded, 'Some of the men who were severely wounded while the battalion was moving in double-quick time, from the left of Brigadier General Cameron's division to the right of the Guards, were burnt to death by the flames from the long dry grass, set on fire by the shells. The men who went out to save their unfortunate comrades were forced back with their clothes burnt, and their pouches blown up on their backs.'[20] If this didn't make retrieval of casualties by exhausted men difficult, the failing light did. Many hurt soldiers lay out on the field or in a dressing station all night until dawn made it possible to get them back to Talavera.

Dr William Fergusson, a Scot, as were so many of the Army Medical Department, was born at Ayr on 19 June 1773. He was surgeon to the 90th Foot for around two years, then served with the 67th for three years and the 5th for a year. He had been stationed at St Domingo, Holland twice and Copenhagen. He remained on the staff from 1800 until 1805, when he was promoted Deputy Inspector of Hospitals, at which rank he served at Talavera. In November 1809 this officer had proven his ability by being appointed Inspector of Hospitals (Portugal only) under Lieutenant-General Sir William Carr Beresford. He obtained his MD (Aberdeen) and FRCP (Edinburgh) in 1812, was promoted Inspector General in 1813, then worked in Guadeloupe in 1815. Retiring on half pay in 1817, he practised at Windsor, was surgeon to HRH the Duke of Gloucester and wrote *Notes and Recollections of a Professional Life* (London, 1846) and other works. He died in 1847. Dr William Fergusson was the senior medical officer at Talavera, having been appointed thus at Oporto. Both he and Guthrie had formerly been recommended for promotion after the crossing of the Douro – the former advised for Inspector of Hospitals, the latter for Staff Surgeon. Parsimony and ignorance of the talents of these two men negated both well-justified appointments.

During Talavera, Fergusson was confined to bed with dysentery, which affected many other combatants during this action. Guthrie not only worked as a surgeon, but also acted as a link-man for Fergusson, conveying messages and orders to other unit surgeons. He was apparently highly critical of two of Fergusson's colleagues – Inspector Franck and a Dr Taggart (I have been unable to identify this doctor). These two 'inhumane' men left the site of the incipient action and didn't reappear for a week. Guthrie, true to his nature, was so angry that he demanded a court-martial of the two doctors.

Although we do not know its location, one of the buildings in the town was used as the regimental hospital for the 29th and Guthrie assiduously collected his own battalion casualties there. Other injured men were scattered indiscriminately in what would be termed general hospitals, where staff surgeons, mates, purveyors and apothecaries came up when it was safe to do so. Guthrie's segregation of casualties into smaller hospitals lay outside normal practice. It did have its benefits. For example the sick and injured were with their own surgeon and comrades; being a battalion hospital meant the lesser risk of contagion and a smaller chance of spreading wound infection; there was commitment of the clinician to patients whom he knew and the dispensing of supplies and medication was simpler. This part of Guthrie's practice and administration was to get him into trouble later. In general terms the mortality in smaller hospitals, given competent staff, was three to four times lower than in larger hospitals.

Guthrie's two assistants did much of the routine legwork. The battalion casualties after Talavera numbered six officers and ninety-eight men wounded, of whom, probably twenty would die and another ten to twenty would remain in hospital seriously hurt. Guthrie treated his own patients first before leaving his charges. The death of his patients caused Guthrie to reflect on a rare complication of injury to the diaphragm (the thin muscular sheet that separates the cavity of the belly from that of the chest). He commented:

A soldier of the 29th Regiment was wounded at the Battle of Talavera, and died in four days of the receipt of the ball, which went through the chest into the liver [which is what would have killed him, causing bile peritonitis and bleeding]. I found, on examining the body, an opening in the central part of the diaphragm of an oval shape, the edges smoothing off as if they were inclined to become round; this opening was nearly two inches long, evidently ready to allow either the stomach or the intestines to pass through it on any exertion.[21]

He noted that, had the unfortunate man survived, the hole in the diaphragm would have been a problem, in so far as, had the soldier stressed himself at any time, the abdominal contents would have been forced up into the chest. If the blood supply of those organs was then to be compressed, then there was a severe risk of gangrene of the organs, with fatal peritonitis.

Fatigue parties, allocated by battalion for burial duties, were given the task of breaking the hot rocky ground, which was so difficult that funeral pyres were made. The stench on the next day was intolerable and local inhabitants were ordered to assist with the French interments. Not a few wounded Frenchmen were surreptitiously slain and plundered by soldiers and civilians, until fired on by British troops. If the evacuation of the casualties was tardy then their reception in town was ramshackle, a common enough problem in these early days of the war, when the Army Medical Department was transiently overwhelmed. Two accounts bear witness to this – the first an anonymous sergeant of the Guards, the other Augustus Schaumann, a Commissary officer:

> great numbers of wounded on both sides lying on the field, their cries & groans were most piercingly grievous however at daylight all the assistance that could be, was given & parties were sent out from every Corps to collect them & bury the dead. This was a part of service by no means pleasant; mangled Carcases [sic] and broken limbs, was a Spectacle truly shocking & notwithstanding the utmost tenderness was used, the removal of the wounded occasioned the most piercing shrieks – It was my lot to go with a Corporal of the company to the general Hospital in Talavera, & I beheld what I never wish to see again – the road [about a mile] leading to the town was literally covered with the wounded, & wounded men dying whilst being carried there. Every street in the town was filled with them & absolutely impassable for no place had been prepared for their reception, & the Spaniards would not admit them into their houses, not even the Officers who had been billeted on them previous to the Action, without the interference of the Alcade.

On his errand Schaumann noted grimly,

> in the town I passed a convent, where the wounded were having their limbs amputated and dressed. Never shall I forget the heartrending cries which could be heard coming from the windows in the front of this building; while from one of the windows the amputated arms and legs were being flung out upon a small square below. In front of the door lay the wounded, all of whom had been deposited there as fast as they arrived, awaiting their turn. Many of them were already dead.[22]

Often it seems, being witnesses to hasty, essential and crude surgery on the awake patient was anathema to even battle-hardened men. Guthrie had now to tend the cases in his own hospital. H Everard, the historian of the 29th, stated, 'The town of Talavera now became crowded with wounded, those of the 29th, through the energy of Dr Guthrie, were however soon lodged.' Being an experienced, dextrous and skilled man, he would later be working with other battalion surgeons, giving advice, lending instruments, medication and bandages. Interestingly, we have no evidence of any triage (priority case selection) amongst those desperate in anxious and painful queues. Many would die waiting.

Threatened by Soult and Victor and with the Spaniards having suffered severe reverses in late 1809 and short of provisions, Wellington retired westwards. One of the other outstanding reasons for Wellington's retrograde was the lack of mates for his battalions. With untried Portuguese battalions and autumn illness weakening his force, retreat seemed his only and most sensible course.

Marshal Soult marching south would have taken Wellesley's depot of stores and sick and wounded at Plasencia, en route to Portugal. Sir Arthur had to leave the hospitalized patients to the care of General Cuesta, whilst he made sure of a movement towards Portugal. It was anticipated that Victor would enter Talavera in the first week in August and, with now 45,000 French before him, Wellesley escaped by crossing the Tagus on 4 August, at the bridge at Arzobispo, securing the bridge at Almaraz. Marching via Truxillo, Merida and Badajoz, Guthrie moved on with his battalion, leaving injured men (around 1,500) in Talavera, under the care of three surgeons, Mr Somers Higgins, Mr McDougal and five assistants, including the celebrated James Goodall Elkington and assistant surgeon Curby (of the 29th), taken previously at Plasencia. Guthrie's abandoned charges were Curby and Lieutenant Stanhope and twenty-seven severely injured privates. The latter were all to die. The two officers were sent to France. No doubt due to the non-combatant and humanitarian role played by Curby, he was released or exchanged then rejoined his regiment later in the year. Marshal Victor, after entering Talavera on 6 August, was witness to looting and placed guards at the hospitals and saw to the provisioning of the Allied casualties.

Having lost the staggering number of 500 men en route from Talavera, about 2,000 casualties, by hook or by crook, struggled and sweated in pain along the poor road to Truxillo (the birthplace of Pissaro). A biographical sketch of Guthrie makes the comment: 'The retreat of the British army across the Tagus at the bridge of Arzobispo was disastrous for those wounded who tried to accompany their regiments in preference to remaining prisoners at Talavera.'[23]

Guthrie marched with the 29th to Deleytosa, then on to Jaracejo and Medellin, from where it trudged on towards Merida on 26 August. Tired and thin, with patched worn clothing, the old 29th had a 'perfect order and cleanliness of their arms, ... steadiness on parade', 'firm and free marching'. The battalion was described by Wellesley in a dispatch of 12 September as, 'the best Regiment in this Army'.[24] The 29th, in Hill's division, were stationed in Puebla de la Calçada, situated between Merida and Badajoz. The sick and wounded went off to Elvas, where assistant surgeon Evans of the 29th was to assist with their care – what had happened to Guthrie? Apparently, most of the more severely wounded except those of one battalion had reached the convent of Deleytosa near Truxillo.

Conditions in this convent were far from good and a soldier called Richard Cooper was an in-patient there, suffering with dysentery. He described his plight, 'My case was pitiable, my appetite and hearing gone; feet and legs like ice, three blisters on my back and feet unhealed and undressed; my shirt sticking in the wound caused by blisters ... and worst of all nobody seemed to give a straw for me.' Sadly his impressions of Elvas and subsequent convalescent depôts were little better. At Elvas, Cooper was one of twenty men in a small room, with no ventilation – eighteen died. At the next hospital, he was accommodated in a charnel house and finally, at the dilapidated miserable unit at Celorico, he had no towel or soap and lived on ration biscuit, salt pork and wine.[25]

The convent at Deleytosa was a medical staging house, an intermediate hospital where much surgery was undertaken. Guthrie doled out experienced decisions and selective, conservative surgery. He was appalled at the unnecessarily mutilating surgery carried out by some of his colleagues. He named the hospital as the 'slaughter-house of the wounded of the British army, from the loss of life which took place through the want of previous care and defective surgical knowledge'. The principal problem in Guthrie's mind was the high rate of amputation of both arms and legs. Wounds by now would be dreadfully septic and he saw a good few sink after operation for this reason. Experience had brought him the understanding that many limbs could be saved through less aggressive surgery. Such was his integrity that he was prepared to lose friends over this matter. His biographical sketch goes on, 'It was here [Deleytosa], that Mr Guthrie, whose opinion was considered valuable, from the service he had at that time seen, formally protested against the amputation of several arms which had been condemned for gunshot fracture. His decision [advice] was followed, but not forgotten for years by one or two persons, however it might have been forgiven.'[26] As so often in such campaigns the problem was both disseminating new ideas and convincing surgeons of lessons learnt through experience. By 1814, clearly some surgeons were still not following Guthrie's teachings,

At the last battle in France, Toulouse, the late Lord, then Sir Hussey Vivian, commanding the cavalry, had his left arm broken by a musket ball, and was advised by the surgeons present to have it amputated. This he refused until he saw some persons of more experience, and Mr Guthrie, then in charge of that part of the army engaged on the right bank of the

Garonne, decided it should not be removed. Many years afterwards, when Lord Vivian presented him to his second wife on her marriage, he did it with the compliment: 'I introduce you to Mr Guthrie, to whom both you and I are indebted for the arm on which you are now leaning.'[27]

In later years as the Crimean War loomed ahead, Guthrie taught that the removal of an arm was rarely if ever needed, except after wounding by cannon-shot. 'The elbow-joint has been cut out, the head of the bone has been sawed off from its connexion [sic] with the shoulder, any portion of the middle part removed, but not the arm itself excised, not even if its principal artery be injured unless mortification [gangrene] has taken place.' The point is that Guthrie would go to any lengths, even leaving a numb or unstable arm as a partly useful limb than randomly amputate without thought. Bold enough doctrine for these times.

In late August, early September, Guthrie joined the battalion at Puebla de Calçada, situated on the plain of the Guadiana, and it was here that a 'bilious remittent fever' struck the brigade. This could have been malaria or typhoid. Medical facilities here were deficient. We know that, later, by 1 November, 290 of 439 rank and file of the battalion were (present or absent) sick.[28] Guthrie must have laboured furiously over this outbreak. It was reported that 'the corps under the care of Mr Guthrie, with an equal number of men and sick, had only a line of graves half as long as the other two [battalions]'. What is fascinating is that this was achieved, 'by discipline, not physic – prevention rather than cure'.[29] Clearly what Guthrie had done was to segregate batches of men and ensure disease containment, a policy that would later massively enhance Wellington's strike force in 1813.

Two things then happened to Guthrie. The first event was not so fortunate. Simply worn out by his efforts, Guthrie went down with a serious fever (typhoid or malaria). He was conveyed in great discomfort from Portalegre, to which Hill had been ordered, on to Abrantes in a bullock-cart and there, it was supposed, he would die.

We have an amusing detail of Guthrie's self-medication during the illness. His biographical sketch relates:

It was the fashion to give [quinine – containing Peruvian or Jesuit's] bark in these fevers, and the inspector-general, in taking his last leave of Mr Guthrie, as he supposed, inculcated the necessity of his taking it; he obeyed, although against his own practice and feelings. It made him so much worse, that he desired the regimental nurse [a wife or an orderly] whom he fortunately had kept with him, to buy, if possible, a couple of dozen lemons, and slice them into a pitcher of water fresh from the spring. It held two gallons. This he drank during the night, with the effect of causing a profuse perspiration for several hours, after which his fever left him, but with feet so swollen and legs so weak as to be unable to walk for several weeks.[30]

The second issue concerned his career. After at least one recommendation for promotion to the rank of staff surgeon, a further effort had proved successful, on the basis that there was no one else suitable for the post! It always seemed that Guthrie's career was continually hampered by his youthful entry into the service. We know that Joseph A Stanford was listed as surgeon to the 29th from 4 January 1810, having transferred from assistant surgeoncy in the Buffs. It was on this same date that Guthrie was appointed to the staff of the Army Medical Department.

On 23 November Dr Fergusson was appointed Inspector of Hospitals to the Portuguese army and Inspector James Franck was appointed head of the British Medical Department. Franck had been Physician to the Forces under Sir Charles Stewart in Corsica and had served in Egypt. He had Wellington's confidence but possessed neither the initiative, administrative ability nor personality of his great successor, Dr James McGrigor.

Sometime in the spring of 1810 Guthrie was posted home for the recovery of his health. He must have been in a particularly low state for this sick leave to be allowed. We know he returned to Lisbon in the winter of that same year, thus being away from service for around six to eight months. While he was away, the contest at Busaco had taken place on 27 September and Marshal Massena had advanced to Lisbon, now solidly protected by Wellington's Lines of Torres Vedras. Wellington's strong defences defied Marshal André Massena, whose force soon riddled with starvation and illness was forced to retreat. So a victory for the British Commander-in-Chief, which cost the French around 25,000 men, vindicated Wellington's strong policy of withdrawal. In the middle of November 1810, Massena withdrew to Santarem to refresh, feed and care for his broken force – also to await reinforcements.

On Guthrie's return at this time, he was to take up appointment as Staff Surgeon to the 4th Division under the Hon. Sir Lowry Cole. He purchased a horse and a mule in Lisbon, also hiring a servant, who promptly ran off with Guthrie's blanket and evening meal! A kindly assistant surgeon (whose name he had forgotten) provided him with some food then, lent him a blanket. The assistant surgeon's soldier-servant stood guard over the animals. Progressing on the following day, our surgeon noted, 'The country was desolate; dead horses, asses and men lay about in all directions and there was little to be obtained of any kind.' The loan of the blanket presented a problem. It was, 'almost a fatal a gift as the shirt of Nessus [a centaur that, by dipping a garment in its blood, fatally poisoned Hercules]. From that time I ceased to sleep, my flesh seemed to be creeping and crawling all night, I became spotted all over, and wondered what could be the matter with me.' Reaching Coimbra, he billeted himself on a priest and one of his nieces that kept the house. She and her servant got rid of many large fleas and Guthrie found his now clean blanket and clothes hanging out in the sun to dry. Travelling on, he almost drowned crossing the Guadiana at Jerumenha. From here to the end of 1812, he was to further establish his growing reputation as a senior military surgeon.

'All the Fiends in Pandemonium' – Albuera

Guthrie was now serving with Sir Lowry Cole's 4th Division and so had advisory, technical and organizational roles, in addition to being responsible for the management of senior battalion and staff sick and wounded. The 4th Division like some others was heavily committed throughout the war, which offered so much opportunity to someone of Guthrie's ability. On his return, he accompanied the division in the 'the first little affair of Campo Mayor'. The French had taken Badajoz and Olivenza and Cole's Division (with some additional dragoons) had reached Portalegre, north of Campo Mayor on 22 March, on which day Beresford set out south. The 4th had had a gruelling march to reach Portalegre and were allowed to rest for two days. The whole army was before Campo Mayor on 25 March.

A brave old Portuguese major had defended the neglected and untenably defensible town and held out for six days, at first refusing surrender, so giving time for Beresford's force to arrive. Mortier was not expecting Beresford and had detailed General Marie-Victor Latour-Marbourg to disable the fortress. The latter commander had two regiments of hussars (2nd and 10th) and a dragoon regiment (26th) with him – also the 100th of the Ligne and some artillery, around 2,400 men in all. As Beresford advanced with the 2nd and Portuguese Divisions, the 4th trudged along as reserve in the rear. Guthrie travelled with the divisional staff. Beresford's cavalry support was thinner than it should be for a force of around 18,000 men – merely 1,500 sabres – commanded by Brigadier-General Robert Ballard Long. The 13th Light Dragoons with the 1st and 7th Portuguese cavalry in support, crashed into the French horsemen and, having sent the French dragoons flying, set off on a reckless pursuit. The upshot in terms of Allied losses was ninety killed and wounded and seventy-seven taken prisoner. The French losses from Captain Andrew Cleeve's guns and the cavalry were around 200 men. While the 2nd Division with Hamilton's Portuguese marched on to Elvas, the 4th Division and Guthrie rested for a day in Campo Mayor. Whilst helping with the injured, Guthrie's surgeons would also be looking after rheumatics and sore and broken feet.

We are reminded of the *sequelae* of sabre cuts inflicted by the notorious Le Marchant 1796 pattern light cavalry sabre in a distressing anecdote of this action.

An eye-witness to the action reported:

> Yesterday, a French Captain of Dragoons brought over a trumpeter, demanding permission to search among the dead for his Colonel; ... The Captain was a fine young man, and had his arm in a sling. Many of us went with him – it was a truly bloody scene, being almost all sabre wounds, the slain were all naked, the peasants having stripped them in the night; it was long before we could find the French Colonel – he was lying on his face, his naked body weltering in blood, and as soon as he was turned up, the Officer knew him, he gave a sort of scream and sprung off his horse, dashed his helmet on the ground, knelt by the body, took the bloody hand and kissed it many times in an agony of grief; it was an affecting and awful scene ... The French Colonel I have already mentioned, was killed by a corporal of the 13th; this corporal had killed one of his men, and he was so enraged, that he sallied out himself and attacked the corporal – the corporal was well-mounted and a good swordsman, as was also the Colonel – both defended for some time, the corporal cut him twice in the face, his helmet came off at the second, when the corporal slew him by a cut which nearly cleft his skull asunder, it cut as deep as the nose through the brain.[1]

The 4th Division had marched from the Lines to Espinhal and then to Portalegre, 6–25 March. Cole, no doubt urged on by our staff surgeon, insisted on his men being re-shod before moving on. There were no shoes at Elvas, so the delay, whilst awaiting a supply convoy from Lisbon, would hold up the division for a week. This logistic failure possibly cost the Allies dear, since the town of Badajoz, being incompletely repaired, would have been an easier prey for Beresford. This was the second time (the first being during the retreat to Corunna) that shortage of footwear had caused significant problems to the British army.

Guthrie was present at the siege of Olivenza, a poorly defended town, whose magazines and sick had not been moved out by the French. The town held out for five days, surrendering on 14 April. The ill-shod 4th Division and Guthrie had been left behind to see to this. One logistical problem for Guthrie was to deal with ninety-eight French patients, left in charge of sixteen surgeons, a very generous medical provision. Survivors were fed back through the chain of hospitals to Lisbon, where most would be returned prisoners of war. The shoes for the division had arrived on 14 April, so Guthrie now marched south to join the rest of the army. Badajoz was to be invested and Wellington had arrived at Elvas on 20 April. Having reconnoitred the fortress and town on the 22nd, he directed that the outlying defensive positions – the Pardaleras, the Picurina (both on the south bank of the Guadiana) and the strong fort of San Cristobal on the north – were to be reduced before a main assault on the town.

The town was commanded by a French engineer, General Baron Armand Phillipon and defended by his 3,000 troops. Whilst the rather inadequate siege artillery was assembled and upon the day of Wellington's departure from the area, on 25 April, the rain fell in torrents and Beresford required a further secure passage over the Guadiana, which needed to be established in case of a retrograde manœuvre by the Allies. The 4th Division was despatched to assist with this precaution. Meanwhile the first siege of Badajoz was off to an inauspicious start. On 8 May the trenches were opened, but work was dogged by rocky ground, forays by the French and poor weather. Casualties from the assault on San Cristobal were high and fell mainly on Guthrie's unit. Over 6–12 May there were around 530 British and 200 Portuguese wounded for the battalion surgeons and himself to sort out. Of the former all but seven were from Colonel James Kemmis's brigade (3/27th, 1/40th and 97th Foot) of the 4th and most of the Portuguese injured were from the 17th Line and artillery. On 10 May, news arrived of the movement of a French army from Seville of more than 20,000 men. This force under Marshal Soult caused Beresford to request concentration of the Spanish and Allied forces at a village eleven miles or so south of Badajoz, at Albuera (meaning the village/place of mills). The siege of Badajoz was postponed, and the siege artillery sent back to Elvas. So the bloody capture of the town was delayed fortuitously under the threat of an approaching relief force. Wellington had anticipated such a problem and it was now up to Beresford to rout the approaching French army, commanded by Soult.

In the north, Massena the old 'Fox', anxious to regain his reputation after his traumatic ejection from Portugal, was to make a stringent effort to relieve Almeida and brush aside any British assault on the town. Wellington had been back to deal with this threat since 29 April with a force of around 37,000 to face Massena's advancing army of 48,200 men. It was at this time that Wellington partly blamed maladministration of the hospitals for the reduced size of his force (by delaying the return of convalescents to the line), composed principally of the 1st, 3rd, 5th, 6th, 7th and Light Divisions.

On 5/6 May the Battle of Fuentes de Oñoro was hard fought to prevent access of the French to Almeida. There were 192, 958 and 255 Allied troops killed, wounded and taken respectively, 1,405 in all. The ratio of killed to wounded was thus 1:5 – a lower ratio than usual, as will be seen when compared with the action that was to follow at Albuera. On the French side, the comparable figures were a total of 2,192 with 267, 1,878 and forty-seven dead, injured and taken, a kill to wound ration of 1:7. Massena had failed in his objectives and with this, his ultimate failure in Iberia, the Fox was retired from command and it would be Marshal Jean de Dieu Soult who was to provide energetic but limited tactical opposition to the Duke until 1814. The Marshal had arrived at Seville, to join his Army of Andalusia on 14 March. With General Thomas Graham (later Viscount Lynedoch) no longer a threat after the action at Barrosa, he could now march to the relief and support of Badajoz, where so many soldiers of both sides were to suffer death or agony during the three brave but costly investments.

After the first abortive siege of Badajoz, the 4th Division along with our surgeon and some of General Xavier Castaños's infantry were the last to leave the parallels to cover the retiring main force, marching off to face Soult. A worthy old Scots staff officer, nicknamed 'Randy Dandy' actually moved to Albuera, having forgotten to withdraw the last of the pickets, and rode hell for leather and retrieved them. Fortunately Phillipon and his garrison neither pursued them nor set out to join Soult![2]

Wellington had actually previously suggested Albuera as a possible site of engagement to arrest Soult's force. Sadly, it would be Wellington's absence which would punish the army so dearly on the 16 May. This underpins the benefit of minimizing casualty rates by careful deployment of forces under an astute commander. As Guthrie's biographer emphasizes, 'The soldiery were always contented when on the field of battle, provided, as they said, they always had that long-nosed patrone of theirs with them.'[3]

On 10 May, Soult's 23,000-strong force set off on the 120 or so miles to relieve Badajoz. Arriving on the 13th at Valverde, a town which was soon to be heavily utilized by the Army Medical Department, Beresford moved the seven miles eastwards to the village of Albuera. Two Spanish forces under General Joachim Blake and Castaños were to link with Beresford's two divisions. The latter took a while to arrive. William Stewart's 2nd Division consisted of more than 5,400 of all ranks, but Lowry Cole's 4th Division only just more than 2,100 British men (some of Kemmis's brigade had not been able to cross the flooded Guadiana river). This is relevant, since Guthrie was said to have been the only British staff surgeon available on the field of Albuera. Had Beresford ordered one staff surgeon of the larger 2nd Division to remain at Elvas or Valverde? Whatever the explanation for the absence of a senior colleague, this made Guthrie the Principal Medical Officer on the field. This was a devastatingly thin provision for the bloody action that was to follow.

So, the 4th Division with British and German soldiers, bolstered up by Portuguese and Spaniards, moved tardily into position. Two native guides, appointed by the Quartermaster General, who had been entrusted to point the division towards Albuera, had fallen asleep at a critical fork in the track, thus Stewart wasted one hour marching towards Jerumenha. Guthrie, riding with Cole's staff through the night, should have been at Albuera at about six in the morning. It was said that Cole and his staff, at the head of the 4th were 'one mile distant from the nearest soldier under the orders of Marshal Beresford' when they heard the first gunfire – around 8am.[4] The staff and Guthrie closed up the men marching behind and rode onto the field. Guthrie and Cole trotted over to confer with the

Marshal. Some artillery was then in place at the village, anticipating a frontal assault by Soult's men. Guthrie, attired in a blue boat cloak, moved up alone to the left of the 'German artillery', i.e. Cleeve and Sympher's batteries. He had wished that, being dressed in a blue garment, he might not be 'fired at in particular'! He set about estimating the strength of the apparent French ranged before him, a task at which he was apparently most expert.

What, from the surgeon's point of view were the conditions on the field Guthrie had to consider? The weather was deteriorating and the grey clouds were to precede miserable rain and hail. The previous night, the Allied soldiers had stripped the poor village of anything combustible, timbers, doors, thatching, etc., an issue that would cause considerable suffering to the wounded on the 16th. The vegetation was different to that which the visitors see today. There were then more vines and olive trees and thus improved cover for French deployment. The terrain was otherwise open with undulations scarcely worthy of being called hills, but to the enemy combatants still there were slopes to climb.

Guthrie set up a dressing station/field hospital in the village, where he and some battalion surgeons would perform early arrest of haemorrhage and other life-saving procedures. Junior and full battalion surgeons would attend to their duties in the front, but as usual there was a limited degree of help that could be given on the spot – water to drink, bandaging, extraction of easily removed debris from wounds – the optimum course of action would have been for the wounded to be brought into the village. Since later in the day there were overwhelming casualties, restricted shelter and just not enough bearers or fit men to help move them, many wounded had to be treated out on the battlefield.

There was one interesting surgical conundrum for our surgeon to address, before the main French assault. It came from the regimental surgeon of the 29th – Guthrie's old unit – part of Major-General Daniel Hoghton's brigade. They stood, early in the action, behind Major-General Charles von Alten's men and the village. At this stage, Mr (later Dr) Joseph Stanford, a surgeon of nine years' experience, approached Guthrie, wishing permission to

> cut off the leg of one of the artillerymen just struck by a cannon-shot, from a French battery, which had halted, unlimbered, and returned the fire of the German guns, with the hope of distracting their attention. Mr Guthrie desired (merely) a tourniquet to be applied, if necessary, and that the man should be left in sight in a hut to the rear. This being done, Dr Stanford returned, saying the man earnestly prayed that his leg might be cut off. This Guthrie again refused, saying, 'These gentlemen below,' pointing to the French, 'do not mean to make their serious attack here; it will be over there,' (pointing to some hills on the right) 'where you now see nothing, but of which, if the French get possession, we shall be killed or taken to a man.

On those hills the two British divisions must win the battle. Leave not your regiment for an instant or you will not see it again.' Dr Stanford thought it harsh, shrugged his shoulders, and walked away, possibly descanting on the evils of a little brief authority. In a few minutes the 2nd and 4th divisions were in march [sic] for the hills designated. They were too late, the French were before them and the contest was desperate. Dr Stanford's regiment [the 29th] went in action 410 [actually 507] and came out 95! [more probably 171].[5]

Whether Guthrie had correctly predicted or observed the ensuing and all-important French out-flanking manœuvre by General Jean Girard and General Honoré Gazan's division and Latour-Marbourg's cavalry is conjectural, but he rightly ordered the 29th's surgeon to be immediately ready to attend to and direct movement of the victims of the serious French onslaught. Mr Guthrie then placed himself 'on the plain a little in the rear of the two British divisions of infantry with the cavalry on the right'. Interestingly, he was clearly directing medical operations, near to the engagement at an early stage of the action, at considerable personal risk. It proved impossible to keep out of the way of shot or shell and Guthrie's assistant staff surgeon Bolman was struck on the chest by a round shot, which passed 'through him'. I can find no record of this unfortunate surgeon – he may have been attached to the King's German Legion. Guthrie was now deprived of all experienced surgical staff and had only the battalion surgeons to help.

In a nutshell the bloody conflict at Albuera consisted of an all-day diversionary attack by General Godinot on the village, which pulled in some of Beresford's troops and artillery. Around an hour and a half after the assault on the village started, a strong force of experienced French infantry under Girard and Gazan, supported by cavalry, moved initially under cover of olive groves, over two small converging streams, to roll up Beresford's right flank to the south. A massive assault by 19 French infantry battalions and 3,500 cavalry was to be met initially by inadequate Allied cavalry support and some hastily organized Spanish infantry units with General Stewart's division headed by Colborne's brigade running up to support the Spaniards. This was the beginning of a prolonged and desperate fire-fight. The rain now began to fall and the strong support for the Spaniards by Colonel John Colborne's unit was to be negated by rain interfering with musketry and a serious assault by General Latour-Marbourg's cavalry. Seeing the Allied right flank exposed and realizing the effect of the rain on infantry firepower, Marbourg charged the flank of the British infantry in line from the side and rear, with the Polish 1st Lancers of the Vistula Legion and Hussars. Many defenceless men were ridden down, lanced and then often repeatedly stabbed on the ground. This particular attack and the severe close action of musketry/case shot fire at 20–90 yards would account for a higher than average kill to wound ratio (around 1:1 in the

3rd and 1:2 for the 2/48th) in some infantry battalions. Whilst Hoghton and Colonel Robert Abercrombie's brigades came forward to carry on the harsh exchange against the two French divisions, the slaughter continued.

The problem was that both Soult and Beresford's moves were less resolute than expected, Soult did not push harder on the Allied right, delaying General Werlé's assault, while Beresford had not strongly reinforced his beleaguered flank. Beresford's error was belatedly (around one hour after the commencement of the battle) rectified by General Lowry Cole, who made the decision to advance the one mile or so forward to save the day. Cole's division consisting mainly of Colonel William Myers's brigade (about 2,200 bayonets), soon assisted by General William Harvey's Portuguese brigade (2,927 men), engaged Werlé's infantry.[6] Brushing aside a flank attack by four regiments of French Dragoons, the Portuguese under William Harvey proved to Myers that they had great metal. Soult's last significant onslaught was to shatter on the steadfast firepower of the fusiliers – French columns or 'ordre mixte' would be at an extreme disadvantage against spread British line volley fire. With distressing casualty rates, the fusiliers ('that astonishing infantry') took great punishment but advanced with volley and bayonet until the French assaults began to melt away. Hoghton and Abercrombie's battered brigades reduced the two exhausted French divisions of Girard and Gazan further. A general withdrawal by Soult heralded a bitter Pyrrhic victory for the Allies. 'For relentless intensity of killing over a small area of ground, there would be no other Peninsular battlefield that looked as shocking as the field of Albuera', Fletcher correctly summarizes, 'but for sheer bloody slaughter none could compare with the nightmare of Albuera'.[7]

The overall Allied casualties were around 5,900 of 35,000 (17 per cent). The French had casualties of around 6,000 of a fighting force of 24,000 (25 per cent). Colborne's brigade lost 1,413 out of 2,066 men, a 68 per cent attrition rate (the 3rd, 2/48th and 2/66th Foot had 85, 75 and 61 per cent casualty rates respectively). The issues contributing to such a traumatic fight with enormous casualty rates were the inadequate anticipation and assessment of Soult's flanking movement, the intensity of the close fire-fight, lack of preparation to receive cavalry, the weather and the infliction of multiple injuries by lancers.

Before battle, the battalion surgeons had let their respective commanding officers know where the regimental aid post would be, scattered areas in the open ground, near any tree or rock or ruin. They directed as many away from there as soon as feasible, but before long the local surgeons would be totally swamped by hurt men and in the evening the majority lay out on the damp ground waiting for death or succour.

It is worthwhile considering the tasks and conditions which lay before our medical colleagues after this sanguinary encounter. Here is the account given in Guthrie's biography:

Rain came down in torrents; the lightening was more terrific than the flashes of the guns, the thunder louder; and what with the noise of the cannon, the shouts of the combatants, the cries and moans of the wounded, the outcry and exclamations of some flying Spaniards, and the darkness of the day, it might have been thought that all the fiends in pandemonium were taking their holiday. At three o'clock the fight was over, and Mr Guthrie found three thousand wounded at his feet, with four wagons only for their removal, and not an article for their relief, except such as might be contained in the panniers of the regimental surgeons; the nearest village of Valverde being seven miles off. The ignorance of the British nation of the fate of those who fall for its honour, as it is called, is inconceivable; it is only equalled by the utter carelessness of almost every one on the subject; and the miseries the unfortunates who are badly wounded undergo, on most occasions, from a neglect which might generally be obviated, is a disgrace to, and a condemnation of the people who are desirous of being considered amongst the most humane and charitable in the world. It is after a great battle that the work of doctors begins. Tired, like everybody else, with the labour of the previous night and day, the dangers of which they are in great part exposed to unless they absent themselves, they are called upon to work in a way of which few people have any conception. Nine tenths of the wounded, for the first three or four days, lie on the bare ground; the doctor has to kneel by the side; his back is bent until he cannot straighten himself; his mental and corporeal powers are equally strained to the utmost; and it is not surprising that under such circumstances, wanting almost everything, even food, the doctors should often think their own lives worth nothing.[8]

Fatigue parties buried the dead in mass graves. Those just alive or dead were stripped and robbed by Allied troops. An eye-witness, a soldier of the 27th, painted a poignant image of the naked dead, 'their bodies disfigured with dirt and clotted blood, and torn with the deadly gashes inflicted by the bullet, bayonet, sword or lance'. Some would not suffer the more fortunate instantaneous death, 'Those who had been killed outright, appeared merely in the pallid sleep of death, while others, whose wounds had been less suddenly fatal, from the agonies of their last struggle, exhibited a fearful distortion of features.'[9]

The desperation to slake thirst was again evident after this conflict. The same witness as above noted a concentration of casualties:

A few pirches [sic – a perch is a distance of five and a half yards] distant was a draw-well, about which were collected several hundreds of those severely wounded, who had crept or been carried thither. They were sitting or lying in the puddle, and each time the bucket reached the surface with its scanty supply, there was a clamorous and heart-rending confusion; the cries for water resounding in at least ten languages, while a kindness of feeling was visible in the manner this beverage was passed to each other.

Although Guthrie had been out on the field earlier on this bloody day, he would soon have to find shelter and treatment for the worst injured, at least as many who could get there, some in the village, which was at one stage entered by Godinot's infantry until they were evicted by Alten's men and a Portuguese brigade. He had to prioritize transport and surgery, no doubt working and coordinating the efforts of many, less experienced Allied battalion surgeons. For the first day Guthrie remained at Albuera to direct, operate and help evacuate the injured men. He then based himself at Valverde, seven or so miles away. Casualty clearance was slow and while Guthrie had only four spring wagons, we know that the French had many more vehicles for removal of their wounded back to Seville. Thus it is not surprising that Moyle Scherer of the 2/34th returned to the field on 20 May, four days later, and noted that the few aid posts at Albuera were still packed with broken men: 'the small chapel at Albuera filled with French wounded, very great numbers of whom had suffered, and who lay on the hard stones, without even straw, in a dirty, comfortless state; all of which was unavoidably the case, for we had nothing to give them on the spot, and, owing to the want of conveyances, they were forced to wait till our people had been carried to the rear'.[10] Many men were carried straight to Elvas, where some would be also sent from Valverde. At Elvas a few notables are interred and the graveyard, high up and overlooking the road to Badajoz, sits peacefully adjacent to a small chapel, where no doubt many a funeral service or requiem was held.

The casualty rates at Albuera reflect the appalling waste of life when tactics on the field are ill conducted. The history of the Worcester Regiment wistfully recalls this on a visit by Wellington to some soldiers of the 29th, convalescing at a ward in the hospital in Elvas. The Commander commented, 'Oh, old 29th, I am sorry to see so many of you here!' One or more replied, 'Oh, my lord, if you had only been with us, there would not have been so many of us here!'[11] Perhaps Wellington preserved more lives than his surgeons.

Guthrie records many examples of injuries suffered and treated after this battle. The wounds managed by him and his colleagues were in the main those received from small arms fire, case shot and lance tips.

Private Barnes of the 29th Regiment was shot in the right thigh behind and above the knee. This shattered the popliteal (main) artery and the soldier lost three to four pints of blood. When the poor man's blood pressure plummeted, the bleeding slowed and ceased. The wound was bound and he lay on the field for two days. After this, he was hoisted in a blanket by four men and carried on a poor road to Valverde. He was considered a minor case, but Guthrie was requested to see Barnes's toes since they were turning black (i.e. 'mortification' or gangrene had set in). As the main artery was damaged, there was insufficient blood passing down the limb. Eighteen days later, the demarcation between living and dead flesh was obvious and he was moved to Elvas on a bullock-cart. Just as he was moved off, the haemorrhage recommenced. This was controlled by pressure and he was taken to Olivenza, where Guthrie directed that an above knee amputation had to be performed. Guthrie requested that the removed limb should be sent to him for examination. He found the blood vessel completely divided and the ends separated by an inch. The upper end had contracted and, as was usually the case, was shaped like the neck of a claret bottle – firmly closed by a firm clot. The lower end was more thinly covered by clot, excepting one small area, which was clearly the part which haemorrhaged after the tenuous covering was dislodged by the rough motion of the transport.

A French infantry sergeant of the 64th Ligne, Baptiste Pontheit, with a similar wound was not so fortunate at Albuera. He was shot high in the front of the thigh. He also bled profusely. This ceased and he went on well until 26 May. He felt something in his thigh give way. After losing half a pint or so, of blood, he pressed on the wound, to control the bleeding. A tourniquet was applied, but after release on several occasions, fresh arterial bleeding recurred. Compressing the femoral artery in the groin, Guthrie cut down on the main artery and vein and tied them above and below the wounds in the vessels. The leg was cool and clearly once again lacked enough blood supply. Warm flannels were applied and brandy given. After eating a tolerable breakfast the next day, he felt some calf discomfort and, although the calf was warm, the foot remained cold. The gangrenous changes spread up the leg and the sergeant died on the fourth day after surgery. Guthrie continued to emphasize the importance of the proper management of injuries to blood vessels: gentle proper pressure on the main artery above the injury, control of bleeding by tying off the vessels above and below the wound and choosing the proper time to intervene, when conservative measures were likely to fail. However, some limbs just could not survive with such a major interruption of their blood supply. It would be 150 years before reconstruction of severely damaged blood vessels could be undertaken.

And then there were the injuries caused by the lances. Guthrie describes the management of several.

A non-commissioned officer, of the 2nd Division of cavalry, was wounded at the battle of Albuhera, on the 16th July[sic], 1811, in several places, by the lances of the Polish cavalry; one of these penetrated the left side of the chest behind, immediately below and in front of the inferior angle of the scapula [shoulder-blade]. He spat and coughed up blood, and lost so much [blood] from the wound, that he became insensible, the bleeding having been stopped by a part of his shirt being bound upon it tightly by means of his woollen sash. Brought to the village of Valverde, my attention was drawn to him some days afterwards, in consequence of the difficulty of breathing having increased, so that he was obliged to be raised nearly to an upright position, as well as from his inability to rest on the part wounded, round which a dark-blue inflammatory swelling had taken place, the wound having been closed. An incision being made into it, a quantity of bloody purulent matter, and clots of blood flowed from it. The incision was then enlarged, so as to allow of a direct opening into the cavity of the chest, which was kept open. The relief was immediate. He was removed to Elvas, apparently doing well, some three weeks afterwards.[12]

Guthrie shortly after discussed an identical case from the 3rd (East Kent) Foot, who made an equally satisfactory recovery. Whilst Guthrie often closed chest wounds to reduce breathing difficulties, sometimes this manœuvre was only of transient benefit, since accumulated air, blood or pus would require an exit.

One other chest injury received at Albuera serves to point out an interesting complication of rib cage and lung damage. An unknown infantryman was wounded in the right chest by a thrusting sword wound under the shoulder-blade. He apparently suffered little after this until

the whole side, as well as the body and neck, began to swell and impede his breathing, which was effected with some difficulty, and with any ease only when sitting up. The external wound was enlarged [with a scalpel], until I could distinctly hear the air rush out, and see the part where the weapon had penetrated between the ribs; upon which he declared himself relieved, when the wound was closed by compress and bandage. It did not unite however; active inflammation of the cavity of the chest ensued, requiring frequent and considerable losses of blood [i.e. bleeding the patient] for its suppression. At the end of three weeks the man was sent to Elvas, in a favourable state for recovery.[13]

Here, the sword cut had penetrated the rib cage and clearly injured the delicate spongy lung tissue underneath, which resulted in an air leak. The air then escaped into the chest cavity and some partly forced out into the muscles, fat and skin of the chest wall through the wound. Air forced into these tissues causes puffing up of the torso and neck and sometimes limbs. Such swelling is crepitant (i.e. crackles with the air in the tissues) and gives the patient the present-day nickname of the 'Michelin Man'.

Guthrie mentions that when the chest was shot through with missiles, occasionally wadding, pieces of clothing, splinters of bone and even musket balls had been coughed up! This could only occur when the lung itself is damaged and the piece of debris carried into it has eroded into a larger airway tube (bronchus).[14]

Abdominal wounds posed a massive challenge for battle surgeons, since without general anaesthesia and muscle relaxation, the patient's abdominal cavity could not be opened sufficiently for access and repair. Also, the general support for the patient that we have today was unavailable. Internal bleeding and peritonitis from damaged internal organs usually ended the patient's existence. However, not all abdominal injuries were fatal. Captain Tarleton of the 7th Fusiliers

> was struck on the left iliac region [lower abdomen] by a large flat piece of shell, at the battle of Albuhera [sic], in 1811. The surface [of the abdomen] was not abraded, although the iron caused a very severe and painful bruise; the whole of that side of the belly became quite black, and the remaining part much discoloured. Some months after he drew my attention to the part, and I found that the whole of the muscular portion of the wall had been removed by absorption to the extent of the immediate injury from the piece of shell, the tendinous [thinned out scar tissue] parts alone remaining under the integuments [skin and fat of the belly wall]. These protruded on any effort, constituting a circular-shaped ventral rupture, with a large base, which required the application of a pad and bandage for its repression.[15]

The piece of shell had struck the abdominal wall with such force as to cause bleeding and disruption of the muscles. When healed, the wound area was so weak that a large bulging hernia resulted.

An unknown soldier of the 2nd Division received several stabs from a lance in various parts of his body and one of these was inflicted while the man was lying hurt on the ground. This stab wounded the lower part of his abdomen. Through the wound some intra-abdominal fat protruded. Naturally and correctly Guthrie replaced the fat, which was 'plugging' an injured artery in the abdominal wound (the inferior epigastric vessel). When the fat was pushed back into the abdominal cavity, the artery lying in the wall of the belly bled vigorously. Guthrie ligated the vessel and stitched up the skin of the abdomen (abdominal muscles were not sewn together, as today) with a running stitch.[16]

A remarkable case of survival was that of a soldier of the 48th, who was hit from short range by a musket ball, which passed under his right ribs and exited the other side, i.e. it had passed right through the man's liver. From the leakage of blood and bile and the ensuing peritonitis, the man's case was rightly assessed as being fatal. Issuing blood and bile from his wounds, he was brought to Guthrie at Valverde, 'the next day, he was bled largely several times; the wounds were dressed simply, and he was kept perfectly quiet, and his bowels gently open. The skin became of a yellow colour [jaundice], his strength failed under the treatment, and he became thin, and looked ill. At the end of three weeks he was sent to Elvas, where he gradually improved, and was forwarded thence to Lisbon and to England, with his wounds healed.[17]

Most abdominal cases were not so fortunate. A moving case of a certain French infantry Captain Negre raises the dilemmas of euthanasia. He

> was struck on the left side [of the abdomen] above the hip … by a musket-ball, which went through the upper part of the sigmoid flexure of the colon [the left-sided part of the large bowel], and came out behind, injuring apparently the fourth and fifth lumbar vertebra. As urine came out through this opening [the one at the back], the ureter [the fine tube leading from the kidney to the bladder] or the lower part of the kidney must have been wounded, and as he had lost the use of one leg, and much of that of the other, the spinal Marrow [canal] must also have been injured. He was left on the field of battle, supposed to be about to die, and was brought to me, to the village of Valverde three days after in a most distressing state. The inflammatory symptoms had been and were severe; the pain he suffered on any attempt to move him was excessive; the discharge of faeces from the anterior [front] wound, and of urine from the posterior one, and by the usual ways rendered him miserable, and he at last implored me to allow the box of opium pills, of which one was given at night to each man who stood most in need of them, to be left within his reach, if I would not kindly do the act of a friend and give them to him myself. He died at the end of ten days, after great suffering, constantly regretting that our feelings as Christians caused their prolongation.[18]

One issue remains clear, there was often a shortage of opium, or at any rate, a rather parsimonious prescription of this drug.

Guthrie and his minions slaved on at Valverde, where 'The worst cases of the wounded were principally brought, the scene was dreadful.' Here I think it important to emphasize that, with few bearers, nurses, orderlies and suitable and sufficient receiving facilities, coupled with a massive under provision of surgeons, the organization and situation must have been, for a while, hell on earth. Guthrie was overwhelmed. Working round the clock with around 3,000 casualties, dispensing as much surgical skill as his energy would allow, he seems most unfairly to have gone unrewarded. His biographer commented:

> His iron constitution enabled him to set an example the few medical men who were present endeavoured to follow. From five in the morning until

eleven at night their labours were incessant, under the most painful circumstances. At the end of three weeks they were nearly worn out they had obtained, however, the grateful thanks of all who survived, the blessings of those who felt they were about to die. Their [the surgical staff's] reward was otherwise curious. Some gentleman who the adjutant-general placed confidence, was pleased to report to him that the wounded had been greatly neglected by the doctors; and the adjutant-general thought it right to signify his displeasure accordingly, which was duly forwarded to Mr Guthrie at Valverde, as well as to Olivenza, Jurumenha and Elvas, where the wounded might have been collected. When this paper was read to the wounded officers, they were exceedingly indignant, and signed another denying its truth, and expressing their gratitude, in their own names, and that of their soldiers, for the attention they received.

What had happened? Had the above informant, unused to the severities of surgery, witnessed and resented the unfortunate demise of a colleague amongst the shambles of the field hospital? Had someone objected to Guthrie's tendency to hoard and isolate his own casualties, rather than move them to Elvas? At any rate, Guthrie 'forwarded this, with the request that the vilifier of himself and his officers might be punished. The adjutant-general acquitted the medical men at Valverde of neglect, but objected to the word vilifier and would not give him up.' Stung to the core, as would be any practitioner at such a slur, 'Mr Guthrie persisted that vilifier was the proper term to apply to such a person. The adjutant-general was impracticable, and the doctors were obliged to submit, receiving the assurance that the report of misconduct or neglect did not apply to Valverde. Medals, promotion and thanks were bestowed on staff-officers and others commanding regiments; the doctors narrowly escaped a reprimand!' Perhaps, like many professional men, working on tough and unglamorous issues, Guthrie and his fellows would merely seek consolation in professional achievement. 'The only satisfaction Mr Guthrie obtained from labours unequalled in the history of any surgical services, was that of laying the foundation for those changes in the principles and practice of surgery which he has since had the honour and happiness of establishing.'[19] His efforts were recognized: he received the Spanish officers' Gold Cross medal for the battle.

Thus, on rather an unhappy note, Guthrie's part in the difficult action at Albuera terminated. Soult was seen off and Badajoz now had to be taken.

To the north of the scene of this carnage, the able General Phillipon had not been idle after the first siege of Badajoz had been raised by Beresford. There was repair, revictualling and stringent efforts made to undo and destroy all the siege works carried out by the Allies. The second siege of Badajoz took place from 18 May until the Duke called it off on 10 June.

Either at this second attempt at Badajoz or possibly at the first siege, Guthrie had the honour of having a round shot fired at him personally from the walls of the city! This was probably somewhere near the Santa Maria bastion. He was 'riding alone on the road in front of the town, at which he was looking; he saw the flash, and was amazingly astonished on finding a large round shot pass over between his back and his horse's tail. The compliment was great, and he felt it impossible not to take off his hat in acknowledgment, and then ride away at a good canter.'[20] At the third and final siege Guthrie would find himself sleeping and working at almost the same spot where the wasted shot from the French field piece had had the temerity to try and destroy him previously.

During the second siege of the town, there were occasional sallies by Phillipon's men on those pickets and troops surrounding the place. Guthrie was involved with two casualties after such an attack:

> A Portuguese caçador on piquet was wounded at the second siege of Badjoz, in a sally made by some French cavalry. He had three or four trifling cuts on the head and shoulders, and one across the lower part of the belly on the right side. He bled profusely, and when brought to me had lost a considerable quantity of blood, which came through a small wound made by the point of a sabre. This wound I enlarged [cut open a little] until the wounded but undivided artery became visible; upon this two ligatures were placed, and the external wound was sewed up. The peritoneum was opened to a small extent, but the bowel did not protrude, and the patient (not being an Englishman, and therefore not so liable to inflammation [i.e. infection]) recovered after being sent to Elvas.
>
> A soldier of same regiment, cut down at the same time, died as soon as he was brought into camp, having been severely wounded in the chest and abdomen. He was said to have died from haemorrhage, from a wound in the belly, two inches in length, made by one of the long-pointed swords of the French dragoons. I had the curiosity to enlarge the wound [after death] and found one of the small intestines had been cut half across, another part injured, and that the blood came from an artery which had been opened by the point of the sword in going through the mesentery [a fatty sheet which anchors the bowel and brings its blood supply], which wound had caused his death.[21]

These two interesting cases presented from the second siege, exhibited the lethal potential of the long pointed French cavalry sword, when compared with the slashing action of the heavy British cavalry sabre. The first man had a fairly small but potentially dangerous wound of a blood vessel in his belly wall. The artery had not been completely severed. If there was complete division of the vessel, there was a chance of the vessel shutting itself down completely, with cessation of haemorrhage. Guthrie understood the danger of an incompletely divided blood vessel and correctly tied the artery above and below the defect. The second man had a fatal outcome again from bleeding, this time from a small intra-abdominal blood vessel, which today would be simple enough to manage, via proper abdominal access. This case reminds us, in what data we have from this and later wars, that injuries of the small intestine tended to have a higher mortality than those wounds of the large intestine.

Wellington aimed to reduce the fort of San Cristobal and the castle in the town. Breaking ground for the digging of trenches was difficult and the Allied cannons concentrated on breaching the walls of the castle and San Cristobal. No doubt Guthrie had to manage injuries from cannon shot and trench construction. When a practicable breach had been blasted, on 6 June, a forlorn hope and storming party of around 100 men were fiercely repelled with ninety-two casualties. A second attack on the same breach took place at dusk on 9 June. The size of the storming party was doubled, with other support. This assault failed likewise, with a further 139 casualties. A truce the following day allowed collection of the immobile casualties. Ian Fletcher makes the point that Soult's attempted and aborted relief of Badajoz might well have proved unnecessary, since Phillipon had held out so strongly without assistance.[22]

On 1 August, Cuidad Rodrigo had been invested, but a superior force under Marshal Marmont forced Wellington to retire to the Coa River. During this withdrawal, Guthrie, in retreat with 300 casualties, near Alfaiates, came upon Dr James Franck, the head of the Medical Department in a sorry state.

> I found him sitting on a pannier by the roadside, and apparently keeping guard over some twenty or thirty others arranged in a semicircle round him. He was one of the best men in the world, but having slept out all night, looked as unhappy as need be for a man not used to it, and not a little frightened withal. It was impossible to avoid laughing when he quietly said, 'I am here taking care of the medical stores of the Army whilst the apothecary is watering the mules lest the muleteers should run away with them. I have seen a great many wounded passing; are they yours?' I bowed, and asked him if he had told them where to go. No, he had not interfered, for he did not know where to go himself. I assured him that the French would be up in half an hour … I ventured to recommend Saburgul [sic], as it would be in rear of the position of the Army was about to take up, but that I should, with his permission, stop at Alfaiates with my wounded. I also ventured to add that the contents of some of the panniers would be very acceptable; might I take a few things out? 'O yes, I might do as I liked, take anything you please.' 'And you will not disown anything I do?' I added. 'O no, provided you do not disobey orders.'[23]

This does not show Franck at his best. A few weeks later he was invalided home. In October the army went into winter quarters. The 4th Division was sickly – half its strength was hospitalized.

Britain and the Commanding Officer of her army in Iberia badly needed to move on. The only way forward was to crack two incredibly tough French-held Spanish nuts – the fortresses of Cuidad Rodrigo and Badajoz – only then could the army push out. There was soon again to be much heartache for Wellington and work for his surgeons.

Bloody Sieges

The year 1812 was a momentous one in the war. First, many brave French soldiers and mercenaries were to die or become prisoners in the totally catastrophic expedition to Russia in the summer and winter of that year. Whilst around 250,000 Frenchmen and their adherents were locked into Iberia nurturing Napoleon's 'Spanish ulcer', there were around 500,000 men of the Grande Armée trudging either in extremes of weather or in the grip of contagion across Europe to and from Moscow. As in the 1914–18 War (until 1917) Russian involvement reduced the potential onslaught by our enemies on other fronts. Secondly, this year marked the Allied breakout into Spain and the 'end of the beginning' after the Salamanca campaign.

The winter campaign ended in the capture of the fortress of Cuidad Rodrigo. Guthrie was to play a large part in aiding men lying injured on the walls and ground round about, also playing a major role in the surgery after the action – 'half the surgical duties of which fell to the lot of Mr Guthrie'. He had charge of the 3rd and 4th Divisions and initially had set up a field hospital in the rear of the trenches.[1]

Before long, the organization, efficiency, scrutiny and the morale of the Army Medical Department were to change. This would all be grist to Guthrie's mill. Throughout the campaigns, he held professional integrity and reputation above any sort of accolade (except perhaps promotion!). It would be in this year that he would be belatedly be elevated from staff surgeon to the rank of (brevet) Deputy Inspector of Hospitals by his parsimonious superiors. Wellington had withdrawn behind the River Coa in November and spread his army for easier victualling. Bonaparte had withdrawn around 60,000 officers and men for the Russian invasion. His Iberian Armies of the North, Centre and Portugal being redesignated, reduced and in some disarray, Wellington seized his chance and with 35,000 men and seventy pieces of ordnance and ammunition at Almeida (only thirty-eight of which were brought up for lack of draught animals), he commenced a move to invest the town of Cuidad Rodrigo on 8 January.

On high ground above the right bank of the River Agueda, the 30foot-high ramparts of the town were surrounded by a *fausse-braye*. Garrisoned by only around 2,000 men under General Barrié, the town contained a large artillery park of over 150 pieces.[2] Outside the walls on the side of the town opposite the river, were two fortified convents in the suburb of Francisco – St Francisco and St Domingo. Another convent – Santa Cruz – was situated on the side of the town near the river. Between these two areas were two ridges, the Tesons, the lesser one 150 yards from the walls, but lower than the ramparts, the greater Teson, higher than the ramparts, was 600 yards from the town. Holding the two ridges meant parallels being dug and then batteries could set up to breach the walls. Eight hundred carts were built and commandeered to bring up ammunition from Almeida.

On the evening of 8 January, with two companies from each of the regiments of the Light Division, Wellington ordered the storming of the Renaud redoubt, guarding the great Teson, achieved with the loss of around twenty-seven men. By dawn, a parallel 3foot deep, 4foot wide and 600 yards long had been hewn out. On 9 January, this was occupied and 1,200 men laboured to dig in three counter-batteries of eleven guns each. The 4th Division relieved the trenches the next day and, under sustained fire from the town, constructed a communication from the trenches to the batteries.

On 11 January, the 3rd Division took over the siege works. Cold weather and sustained fire from the besiegers made life tricky for the riflemen, who were digging pits from which to pick off the French gunners. The whole army was now brought up and posted along the Coa River, some in villages but many having to sleep, freezing, in the open. It was now time to cross the Agueda. Regimental hospitals were set up in small houses or marquees. On 12 January a key event occurred for Wellington's army – the timely arrival of Dr James McGrigor in Iberia. With a staff of a physician and secretary, Dr John Forbes, and three clerks, McGrigor would soon commence the long overdue resuscitation of the Department.

The Santa Cruz convent was taken and, on 14 January, batteries containing twenty-eight guns were ready. These emplacements were attacked by a sally out of the town of 500 men of the garrison – all that Barrié could spare. The sortie was repulsed. At 1630hrs the bombardment started on the *fausse-braye* and ramparts and on the San Francisco convent. Answered by fifty French field pieces, there was a mighty commotion. As evening fell the 40th Regiment took the convent. The two breaches (greater and lesser) were opened on 15 and 16 January, the battering sometimes interrupted by mist. By the 17th, the curtain wall was falling in great cantles, but the besiegers were continually subjected to a brutal return of fire. The convents provided shelter for the surgeons and their charges.

By 18 January the great breach was practicable in the centre and, on the following day, the assault was ordered by the 3rd and Light Divisions and Portuguese troops under Major-General Dennis Pack. The latter, along with Lieutenant-Colonel O'Toole's 2nd Caçadores and the light company of the 83rd, were to mount feints and attempt escalades on the opposite side of the town to the main attack, at the Santiago and Castle gates respectively. The attack was set for 1900hrs. On the extreme right of the parallels, two battalions of Colonel John Campbell's brigade (the 2/5th and the 94th) were to leave the shelter of the Santa Cruz convent and approach the great breach from the right by the *fausse-braye* and ditch respectively. Major-General Henry MacKinnon's brigade (the 1/45th, 74th and 1/88th), preceded by 180 sappers carrying hay bags, was the main assault force, supported by the Portuguese as divisional reserve. The lesser breach was to be stormed by General J Ormsby Vandeleur's and Colonel Andrew Barnard's (reserve) brigades of the Light Division under Robert Craufurd. The main party was subjected to musketry and canister as it struggled forward from the parallels where it met the 2/5th and 94th, who had preceded them at the breach. Two discharges from a pair of 24-pounders loaded with canister, one each side of the breach, and an explosion of some powder bags left in the debris of the breach by the French caused transient carnage to the head of the column. The impetus of the assault was again impeded, this time by the 16foot drop over the lip of the breach into the town. A cut across the sides of the wall at each end of the breach was surmounted by a parapet with the two guns mentioned above. These cuts were crossed and the men poured onto the ramparts. As this happened, a massive explosion from a detonated mine, placed under a postern at the upper wall, took place. The senior brigadier of the 3rd Division, General MacKinnon was hurled skyward, his broken burnt corpse was thrown a distance away.

This assault gave rise to burns, fractures, concussions and musket and canister shot wounds. One of the assistant battalions surgeons would go in after the storming parties for dressings, rescue and to control bleeding. Guthrie had set up brigade dressing stations in convents or other appropriate buildings.

The Light Division had successfully stormed the lesser breach before the main assault was over. Vandeleur's brigade was headed by a forlorn hope of twenty-five men under Lieutenant Gurwood, succeeded by George Napier's 300 stormers. As the column crashed into the lesser breach, a single field piece discharged canister into the mass of men. Several officers were hit. George Napier had a mangled arm, Colonel Colborne, commanding the 52nd, received a ball in the shoulder, which was to cause him much trouble. Around this time, General Robert Craufurd, probably standing on the glacis exhorting his men into the assault, received a ball into his right chest. Vandeleur was also shot down. Sweeping along the ramparts in both directions, some men moving to the right met the Frenchmen retreating from the great breach.

The town garrison surrendered and then the inevitable looting and drinking began. There was little of the barbaric behaviour that would follow the capture of Badajoz and San Sebastian however, and by daybreak the town was controlled. When the assaulting parties moved out, the 5th Division moved in to repair the town. As the tired regiments moved away, Ned Costello related, 'some with jackboots on, others with white French trousers, others in frock coats with epaulettes, some even with monkeys on their shoulders, we met the 5th Division on their way to repair the breaches. They immediately formed upon the left of the road, presented arms and cheered us. I was afterwards told that Lord Wellington, who saw us pass, inquired of his staff, "Who the devil are those fellows?"[3]

Wellington had done well to take the town in twelve days, but the cost had been relatively high. There were two meritorious dead generals, 1,111 dead and wounded, half of whom (562) had fallen in the storming. The 3rd Division had come off worst.

Through the night and the next few days, the dispersal and treatment of the casualties kept Guthrie and his colleagues busy. He had been allocated responsibilities for half of the surgical cases in addition to being charged with recovering all the casualties from the parallels, town and breaches. The orders were to collect the badly wounded and ill men into several buildings in the town and use these and the French hospital as general hospitals. Guthrie had a problem with this directive. By rights, all outlying casualties should have been taken into the general hospitals at Cuidad Rodrigo, or sent to others, miles away. Guthrie, despite depriving the wounded men of some available facilities in the main hospitals, knew there were serious disadvantages in herding large groups of wounded men together in the depths of winter. Fever, especially typhus, could decimate the chance of survival for men weakened by haemorrhage and infected wounds. So he scattered his patients around outlying villages and buildings in Gallegos and Aldea del Bispo, which he had already set up as smaller regimental hospitals. This was a repetition of his organization after Talavera. For the reasons given above, Guthrie felt that this wider dispersal of casualties was one of the factors keeping an army effective in the field. There were complaints and Guthrie had to appear before the Adjutant-General, who told him that he 'had a far greater number of sick with his than with any other division of the army, contrary to orders, which ought to be obeyed. He [the Adjutant-General] yielded this time to the proofs adduced of the advantages resulting from this mode of proceeding, but declared, that if any evil consequences ensued, the responsibility must rest on Mr Guthrie not on him.'[4] Guthrie's arguments were unassailable and the senior staff officer had had to give way, with little understanding and bad grace – not the way to support a respected professional colleague.

Guthrie, being a senior and experienced man, was called in as a 'second opinion' on several cases. Colonel Colborne (later Lord Seaton) was badly hurt leading the 52nd into the smaller breach. A ball was deeply situated in his shoulder and could not easily be retrieved. He was concerned at not showing reaction to the pain he felt, which must have been at times severe. He therefore would only give the surgeons limited time to explore his wound, for the purpose of retrieval of the missile. He set up his fob-watch to measure a limit of five minutes for the surgeons to dilate, probe and delve with bullet forceps into the depths of his shoulder.

The second illustrious patient, fatally hurt in this sanguinary siege, who was seen by Guthrie was the somewhat enigmatic Major-General Robert Craufurd. Craufurd met a brave, but rather sad end to his turbulent life at the foot of the small breach, exhorting his Light Bobs on. He had probably turned to his left facing away from the breach when wounded. Shot through the soft tissues of the back part of his right shoulder and armpit, the ball entered the chest. The ball had not exited the thorax and was clearly lodged in the spine or chest cavity. Air and blood had escaped into the general's chest and caused him pain and difficulty in breathing. Staff Surgeon Robb, who had been surgeon to the 'Corps of Rifleman' – afterwards the 95th – for nine years, since he had been on the staff would have known Craufurd well. He was a capable surgeon and eventually became Inspector General in 1830. He asked Guthrie's opinion. Guthrie found the slit where the ball had entered Craufurd's chest almost too small to account for its entry. For the next few days, Craufurd was in extreme discomfort and was to suffer much, feverish, breathless, in pain and restless. Guthrie seeing the patient within the hour of wounding recounts 'when, from the general anxiety manifested, I was satisfied with the severity of the injury. The symptoms were not at first urgent [often the case with severely injured people]; but their continuance and augmentation, in spite of the most rigorous antiphlogistic treatment [i.e. anti-inflammatory management; bleeding vigorously, a cathartic, emetic, a low diet and also opiates], led, in a few days, to his death.' Everyone, including curious surgeons, would want to hear the findings at post-mortem (the 'examination' or 'dissection'). Guthrie examined the corpse:

> On examination of the body, the ball was found lying on the diaphragm; the cavity of the chest contained a very large quantity of turbid serum; false membranes had formed on the lung [layers of deposited infected serum and thickened, inflamed lining of the lung, the pleura], which was compressed towards the spine, and at the upper part retained the mark of an injury as from a ball which had not force enough to penetrate and lodge.

From this account, it sounds almost as if this was a spent missile which had broken through the ribs, caused some bleeding, but most obviously a collapse of the lung and accumulation of fluid and air on that side of the thorax. The most significant issue in Craufurd's demise was the thickened and turbid serum in the thorax. The collection of infected fluid in the chest is named a pyothorax and the sepsis from this had caused the uncomfortable death of this gallant, controversial and tough British general. Despite many a harsh word or command and sometimes ill-judged and brave acts, the Commander-in-Chief and the army were mortified by this man's demise. He was buried at the base of the lesser breach, where wistful memories of his colourful past still waft over the visitor to the site. With hindsight I wonder why a trocar and canula (a metal tube and its introducer) had not been used to drain off the fluid, which just might have avoided Craufurd's mortal end.

Guthrie was asked to see yet another illustrious casualty, Major George Napier of the 52nd, who had led the storming party into the lesser breach. Napier relates his wounding at the storming, 'When about two-thirds up [the breach] I received a grape shot which smashed my [right] elbow and great part of my arm.'[5]

The Prince of Orange, serving then with Wellington, offered his sash to bind up and support the wounded major's arm. He then wended his way to a ruined convent (most likely that of San Francisco), where he found the surgeons busy. George, like Lord Nelson after the assault on Tenerife in 1794, knew what had to be done:

> It soon came to my turn [even he had to queue!] to have my arm amputated, and I then reminded my friend Walker [assistant surgeon Thomas Walker of the 52nd, June 1805 until September 1812], who was there, of his promise to me a few hours before, and begged he would be so good as to perform the operation [interesting that Napier clearly had confidence in a mere assistant surgeon]: but he told me he could not, as there was a staff surgeon present, whose rank being higher, it was necessary he should do it, so Staff Surgeon Guthrie cut it off. However, for want of light [it must have been round about or after nightfall], and from the number of amputations he had already performed, … It was [a] long time before the thing was finished [suggests a selection based on severity of wound rather than seniority], at least twenty minutes [not an unrealistic time for an amputation], and the pain was great. I then thanked him for his kindness, having sworn at him like a trooper while he was at it, to his great amusement[!], and I proceeded to find some place to lie down and rest.[6]

This wasn't the only wound suffered by George, he had been struck in the shoulder by a shell splinter, during the siege, on the 16th. The stoic Napier family made a significant impact and reputation for themselves during the Peninsular Wars, if for no other reason than for their suffering. George had already received two wounds by 1812. On 27 September at Busaco, when a French infantryman, lunging at him with his bayonet, let off his loaded firelock, discharging the contents into just under his hip, fortunately only a soft tissue injury, from which he clearly recovered to receive his next wound at Casa Noval, on the Ides of March 1811 – a shot in his right wrist, which completely shattered it and forced him to the rear. Again recovery clearly occurred, but presumably not without severe pain and, ultimately, a stiff and arthritic joint.

It is worth recalling another of the Napier brothers' injuries. Major Charles Napier, whilst in action at Corunna, having seen the occupation of the village of Elviña, pushed on, exhorting the 50th ('the dirty half hundred'), ahead of the 42nd Foot, careered on through the village, not having the back-up that he had hoped. Somewhat isolated and while exhorting his men on, he broke out of cover and exposed himself to French musketry and case. Running on, he was finally brought down: 'a musket ball just then broke the small bone of my leg [the fibula] some inches above the ankle; the pain was acute, and though the flesh was not torn, the dent remains in my flesh to this day'. Cornered against a building, 'just as my spring and shout was made the wounded leg failed, and I felt a stab in my back [with a French bayonet] … they struck me with their muskets clubbed, and bruised me much'. Apparently, an Italian officer, in the pay of the French, arrived and 'at that moment a tall dark man came up, seized the end of the musket [i.e. Charles's firelock] with his left hand, whirled his brass-hilted sabre round, and struck me a powerful blow on the head … it fell exactly on the top, cutting into the bone, but not through it'.[7] Charles encountered more trouble on 27 September 1810, at the defence of the ridge at Busaco, where a bullet had entered his cheek on the right side of the nose and lodged in the left jaw, near his ear. From brother George's account, 'I found Charles in bed very ill, his face so dreadfully swollen that I could see neither eyes nor nose … the ball … had lodged in the jawbone of the opposite side, from whence it was extracted with much difficulty, great part of the jaw coming away with it, as well as several teeth.'[8]

But to return to Guthrie's cases at Cuidad Rodrigo. An unidentified soldier involved in the siege received a wound, consequent on the bursting of a shell. Brought to Guthrie, soon after, the surgeon noted that, 'The axillary artery [main blood vessel to the arm in the armpit] becoming brachial [i.e. as it came to the arm, leaving the armpit], was torn across, and hung down lower than the other divided parts, pulsating to its very extremity. Pressed and squeezed in every way between my fingers in order to make it bleed, it still resisted every attempt, although apparently by the narrowest possible barrier, which appeared to be at the end of the artery, and formed by its contraction.'[9] Although there was a tiny and insignificant clot plugging the end of the torn vessel, the reason that the bleeding had ceased was as a result of a normal bodily defence mechanism. The local stimulus to control haemorrhage was an intense contraction or narrowing of the muscular layer of the damaged end of the artery caused by local secretion of vasoconstrictors (chemicals that cause the contraction). In this case, Guthrie was bemused by his unsuccessful efforts to overcome this vitally important physiological response to injury (the contraction), which was to save many a life on the battlefield.

Although not the therapeutic philosophy of the day, many wounds were left to heal by 'second intention', which is to say that the wound was not closed with sutures and nature was left to run its course, the open defect gradually filling with serum, coagulum and new blood vessels, which would bring vital nutrients and oxygen to the healing wound. Thus the defect would heal slowly, often resulting in an ugly scar. Such dreadful scars and amputation stumps were, of course, marks of heroism. Guthrie had treated such a patient:

> An officer, whose name I forget, was wounded at the assault of Cuidad Rodrigo in 1812, by a musket ball on the left side and fore-part of the abdomen, near the crest of the ilium [tip of the hip bone]; it made a wound about four inches in length, cutting away the muscles of the abdominal wall so deeply as to lead to the exposure, and, as I feared, to the ulceration of the peritoneum, when the sloughs should separate. Under these circumstances, although not belonging to my division I took him with me from the field to the divisional hospital at Aldea Gallega, some ten miles from the battlefield. Granulations sprang up, however, from the bottom and sides of the wound, which gradually closed in and healed without further difficulty.

It is interesting to note, once again that Guthrie purloined this officer patient from another division![10]

Another case demonstrates not only the remarkable healing ability of wounded men, but also the conservative intent of thinking surgeons at this time. Guthrie was foremost in preserving as much useful tissue as possible. He advised:

> A very extensive destruction of the soft parts, the femur [thigh bone] remaining entire, does not authorise the removal of the limb in the first instance, unless the main artery be also injured. Captain Flack of the 88th Regiment, was struck by a large cannon-shot at Cuidad Rodrigo, on the outside and anterior [front] part of the left thigh, which tore up and carried away nearly all the soft parts from the groin, or bend of the thigh, below Poupart's ligament [at the groin crease], to within a hand's-breadth of the knee. It was an awful affair. He was supposed to be dying, was returned dead, and his commission was given to another. Left to die in the field hospital after the town was stormed, and finding himself thus deserted by his own friends, he claimed my aid as a stranger. I took him five leagues [about fifteen miles] to my hospital at Aldea del Obispo (sic). The femoral artery [main artery to the leg] laid bare for the space of near four inches, in a channel at the bottom of the wound; the whole, however gradually closed in, and he recovered.[11]

One rare and most interesting case treated by Guthrie at this event, was that of a man whose belly was grazed by a round shot.

A soldier of the 40th Regiment was struck by a ricochet cannon-shot, on the last day of the siege of Cuidad Rodrigo. He saw the ball, which destroyed his left fore-arm so as to render amputation necessary, strike the ground a little distance from him, before he was himself injured. He thought from the sort of shock he received, that it had also struck his belly; but this I should not have credited, if it had not been for a bruise across the umbilical region without actual abrasion of the integuments [skin and fat], on which account my attention was drawn to him on the fourth day after the injury, at the hospital of Aldea Gallega. He had been bled on account of complaining of pain, and because of the quickness of pulse and the fever that had ensued, and which was attributed to irritation after amputation [i.e. suspicions of infection]. The belly was swollen and tender under pressure. Calomel, antimony and opium were given: he was bled again and blisters [counter-irritation] were applied. The stump took on unhealthy action [early infection/colour], and he died a fortnight after the receipt of the injury. The abdomen when opened, was found to contain a quantity of opaque serous fluid [i.e. an infected effusion], mixed with shreds of coagulable lymph. The Omentum and intestines were of a dark colour, and loaded with blood, distinctly indicating the chronic state of inflammation which had taken place.[12]

Interestingly in this case, Guthrie advised puncture of the belly cavity with a trocar to drain the fluid, but only if the patient were to survive long enough. This perhaps insinuates that patients acutely ill with accumulations of fluid or air in their body cavities were rarely submitted to tube drainage. Surprisingly, neither Lord Nelson nor Craufurd had been managed in this way. The above case history suggests that the high-energy tangential blow from the iron missile had caused a thrombosis of a major abdominal blood vessel, possibly the superior mesenteric artery, which is the blood supply to the small intestine. If the blood supply had been suddenly cut off, the gut and the patient would die.

Nature's inimical way of coping with trauma was shown in the case of a 'soldier of the Third Division of Infantry', who

was wounded during the assault of Cuidad Rogrigo, by a ball which entered and lodged in the left side of the back, about midway between the spine and a line drawn to the upper part of the crest of the ilium [the bony pelvic ridge above the hip-joint], from which opening the contents of the bowel were discharged. Left among the dead, and those who were supposed to be dying at the field hospital, in the rear of the trenches, I sent him, with all those of different corps who were wounded, to my own hospital at Aldea

Gallega, some ten miles off. Here, under a sufficiently vigorous treatment, of which bleeding, starvation and quietitude were the prominent features, he recovered. On the fifth day the ball passed per anum, and on three different occasions afterwards, portions of his coat, flannel shirt and breeches Foecal [sic] matter passed readily through the wound, whilst the bowels were gently solicited by common injections [enemata] for some time; but the wound gradually closed in, and the man regained his health, and was sent to the rear with a slightly coloured discharge from the wound, not quite free from odour.[13]

This was a well-managed case and clearly the abdominal cavity had walled off the sepsis.

Likewise, there was Captain Martin, his unit unidentified by Guthrie, who survived a remarkably dangerous wound, carrying even today a significant risk to life. Hit by a musket ball just above his pubic bone, the ball passed through Martin's bladder and rectum, from front to back, and exited by shattering the sacral bone. His progress continued,

the contents of both viscera being freely discharged through this opening [behind]. As he suffered but little inconvenience from the urine, very little of which passed by the urethra, that passage was not interfered with in the first instance. Inflammatory symptoms were kept within due bounds, the rectum was carefully washed out with emollient enemata, and his food rendered as light as possible. Under this treatment he gradually improved; the anterior [front] wound first healed, and subsequently the posterior one, leaving him comparatively well, when he left me for Lisbon on his way to England.[14]

Again this event was a great credit to nature and the patient's fortitude.

Guthrie's first attempt at disarticulation (amputation) through the hip joint failed after this siege, and on reflecting on this disappointment, recalled that the attempt by Mr Brownrigg (staff surgeon) at Elvas after Albuera, had also ended fatally. The accolade of success with this monumental operation would elude Guthrie until 1815, after Waterloo.[15] The unfortunate victim was a private of the 23rd, Mason by name. He had already undergone a mid thigh amputation for a wound and then bled, had his femoral artery ligated, bled again and then finally had a further limb ablation at the hip joint. Guthrie was assisted by surgeons Cartan (then assistant surgeon of the 40th Foot, later 15th Light Dragoons (Hussars)) and Loane (assistant surgeon 40th Foot, later surgeon to 94th Foot) and the operation lasted a quarter of an hour![16] Mason sadly passed away seven hours after surgery.

James McGrigor, soon to be a close colleague of Guthrie, perceived great deficits in the Army Medical Department. He had noted in a snapshot letter of 26 February 1812, to the new Army Medical Board that

> On my joining the army ... there were 18,000 men on the sick list. I had 111 effective medical officers of the general staff and ten sick of sixty-seven Corps, of the line and foreign [i.e. Allied battalion surgeons of the line], whose establishment is not 201 medical officers, only 109 [i.e. now including assistant surgeons] are present effective and doing duty. The effective medical staff were surely too weak for the number of sick, particularly dispersed as they were in a great part of Portugal and part of Spain![17]

Guthrie's first brush with McGrigor was not a particularly happy one. The build-up and dispersal of the casualties and sick from Cuidad Rodrigo dragged Guthrie into a scrape. In February,

> the adjutant-general sent for me to know why I had so many sick and wounded and what I meant to do with them. I told him they were much better with me than at Celerico [which never became one of the successful general hospitals], provided they were not in danger from the enemy; and he allowed me to keep them on my own responsibility for moving them when the order for the march to Badajoz should arrive. To do this when the order came, I was obliged to give the division to the senior regimental surgeon, and to go myself with the very last of my worst cases to Celerico, in order that I might ensure attention to them.

When Guthrie arrived, despite his sending a note to the hospital commander concerning the number of patients he was bringing, he found that the hospital was full and seventeen of his cases died, occasioned to some degree by lack of accommodation. This issue and the fact that one of the regiments of Guthrie's division near Cuidad Rodrigo had got the itch (scabies) landed Guthrie with a reprimand from McGrigor. There was no ointment for the patients with scabies. McGrigor had sent to Abrantes and elsewhere for the ointment, and the therapy held up the battalion for three days. When Guthrie reached Elvas, he heard of the affair, and was duly irritated, as he would have handled the issue better than the surgeon he had left with the division! Guthrie's colleagues were somewhat amused at Guthrie's rebuff and soon after Badajoz McGrigor acknowledged Guthrie's efforts, with those of his fellow surgeons, and said that 'he believed that he and I [Guthrie] must be friends'. Guthrie asked that his meritorious acknowledgement should be offset against the episode of the itch! As to the affair of the seventeen dead patients at Celerico, this and other arguments soon convinced McGrigor of Guthrie's correct and appropriate use of regimental hospitals.

During the tour of duty following the siege, Guthrie, rode over the field of the action at El Bodón, around ten miles south-west of Cuidad Rodrigo. This combat had taken place on 25 September 1811. He 'rode over the ground and found the skeletons of those who had fallen. I was curious in looking for the death-wound in each; and in only one case, out of twenty odd, did I fail to see the broken bone which had, in all probability, been implicated in it. Some of these must, I fear, have died of starvation, to whatever nation they belonged. The sun and rain had bleached the bones the vultures had picked clean.'[18]

The now-strengthened key border fortress town of Badajoz had yet to fall after two previous unsuccessful assaults, Wellington, aware of the stretching of Bonaparte's forces and the need to get the two strong fortresses at his back, knew that he had a significantly more hostile challenge this time. His difficulties in this third siege were that he lacked a good corps of sappers and miners, he had a tough able opponent defending the fort, the engineer General Phillipon, and the weather was uncertain. The town garrison was made up of French, Hessians and Spanish defenders – around 5,000 in all. Quite apart from the counterscarps, covered ways and glacis, Phillipon had strengthened and reinforced the defences in a most professional manner – retrenchments inside the walls, mining glacis and stocking up food. Sandwiched between the dammed Rivellas stream (forming the inundation) and the Guadiana, Badajoz fanned out surrounded by a strong curtain wall, eight bastions and a castle.

The Allied army was well on its way to the Tagus by 5 March. By the 15th, the pontoons were over the Guadiana and the following day Beresford had crossed the river with around 15,000 men to invest the fortress. There was a covering force (Hill and Graham) of about 30,000 men.

Dr James McGrigor had ensured that all divisions possessed their full quota of medicines, instruments and stores and also that the depot at Elvas had been properly stocked by the apothecaries and purveyors. Whenever carts could be procured, the less severely ill or wounded men went with their battalions. McGrigor fumed at the delay in the arrival of medical supplies, panniers and medical staff at Elvas: much was not in place by the 14 March. He noted that not a single spring wagon was available in the Alentejo.[19]

The siege train was assembled to help reduce the town, defended also by four outworks, the Pardaleras, San Roque, the Picurina, also the tough San Cristobal fort. Parallels and batteries were set up on the west and southern aspects of Badajoz. The Picurina outwork required capture, since from there batteries could bear on the Trinidad and Maria bastions and the curtain wall between them (these were the assault objectives). On 17 March, 1,800 men broke ground 160 yards from San Cristobal. Their efforts were hampered by severe rain, raking fire from three field pieces set up on San Cristobal and a vigorous French sortie from the town and Picurina on the 19th. Despite trench flooding on 23 March, the San Roque and Picurina outposts had to be subdued and the 5th Division was to invest the town from the right bank. The night assault on the Picurina was to be mounted by 500 men of the 3rd Division under General Kempt. On a fine night, the assault commenced, stimulating a vicious defence. Sweating, desperate men struggled hand-to-hand to gain ditches across ramparts strongly staked against their adversaries. Commandant Gaspar Thiery only surrendered after half his garrison was killed. In one hour British casualties had mounted to 319 (265 wounded). This was an evil omen of the assaults to follow. Despite the fall of the Picurina and the fierce Allied assault, Phillipon harangued his men with threats of their fate on the English prison hulks should their defence of the town be less than robust. A few local buildings and hospital marquees, sent up from Abrantes, formed the field hospitals for mounting casualties, not far behind the assault areas.

On 27 and 28 March, efforts on the parallels and working the new batteries continued, under fire from the town walls. On the 30th, the 5th Division was moved over the river, to reinforce Wellington's force on that side, in case of an attack by a French relief force. This left the Portuguese troops on the right of the river. As forty-eight pieces of artillery hammered the town, the bastions of Trinidad and Santa Maria began to crumble. With the breaches almost practicable and yet some way off, Soult having effected a junction with Generals Drouet and Daricau, time was now of the essence. An assault was planned on 5 April, but Wellington delayed until a breach in the curtain wall between the two bastions could be made on 6 April. The main assault was to be at the breaches. Diversionary assaults by General James Leith's 5th Division and Picton's 3rd were to be made on the eastern (Pardaleras) and western (castle) aspects of the town respectively. The San Roque outpost was also to be assaulted and a feint made on the bridge-head over the river. The main storming was to be carried out by the 4th Division (Guthrie's unit) and once again the Light Division.

The attack was to be at night, which might benefit the assaulting force but could well lead to confusion and difficulties for the casualties and the surgeons. Despite the huge hazards, men begged for a place in the Forlorn Hope and it could be said that around 18,000 men were now straining at the leash to wrest this harsh citadel from Phillipon. General Charles Colville's 4th Division was to take the Trinidad breach and the curtain wall, while Barnard's Light Division was to assault the Santa Maria breach. Both divisions were led by a Forlorn Hope, a storming party of 500 men, armed with axes, bales and ladders, who were then to scramble up the rugged slopes to face Phillipon's destructive defence. The latter employed incredible ingenuity, which would provide much work for the burial parties and surgeons. On the walls, several loaded muskets per man, cheveau-de-frise, animal carcasses filled with burning oil, grape, canister, retrenchments behind the breaches, mines, powder barrels, grenades, pikes and bayonets. Fearful carnage, observed insult and assistance from the town's folk and the intense desire for alcohol and plunder would soon fuel a vengeful cruelty from the Allied soldiery which still throws a sad pall over the town today.

Ten o'clock was the appointed hour. William Napier wrote, 'Dry but clouded was the night, the air was thick with watery exhalations from the rivers, the ramparts and trenches unusually still; yet a low murmur pervaded the latter, and in the former lights flitted here and there, while the deep voices of the sentinels proclaimed from time to time that all was well in Badajoz.'[20]

Picton's assault was led by Kempt as the former was hurt and Kempt also soon fell. The 3rd Division then began the immense struggle to get up the long ladders. Hand-to-hand fighting, falls, crushing and wounds from thrown debris from the castle walls made this harsh combat. The story of Lieutenant-Colonel Henry Ridge and a grenadier officer, Canch, remain heroic as they gained the castle ramparts.

As the firing at the castle walls started to the west, the two main assaulting parties quietly reached the glacis before each of the breaches. Soon the air was rent asunder by musketry, the crash of ordnance and all fire and brimstone that could be imagined. In the dark there was soon great confusion with the Light Division parties running into the Trinidad breach. Swarms of desperate men were soon fighting their way up and clambering over rubble, corpses and wounded comrades. The defences at and for ten feet below the breaches included cheveau-de-frise and planks covered in iron spikes and chained together. These obstacles coupled with intense small-arms fire thwarted attempt after bloody attempt to get through. Men were funnelled into the narrow well-defended gaps. Fireballs highlighted the brave but futile efforts to break in and illuminated the heaving mass of burned, pierced and mutilated men on the breaches. After so many rushes, maybe thirty to forty times up the heaps of masonry, the place stank strongly of spent powder, burned flesh and flaming oil. Between fusillades, the cries of the hurt men must have been heart-rending. All these incredibly brave assaults faltered. There were now more than 2,000 casualties and Wellington ordered the broken parties to retire, possibly for a second wave of assaults.

Inspector James McGrigor, the senior doctor in the Peninsula, with his colleague, Dr Forbes, had had a tent erected near Wellington's.[21] Two spring wagons for movement of wounded men had been allocated per division. After dining in Marshal Beresford's tent, McGrigor and Forbes (the latter armed with the necessaries of surgery, in case the Duke was injured) stood close to the Commander, with the Prince of Orange and Lord March, on a hillock opposite the breach. Report after report of failures at the breaches reached the Duke, who knew well what was being asked of his men and as he watched the assaults go in. McGrigor observed his Commander, 'At this moment, I cast my eyes on the countenance of Lord Wellington lit up by the glare of the torch held by Lord March; I shall never forget it to the last moment of my existence and I could now even sketch it. The jaw had fallen, and the face was of unusual length, while the torchlight gave to his countenance a lurid aspect; but still the expression of the face was firm.'[22]

Meanwhile, unknown to the staff, the 3rd Division had entered the castle precincts, but not reached the rear of the breaches. The 5th Division's men had also clambered over the wall near the San Vincente bastion. The town was now penetrated in two places, the breaches were abandoned and both General Phillipon and Villande, another senior garrison commander, were wounded and retired to the San Cristobal fort. Phillipon had sent out despatches to Soult to prevent his advance.

Not one soldier had penetrated either of the main breaches or curtain wall. One brave fellow who was nearly through the ghastly barricades was found dead with a stoved-in head, lying under a cheveau-de-frise. Each of the two breach-assaulting divisions had around 1,200 casualties. Before the main clearance of the injured and dead from the fort's outskirts at daybreak, havoc was to descend on the town. The battered besieging force was to wreak a terrible revenge on Badajoz that since has had little enough reason to forget and forgive. The reasons for their fury have been explained, but not excused. This debauch would, for three days, make the town unsafe for settling the wounded there.

Next to the Battles of Assaye and Waterloo, this siege clearly deeply affected the Commander-in-Chief and when visiting the blackened and burnt breaches on the 7 April, he wept at the carnage. Many others of his staff must have been so moved.

French casualties were around 1,500 killed and wounded and 3,500 prisoners of war. Allied casualties were 3,752, with around 600 from Guthrie's 4th Division injured.

Where were the surgeons? Were some assistant surgeons sent in to the rear of the storming parties? Possibly, but unlikely since it would be extraordinarily dangerous and also there would be little room or cover to work to any useful purpose at the breaches. Staff Surgeon John Burnall (promoted to the staff from battalion surgeon of the Coldstream Guards in the summer of 1809) and Assistant Surgeon James Goodall Elkington (Assistant Surgeon of the 30th Foot since 1808) did approach the assault areas by placing themselves in a small quarry, a hundred yards or so from the Santa Maria bastion.

Even there they found the lightly wounded hared past the surgeons, no doubt only too grateful to get out of the hell behind them, whilst the severely wounded could not be extricated to the quarry.[23] Elkington noted that the town was taken by 5am and since it was now daybreak, he wandered to the breaches.

A most awful sight. The *cheveau-de-frise* of sword blades let into solid timber were [sic] on top of the breach still standing; platforms of wood with large iron spikes chained lay on the front of the breach. In the bottom of the ditch a deep trench was dug, full of water, and many fell into it during the darkness. The dead and dying lay in every direction, and many, I think, were buried by the débris of the breach as they lay at its foot unable to move. All day we were employed in removing the wounded. I was ordered to do duty at the convent of St André. Many wounded were brought in immediately, but the whole were not for three or four days. Each fatigue party sent in from the front brought a certain number of wounded, but instead of returning for others they went off plundering. There was no control; the goods, chattels, and persons of the inhabitants were alike made free with. My horse and valise were stolen, and it was not till two or three gallows were erected in the chief square that the plundering was stopped. From fifty to sixty females, friends of the Spanish Colonel in whose house I was staying, came under my protection. Our loss during the siege was near 5,000 killed and wounded. I remained in Badajos till April 18, when I was ordered to rejoin my regiment, now on its way to the north.[24]

The breaches were clearly a heart-rending sight and Guthrie saw them too. He noted, '3 dead officers lying dead on the great breach, stripped stark naked in the night by their own friends or their allies. In such a way does war destroy our noblest feelings.'[25] Before they could enter the town, the medical staff had set up marquees (brought up from Abrantes) and tents in front of the breaches, where they could receive the casualties from those blackened, smouldering slopes. Other regimental aid/dressing posts may well have been designated temporarily at the Pardaleras, San Roque, San Cristobal, etc. during the assault. Guthrie's workload was high and from his tents he travailed over the broken bodies of all the principal officers injured from the 1,200 or so casualties of the 4th and Light Divisions. Although much of his work would be taken up with dealing with small-arms injuries, so common in open battle, here at Badajoz there were many other types of injury.

The time had come to mend the shattered army. When considering the wounds, common shell bursts were most effective anti-personal weapons. Guthrie, in one such case, 'had to remove one leg, an arm, and a testicle [a part of the penis and scrotum being lost]. In one of the flesh-wounds in the back part of the thigh and buttock a large piece of shell was lodged, and kept up considerable irritation until it was removed. The man recovered.'[26] A master tailor of the 40th, on the night of the assault on the town, was

> tempted by the approaching prospect of plunder, gave up his shears and armed himself with a halbert [sic] and so joined the stormers. He was punctured just below the right shoulder by a pike tip. The wound bled

copiously and when being received, he fainted and was thought to be less than robust! The pike end had divided his axillary artery [the main vessel to the arm], even though the entry wound was less than half an inch long. By the first of May, the pulse, which had disappeared after wounding, had now returned. An alternative [collateral] circulation had been formed by other smaller blood vessels opening up.[27]

One of the most tragic tales of wounding in the Peninsular War happened to a brave officer of the 5th Division, who was part of the assaulting party near the easterly San Vincente bastion. This case clearly distressed Guthrie considerably. A round shot struck the officer on right side of the head and face.

> It carried away the right eye and the whole face, the left eye hanging in the orbit, the floor of which was destroyed. A part of the lower jaw remained on the left side, but a great part of the tongue was gone. He had lost a large quantity of blood, but was quite sensible. In the middle of the next day he suffered much from the want of water to moisten his throat, which could not be procured. After a distressing delay of three or four hours under a hot sun, a small quantity was obtained, the arrival of which he observed; and whilst I was giving directions relative to its distribution, I felt a gentle tap on my shoulder, and on turning round, saw this unfortunate man standing behind me, a terrific [terrifying] object, holding out a small cup for water, not one drop of which he could swallow. Alone amongst strangers, he felt that every kindness in our power to offer was bestowed upon him, and he contrived to write his thanks with a pencil, which he gave me when he pressed my hand at parting at eleven at night.

Our surgeon's understandable feelings about this patient must have been somewhat ameliorated when he went on to comment, 'I was glad at sun-rise to find he had just expired.'[28]

Sir Thomas Picton, that fiery Welsh commander of the 3rd Division, was hit in the thigh by a spent ball, which deflected up, severely bruising his inguinal [groin] region. The ball must have caused extensive bruising and possibly much muscle damage since he had to return to Britain to convalesce. We have no evidence that Guthrie was involved with his management.

Sir James Kempt was also wounded at the storming of the castle, 'on the inside of the left great toe, by a musket ball which, from the appearance of a slit-like opening, was supposed to have rebounded from the bone, but was discovered a fortnight afterwards flattened and lying between it and the next toe. Inflammation [infection] had ensued, followed by great irritability and numerous spasmodic attacks, appearing to render locked-jaw probable. The spasm soon became general

'The Surgeon Dressing of His Wounds'. (*The National Army Museum*)

(*Left*) Private drill dress, 29th (Worcester) Regiment: officer 29th Foot *c.*1811. (*Courtesy of Colonel J. Lowles and the Worcester Regimental Museum*)

(*Right*) The city, port and bay of Halifax, Nova Scotia in 1832. (*Courtesy of the Library and Archives of Parks of Canada (National Archives)*)

The main road out of Columbeira (left of the houses) and the gully (to the right of the telegraph pole), up which Colonel Lake led his men. (*Author's collection*)

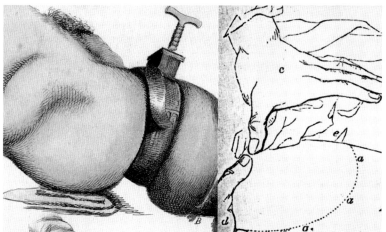

Screw tourniquet in place (illustration by Sir Charles Bell) – to be compared with Guthrie's digital compression of the femoral artery: note the left hand of a surgeon compressing the amputation flap. (*Author's collection*)

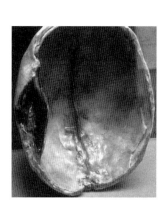

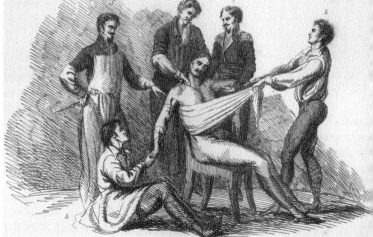

(*Left*) A fatal extradural haematoma – a collection of blood, inside the skull and compressing the brain but outside the protective dura membrane. (*Courtesy of the Royal College of Surgeons of Edinburgh*)
(*Right*) Preparation for removal of an arm (drawing by Sir Charles Bell). (*Author's collection*)

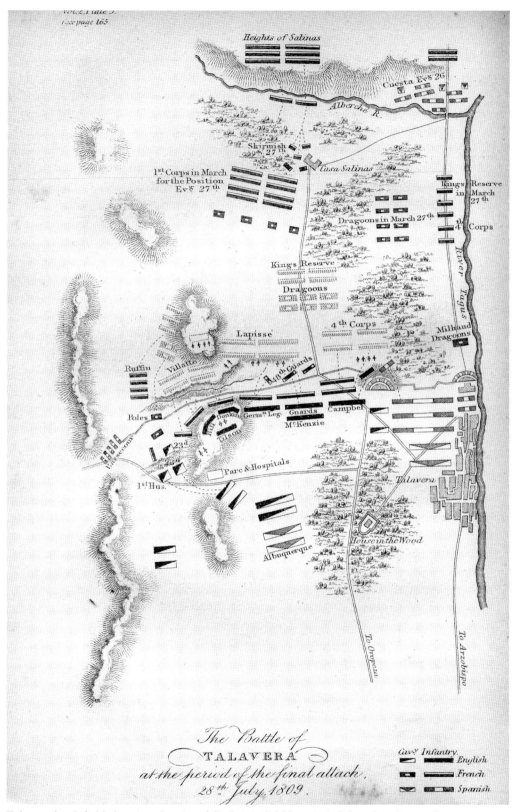

Talavera battlefield showing the site of Guthrie's field hospital. Other dressing stations were situated here – around 700 yards behind the lines. (*Courtesy of Colonel J. Lowles and the Worcester Regimental Museum*)

Ensign Charles Walsh of the 3rd Foot (Buffs) wounded and Lt Matthew Latham, himself later dangerously hurt, concealing a regimental colour during General Latour-Marbourg's cavalry assault at Albuera.
(*Author's collection*)

Graveyard at Elvas, where there are now memorials to the fallen at Badajoz. The small chapel is seen nearby on the right up against the graveyard wall.
(*Author's collection*)

The mine explosion at the great breach during the storming of Cuidad Rodrigo.
(*Author's collection*)

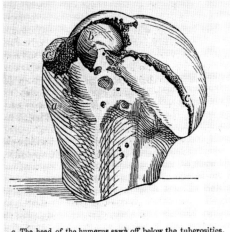

a. The head of the humerus sawn off below the tuberosities.
b. The ball.
cc. Fractures of the head of the bone.

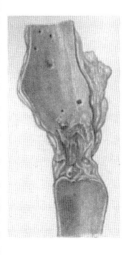

(*Left*) Traumatic limb avulsion; brachial plexus, artery and vein torn across – the blood vessels have vasoconstricted (closed down) after the limb had been torn off. (*Courtesy Captain Peter Starling and the Army Medical Services Museum*)

(*Centre*) Musket-ball wound of the shoulder – a ball lodged in the head of the humerus (upper arm bone) – from Guthrie's *Commentaries*. (*Author's collection*)

(*Right*) Artery damaged by gunshot and although appearing externally intact, the internal structure is occluded by the damaged lining of the blood vessel. (*Author's collection*)

General the Hon. Sir Galbraith Lowry Cole. (*Courtesy Dr J. Cruickshank*)

Cerebral hernia and circular horsehair protective ring. (*Author's collection*)

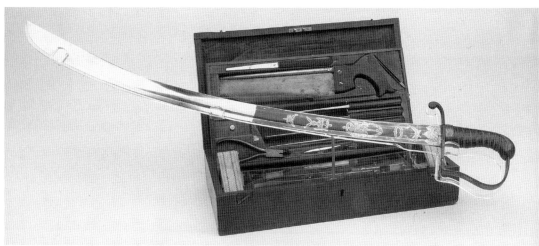

Staff surgeon John Maling's 1796 light cavalry pattern sabre with a capital surgical instrument set. Medical officers at these times were required to carry arms. (*Courtesy the Royal College of Surgeons of England*)

Trepanation of the cranium for a depressed fracture. The circular saw is applied over a relatively stable area of bone to remove a disc of bone for improved surgical access. (*Author's collection*)

No. I.

RETURN of SURGICAL CASES *treated, and* CAPITAL OPERATIONS *performed, in the* General Hospital *at* TOULOUSE, *from April 10th to June 28th, 1814.*

DISEASES AND STATE OF WOUNDS.	Total treated.	Died.	Discharged to duty.	Transferred to Bordeaux.	Proportion of Deaths to the number treated.
Head	95	17	25	53	1 in $5\frac{17}{17}$
Chest	96	35	14	47	1 in $2\frac{35}{35}$
Abdomen	104	24	21	59	1 in $4\frac{1}{3}$
Superior extremities ...	304	3	96	205	1 in 101
Inferior ditto	498	21	150	327	1 in $23\frac{1}{2}$
Compound fractures ...	78	29	...	49	1 in $2\frac{20}{29}$
Wounds of spine	3	3	...	...	1 in 1
Wounds of joints	16	4	...	12	1 in 4
Amputations—					
Arm.............. 7 ⎫ Leg and thigh...41 ⎭	48	10	...	38	1 in $5\frac{1}{3}$
Total......	1242	146	306	790	1 in $8\frac{124}{146}$

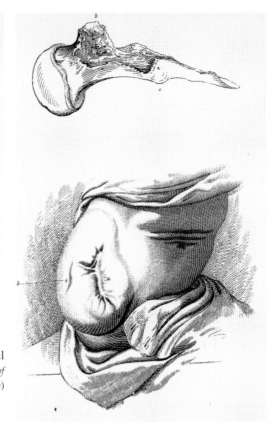

Results of surgery in Surgeon Guthrie's General Hospital at Toulouse: original table from the 6th edition of *Commentaries*. (*Author's collection*)

François de Gay's shattered upper femoral fragment, his wounds after surgery. (*Courtesy of Professor M.H. Kaufman*)

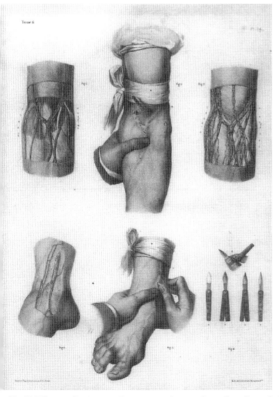

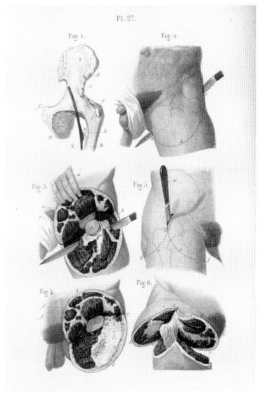

(*Left*) The technique of venesection using the thumb lancet. (*Author's collection*)
(*Right*) A later illustration of a disarticulation of the thigh at the hip-joint. (*Author's collection*)

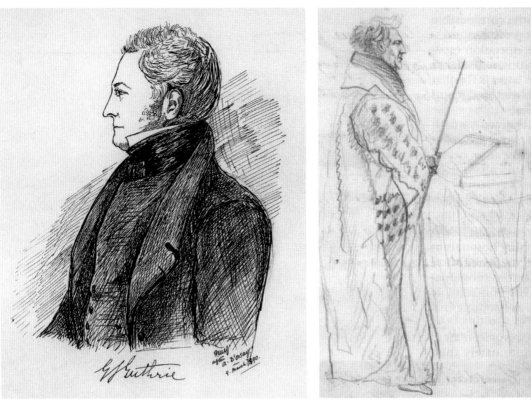

(*Left*) George Guthrie aged around 35 – a sketch presented to the now extinct Guthrie Society in 1890. (*Courtesy of Mr S. Wright*)

(*Right*) A charismatic sketch of George Guthrie lecturing at the Royal College of Surgeons. (*Courtesy the Royal College of Surgeons of England*)

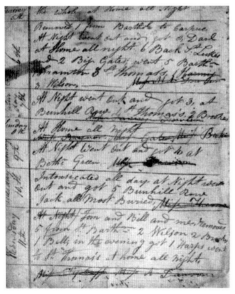

(*Left*) Page of a resurrectionist's diary – Joseph Naples, a former sailor, who had served on *HMS Excellent*. (*Courtesy of the Royal College of Surgeons of England*)

(*Right*) Daguerreotype of Guthrie – this and a photograph of Dr Walter Henry (66th Regiment of Foot) are the only extant photographic images of British Peninsular War surgeons. (*Courtesy of the Royal College of Surgeons of England*)

but tetanus did not take place.'[29] Kempt continued to suffer with spasms, which worsened after he had served at Waterloo and appeared to be set off by exposure of the foot to cold weather. It took six to seven years for him to recover from the symptoms. Wounds of the leg and foot were at particular risk of tetanus because of indriven soil, contaminated with Clostridium Tetani, present in horse manure. Tetanus was a rare occurrence on the whole and there seems little doubt that there were sometimes less severe forms of the infection.

Another example of Guthrie's conservative approach to trauma surgery was that of Lieutenant Madden of the 52nd, who was 'wounded at the assault on Badajos in 1812, by a musket-ball, which fractured the head of the humerus, and lodged in it. The broken pieces were from time to time removed by incisions, together with the ball, and he ultimately preserved a very serviceable arm. He is now a very zealous member of the Church of England.'[30] Ensuing infection would have left a shoulder with very stiff ankylosed (fused) joint.

By contrast, the dangers of delaying a timely amputation after a ball injury were well illustrated by the case of Captain St Pol of the 7th or Royal Fusiliers. He

> was wounded in the ham from behind, whilst in the ditch at the foot of the great breach at Badajos. He fell instantly, and lost, as he thinks, a considerable quantity of blood. On recovering he was raised from the ground, and walked a few paces prior to his being carried to his tent, where I saw him in the afternoon of the next day, the 7th. The leg had ceased to bleed before his arrival in camp. A substance could be felt on the inner side of the patella, which, by the sensation communicated to the finger on moving, appeared to be the ball, which was extracted.

The joint was opened by the ball, a very dangerous wound, and when Dr Armstrong (who had served with the 7th for seven years, promoted full battalion surgeon on 29 August 1811), the battalion surgeon, consulted with Guthrie, they decided that, despite the minimal amount of bone damage (St Pol had walked and the finger of the surgeon had found no splinters), above knee amputation was needed. The captain did not consent and was sent out of his broiling tent to the cool of a hospital in Badajoz on 8 April. Gangrene had set in and the officer's leg was removed by cutting through already devitalized tissue and the application of sixteen ligatures. Eight days later the poor man died. Post-mortem revealed the totally divided femoral artery. Guthrie surmised that a lesser operation on the 16th might have saved Pol's life. In reality, the operation should have been done the day after wounding. Certainly officers' rights to turn down surgery had been respected, but there is little evidence of such refusals being accepted in wounded NCOs and enlisted men.[31]

Two senior officers of the 40th were hit in the chest by firelock balls during the assault, Lieutenant-Colonel Harcourt and Major Gillies:

> the wounds were as nearly similar as possible, from before directly backwards. They were taken to the same tent, and treated alike with the same care by the late Mr Boutflower [by all accounts an able operative surgeon, appointed to the 40th on 8 June 1809, and author of *The Journal of an Army Surgeon during the Peninsular War*; Boutflower had been taken prisoner during the campaign of the Rio Plata in 1807 and had started his career as an assistant surgeon in the Royal Navy in 1805], the surgeon of the regiment, with whom I saw them daily. The inflammatory symptoms ran high in both. In Major Gillies, a tough old Scotchman, they could not be subdued [by bleeding, emesis, antimony and catharsis], and he died at the end of a few days of pleuro-pneumonia [more likely an infection in the blood and fluid in his thorax]. Colonel Harcourt slowly recovered, and died Marquis Harcourt, near Windsor, more than twenty-five years afterwards, suffering little or no inconvenience from his chest, when I last saw him.[32]

One of the real problems with penetration of the chest cavity by missiles was inaccessible bleeding from the artery and vein that lie tucked under each rib – the intercostal vessels. If these vessels were hit by a missile or the sharp end of a broken rib, brisk bleeding would threaten the life of the casualty. The brave General Sir George Walker, with the 5th Division, mounting a rampart to storm a bastion to the east, ran into an ordnance discharge and musketry. The lower costal cartilages (false ribs) of the right side were injured by a musket ball, which passed right through the man's chest. Guthrie looked after him:

> He remained in Badajoz under my care for the first three weeks, with many of the other principal officers who were wounded; and overcame the first inflammatory symptoms in a satisfactory manner. After I left him the wound sloughed, some part of the now [dead] cartilages separated, and one of the intercostal arteries bled; although the bleeding was arrested once by ligature [passed on a needle through the wound] and afterwards on its return, by different contrivances; each time it reappeared his life was placed in considerable jeopardy from it and the discharge from the cavity of the chest, which was profuse. The bleeding was ultimately arrested by the oil of turpentine, applied on a dossil of lint, and pressed on the bleeding spot by the fingers of the assistants until the haemorrhage ceased. He recovered after a very tedious treatment, with a considerable flattening of the chest, and a deep hollow at the lower part of the side, whence portions of the rib, and of the cartilages had been removed.[33]

Major, the Hon. Hercules Packenham, assistant adjutant-general of the 7th Foot, was wounded at the breach by a musket ball which

> deprived him of the use of the thumb and little finger, and partially of the hand; and by another which struck him on the right iliac region passing in just below Poupart's ligament [i.e. just below the groin], and outwardly through the ilium [i.e. traversing the pelvic bone]. Eight pieces of bone came away at Elvas, and eleven more [with the chronic infection], in 1813, in London. He went to Barège [in the Hautes-Pyrénées] in 1814–15–16–17, with the hope that the ball might be loosened and removed, but in vain. A small quantity of inoffensive glutinous [thick mucous-like substance] matter, sometimes streaked with blood, was discharged occasionally from the seat of injury.[34]

Presumably the hip joint was damaged, but surprisingly there was no record of stiffness or difficulty with that joint.

After due consideration, Wellington, at McGrigor's request, agreed to put a mention of the services given by the Army Medical Department in his already-complete London Despatch. The Secretary for State, the Earl of Liverpool, received the following addition to the document, 'Camp at Badajoz, 8th April 1812, My Lord, It gives me great pleasure to in form your Lordship that our numerous [wounded] officers and soldiers are doing well. I have had great reason to be satisfied with the attention paid to them by Mr McGrigor, the Inspector-General of Hospitals, and the medical gentlemen under his direction and I trust that the loss to the service upon this occasion, will not eventually be great.'[35]

This may have drawn a feeling of gratifying warmth from the surgeons. McGrigor explains that the predicaments and efforts of the medical staff after such a fearsome combat, and reflecting the attitudes of commanders and historians, are frequently overlooked and soon forgotten. The Inspector-General wrote:

> From the great number of wounded the labours of the medical officers after the fall of Badajoz were immense. Their duties before and during the siege were heavy upon them. But it is after a siege or general engagement, when the military officer is in comparative ease and with very light duties, that the toil of the medical officer is arduous in the extreme, and the fatigue of the mind is not less than that of the body. While laboriously employed from morning to night, the anxiety he feels frequently prevents the refreshment of sleep at night when, wrapt in thought, and drawing constantly on his professional resources, he becomes careworn and exhausted. It is at these times that his value is felt by the army at large and that by the officers in particular he is caressed, flattered and almost

idolised. He nearly everywhere alleviates pain; in many instances he gets credit for saving life; and on all sides expressions of gratitude and eternal obligation are made to him. From what one sees and hears at such times, one might be led to fancy that the doctor would be cherished ever afterwards. But, alas, those feelings are but too often the feelings of the moment only; they grow fainter and fainter with the lapse of time and I have but too frequently observed that the doctor and his doings have, in a few years, been quite forgotten and when these have become the subject of conversation it has been too often said, 'Well, what more did he do than his duty? Was it not the doctor's duty to have done all this?' I do not say that this is the cold transitory feelings of all military officers for I know bright examples of the contrary in the highest ranks in the army and of civil life who, to their dying day, have honoured as a cherished friend the medical officer, who in battle or in serious illness, was their surgeon or physician. Yet, as the result of close personal observation, during a period of upward of fifty years, I must affirm that too frequently the feeling of gratitude has subsided in time, and even in instances where the attention has been extreme and much beyond what the strict line of duty required of the medical officer. I have indeed known more than one instance where the surgeon, besides visiting the officer three or four times a day, when the great pressure of fatiguing duty devolved upon him, after expending all the bandages he could get from the stores, has torn up his own shirts for bandages and dressings for his patients; while he has furthermore supplied not only all the wine required, but the very eatables from his own stock, and nothing but that constant kind attention saved life.[36]

McGrigor then saw that every church, convent, monastery and public building in Badajoz was fitted out as a hospital and Wellington toured the principal hospitals with him and, 'in going round, he spoke kindly to many of the poor fellows as I pointed out their cases to him, and expressed himself much satisfied with the degree of comfort and cleanliness'.[37] Outside the town, Dr Dickson, the Purveyor General formed a chain of hospitals from Badajoz to Lisbon, at Elvas, Estremos, Alter de Chaô, Abrantes and Santarem.[38] Anxious now to get the army on the move again, Wellington directed the incurables to be transported to Cuidad Rodrigo, if feasible, and to McGrigor he comments in his letter of approbation, 'I assure you that I am very sensible of the diligence and attention of the Medical Department of which I have reported my sense to the Secretary of State.'[39]

So ended two bloody sieges. Wellington, although concerned after this last costly assault, now had the two border fortresses at his back. Secure in that knowledge, it was time to go on. Dr McGrigor's assistant Dr Charles Forbes was, with Staff Surgeon Burnall, left in charge of the general hospital in Badajoz. Between 21

March and 20 April, leaving aside those killed in the siege, 8,925 men were in general hospitals, in regimental hospitals, with 462 deaths (of which 122 died of dysentery; 161 of 'continued fever', typhus; and 146 of wounds – including 17 cases of tetanus).

Breakout

Meanwhile, way to the north, Marshal Auguste Marmont, with 70,000 effectives threatened Cuidad Rodrigo. This forced the Duke to head north, rather than proceed to Madrid or invade Andalusia to confront Soult. The latter Marshal having retired towards Seville, Wellington now marched on towards Beira. Rowland Hill had been sent to destroy the fortified bridgeheads at Almaraz in order to hamper communications between Marmont and Soult. Hill accomplished this on 12 May.

Wellington's force was as strong as it might be – particularly with cavalry and ordnance – and with so many French troops involved in the invasion of Russia, Wellington had few qualms about engaging Marmont. He now had the confidence and cooperation of the Spanish population and *guerrilleros* and also a decent intelligence system. On 13 June, Wellington crossed the Agueda River to march east. By 16 June, he was within six miles of Salamanca. At Wellington's approach, with around 50,000 sabres and bayonets, Marmont retired to Salamanca. Here he had fortified three convents, lying to the west of the city, which barred the bridge at the River Tormes. The Allied army forded the river above and below the town on the 17th, whereupon General Henry Clinton's 6th Division invested the forts and Salamanca rejoiced as the Allies entered the city. Of note, it was on this day that the President and Congress of the United States declared war on Great Britain.

The 4th Division, with its staff surgeon, under Sir Lowry Cole, licking its wounds and minus 600–700 bayonets, had advanced with the Duke to Salamanca in one of four columns and with the rest of the army marched off to encamp on the heights of San Cristóbal, two to three miles north of Salamanca on 19 June.

The division consisted of Major-General George Anson's brigade (3/27th, 1/40th and one company of the 5/60th) and Ellis's brigade (1/7th, 1/23rd, 1/48th and one company of the Brunswick Oels). Whilst the siege of one of the forts – the San Vicente convent – was in progress, on 20–22 June, Marmont with his force of 25,000 men advanced temptingly close, at around 800 yards from the Allies stationed on the San Cristóbal heights, but neither leader risked an assault.

Dr McGrigor was based in Salamanca and one day visited his colleagues – including Guthrie – then he descended a slope to visit the Allied pickets, with the field officer of the day. He witnessed a desertion from the Chasseurs Britanniques and, as he climbed back up the hill, was promptly told by Sir Lowry Cole to go to the rear, since an attack was expected any time. However after a counsel of war, Marmont decided to forego a major assault and withdrew, on 23 June, six miles to Aldearrubia, east and north of Salamanca.

The three now abandoned forts with their garrisons (of about 800 men) – San Vicente, San Gaetano and La Merced – at length surrendered on 27 June after bombardment and being plied with red-hot shot. So far, the Allies had suffered about 500 casualties in the assaults. Seven hundred prisoners and thirty guns were taken from the French.

During these assaults on the forts, Guthrie was clearly closely involved at some stage,

> everybody of all ranks passed along the road quite within range of the [fort's] guns without the slightest molestation, until one very fine day a handsome captain of the Welsh [sic] Fusiliers took it into his head to put on a new red coat, with a pair of large gold epaulettes, and mount himself on a white horse to attract the attention of the Salamanquiñas [ladies of Salamanca]. Mr Guthrie rode by his side, little thinking of the evil intentions of the garrison, when, lo! a round shot dropped under Mr Guthrie's horse's nose on the road, throwing the dirt in his face. Both gentlemen rode off rather quickly, Mr Guthrie protesting he would never again ride by the side of a white horse, the ordinary attribute of a marshal of France, or general commanding, and for which his friend was, it may be presumed, taken. Chance was soon afterwards more successful than the aim of the French artilleryman; the handsome captain fell from a grapeshot, which entered his abdomen on one side, carrying out with it, on the other, several feet of his bowels, which were lying on the ground when Mr Guthrie reached him.[1]

While Guthrie plied his skills in the city, the army prepared to move off to follow Marmont who, knowing of the forts' surrender, had decided to withdraw northeast towards Valladolid.[2] He would cross the Douro at Tordesillas. By 2 July, the advanced Allied troops were near that place, not far from Rueda. The weather was very hot on the march and sometimes it had been hard to find enough water to slake thirsty throats. The countryside was fairly abundant in fruit, crops, straw and forage and no doubt the Allied force was now in reasonable shape. There had been some opportunities to bathe and play during manœuvring, since there was little activity for two weeks or so. As two divisions of Marmont's force had recrossed the Douro at Toro, to the south, so Wellington's force also moved southwestwards. However, the two French divisions had returned over the river and burned the bridge at Toro. The main French force then recrossed the Douro at Tordesillas on

16/17 July, following the Allied force. Guthrie's 4th Division with the Light Division, as a rearguard were halted at Castréjon to the north of the main force. At this place, there was a tale of a casualty of the 4th Division that has been retold in various circumstances. An Irishman of the 27th, who saw a round shot bouncing towards him apparently shouted, 'Stop it boys!' He put out his foot to stop it like a cricket ball. The ball smashed his leg below the knee and Guthrie had no option but to ablate the limb.[3]

There was a good deal of jostling and manœuvring for position by both armies. During these movements, the 4th Division, with Guthrie, were at one time subjected to French fire from batteries set up above them, whilst they moved through a valley.[4] The 40th and 27th Foot were involved in repelling an assault near Castrillo, where the 4th Division formed the left flank. A brigade of French cavalry, a battalion of infantry and some guns were pushed away by Alten's horse and the 3rd Dragoons. This day's action cost Wellington 442 casualties of all ranks.[5] This small action is relevant since there were so many wounded to be transported to Salamanca. Guthrie's biography notes, 'The affairs which took place in the beginning of the campaign of 1813 [i.e. 1812], at Castréjon, and afterwards on the Gareña, deprived Mr Guthrie of the whole of his means of transport, and the Battle of Salamanca left him with many hundred wounded strewn over the field, without the capability of removing one.'[6]

By 19 July, there was some respite, for the marching had begun to take its toll of the troops and place the men under considerable hardship. Not a few expired of heatstroke, keeping Guthrie's battalion surgeons busy. The next day the great parallel march of 20 July took place. Hot and dusty the armies eyed each other suspiciously, Guthrie riding not with the divisional staff, but with his three spring wagons in the rear and, as so many others, wondering when the calamitous action would take place and how far he and his surgeons would be from shelter and water. He found no victims of the sporadic French artillery fire and was relieved that the French gunners left his little group alone. Two nights before the action of 22 July, Guthrie had to pick up casualties from a skirmish involving the 27th and 40th and he shouted to the French, who had retired across a stream, that they should retrieve their wounded. Guthrie remembers, 'Some of the French were unable to move, and fell into my hands; and, recollecting what had happened in the morning [i.e. him not having been fired on], I went forward, and called for them to cross the stream to send for their wounded officers and soldiers, who would be given to them by Sir L. Cole, the general commanding. Several officers and men came forward immediately, without arms: and you cannot conceive how we complimented each other.'[7] Guthrie's surgeons worked all night and packed their convalescents off to Salamanca. As dawn broke, Guthrie washed and ate a 'hearty' breakfast of bread and water. Dr James McGrigor trotted up to 'enquire if I had received his orders relative to the wounded. I told him I had not. He then desired they might go to

Salamanca, whither they had already been dispatched. The cavalry had received his orders, he said, but had not obeyed. He now asked if I had a spring wagon left. I replied, one; which he said he must have for Sir Thos. Picton, who was very ill [three months after his wound]. I remonstrated, saying, it was the only one I had or could get, and that if we had another fight, I could not move a single man.' Guthrie was seething after this and commented with a degree of vehemence, 'He promised faithfully to bear this in mind, and provide for me accordingly, – which, luckily for me, he was not able to do.'

Veering off towards his previous position near Salamanca, Wellington was forced to move south on 21 July, since Marmont's force was heading to cut off his line of communication with Cuidad Rodrigo and Portugal. The Allied force forded the Tormes and took up positions for the night preceding the battle. A violent storm caused some havoc and injuries during the night and afforded little rest for the combatants. This night, Guthrie sought permission to move the divisional sick out of Salamanca, in the event of a reverse and to avert their capture. He rode with a few mules, loaded with bread, corn and spirits and effected this, probably moving them to houses nearer to the army. As he rode back in the storm, he sheltered with a clergyman in his tent, with two young officers, Captain Prescott and Lieutenant Leroux, and their ladies. The divisional commander had sent these two married men back with the baggage a few miles to the rear. Guthrie shared supper with them and in the morning, an early breakfast. At the sound of a distant gun, the young wives' cheeks blanched and Guthrie's horse came to the door. Guthrie suggested the officers remained, but they followed him into the lines and two hours later, both had been shot dead.

On 22 July, across the arid plains, the Allied arrayed themselves around the villages of Los Arapiles and Las Torres, in which field hospitals would be set up. Cole's 4th Division was positioned, near the lesser Arapil, on the Teso de San Miguel, close to the little village of Los Arapiles, where Guthrie's hospital tent and buildings were to be found. The village was defended by light companies of the Foot Guards. Guthrie once more was to narrowly avert death and wrote:

As it was plain we were in for a good pelting, the General sent his aide-de-camp, Captain Roverea, to ascertain where I had fixed the field hospital, that the wounded might be directed upon it. I was at this moment going to the front, and saw my friend Roverea approaching, when my horse stopped and ducked, a sort of gambol I did not think he was warranted to make from the quantity of corn he had eaten. This motion was explained in a moment; a twelve-pound shot, which he had seen, but which I had not, plunged into the loose ploughed field a few feet before him, covered us both with dirt, and hopped calmly but irresistibly over my shoulder. Roverea was so white in the face that I thought he must be wounded; he said no he was not, and eagerly enquired whether I had seen that shot pass. I said I had, and nearly felt it too. 'Well,' said he, 'it nearly took my nose off.'

Guthrie's robust sense of humour was seen next:

It was impossible to resist laughing at this, for my poor friend, although a most excellent, honourable, and upright man, was certainly not handsome; he was short, with a large face, having high cheek-bones, and as small a proportion of nose as was ever allotted to man, so that in profile but very little of it was to be seen. I could not for the life of me help saying, 'My dear Roverea, it might have taken off your head, but I will be hanged if it could have taken off your nose.' Not all the sal-volatile [ammonium carbonate, spirits of ammonia, a stimulant] in the army could have bought the blood more quickly into his face, for he was very tenacious on this point, having been caricatured in England, and he very indignantly replied, 'Sir, you are the only man that would have dared to make such a remark.' He had been shot in the head at Albuhera [sic]; his skull had been fractured, and when delirious, he had thrown himself out of bed, and thought he owed his life to my kindness. He was, therefore, soon pacified, and willingly forgave my joke. He fell honourably, and for his rank gloriously, shot through the same side of the head on the heights in front of Pampeluna [sic].[8]

After some skirmishing on the left of Wellington's line in the morning, the French drifted on to their left, southwards and to the west. They had raced and beaten the Allies to occupy the greater Arapil hill position. Wellington then moved the 5th, 6th, and 7th Divisions behind Cole's near the village, whilst Packenham's 3rd Division (Picton being incapacitated) moved westwards, further back. Around 2pm, having concluded that the Allies were in retreat towards Portugal or Cuidad Rodrigo, Marmont marched his army further, also moving westwards to cut Wellington off. The movement of men and huge dust clouds observed by Marmont and his staff were thought to be Wellington's rewithdrawal, but in fact were thrown up by Packenham's relatively concealed force.

Wellington could hardly believe his fortune – the enemy stretched out in front of him, with General Thomière's division moving ahead to the Duke's right, unsupported, to attack his 'retreating' force. Wellington galloped over to Packenham at about 2.30pm and ordered the attack on Thomière's men, by heading them off. Around 3.30pm, Packenham's men started their destruction of Thomière's division. Soon it was time to attack the French column and Leith's 5th Division moved out to the right of Cole's men. Now exposed to enemy round shot, the attack went in at around 4.15pm. The assistant surgeons moved in with the assault and returned surviving casualties to battalion dressing stations and to the field hospital in Los Arapiles. James Leith's division crashed into General Marcune's men, who formed in squares, many of which were broken. It was now that General Gaspard Le Marchant's brigade of cavalry had its time. It sent Marcune's men in a shambolic retreat, the unwieldy straight blades of the 1796 heavy cavalry sabre producing ghastly wounds on the Frenchmen's heads, shoulders and arms. Unfortunately, the 46-year-old Le Marchant was killed in the assault – the end of a great leader, who had helped to raise the reputation of British cavalry in this war.

Cole's men had moved into the attack to confront General Bertrand Clausel's division at around 4.30pm. There was a furious fire-fight. The French were pushed back, Cole was wounded and, as Pack's support to Cole's left had been repulsed, the 4th were now exposed to flank fire and soon were forced to retire back to the environs of the lesser Arapil. Around 5pm Clinton's 6th Division saved the day and pushed the French attack to the rear. With the support of the little-engaged 1st and Light Divisions the French retreat was assured, covered by a spirited rearguard action. The French retreated over the undefended bridge at Alba de Tormes. Wellington following the French and after the successful cavalry action at Garcia Hernández, arrived at Valladolid on 30 July, entering Madrid in triumph on 12 August.

As dusk fell on 22 July, wounded and exhausted men burnt in the fires, which were caused by smouldering wadding and cartridge debris amongst the tinder-dry crops. What was the cost? Around 5,000 Allied casualties (700 killed) and about 14,000 Frenchmen killed, hurt, taken prisoner or missing. There were many notable casualties; Marmont, Ferey, Leith, Cole, Le Marchant, even Fransisco Sánchez. 'El Cojo' (The Limper) – Wellington's local guide on the field – who survived a leg amputation. So once more the problems for Guthrie and his worthies were plentiful, night was coming in, lack of water and around 10,000 wounded men (4,800 British, Spanish and Portuguese) to dress and move out. The missing transport after the action near Castrillo was now felt acutely. Most men were too exhausted to make efforts to escort the wounded back to the city or even to nearby villages. Casualties lay out untended and, for many, it would be a long painful or fateful night. The following day, some help was on its way. Robertson quotes from Commissary John Daniel's journal and reported that many females from Salamanca had 'prepared a great quantity of lint and rags for the use of the wounded'. They also brought out food and drink and, Daniel goes on, 'and here might be seen the interesting spectacle of Spanish girls supporting from the field such of our wounded as were able to walk, carrying for them their knapsacks and muskets'.[9] Guthrie meanwhile, remained out on the field, scooping up wounded Allied and French casualties.[10]

As the wounded staggered, rode or were dragged in, Guthrie and his colleagues started their grim work of assessment and surgery. Having more than a thousand injured men and his divisional commander to look after taxed Guthrie sorely. He pointed out, somewhat ironically, that 'a wounded commanding officer of a regiment is next to nobody when away from his regiment; but a wounded general of division resembles a sick lion, being very likely to show his teeth and talons on a future day, and not to be neglected until he is dead'. Guthrie was under intense pressure and, presuming on Cole's authority, he reacted to the challenge by ordering

> all the medical officers and all the hospital establishments to join me from the division except two; and the commanding officers obeyed without a murmur, which they would not perhaps have done at such a moment, if they had not known I lived with and wielded the authority of the general on all medical points. My wounded were now safe, but the afternoon of the second day had arrived and we were alone on the field of battle without even a bit of bread; not a man had stirred [i.e. left the field station], for I had kept the slightly wounded to assist the bad cases, and would only move as a whole. Sir James McGrigor could do little beyond acquitting me of blame, for the Spaniards promised everything, but as usual, did nothing, and he could only speak to them through an interpreter.[11]

Guthrie is clearly sensitive to McGrigor's presence and directions, perhaps the reaction of a veteran surgeon, who 'knows the ground', and the new inspector, endeavouring to get the best out of his department.

As noted, Guthrie's most illustrious case at Salamanca was Sir Lowry Cole. Leading the 4th Division into their ill-fated advance, he had been struck by a musket ball, 'immediately below the left clavicle [collar bone]; a part of the first rib came away, and the artery at the wrist became, and remained, much diminished in size'.[12] The ball had almost completely disrupted the large (axillary) artery. Guthrie noted, 'There was the sixteenth part of an inch or less between him and immediate death.' The reason for the loss of pulse at the wrist was damage to the vessel's structure as the ball shattered the rib, just below it, so disrupting the inner lining (intima) of the large artery so that blood could no longer flow down the blood vessel (a fact recognized by Guthrie).

Fortunately there is a rich network of smaller blood vessels near the armpit and shoulder-blade, which open up as 'collaterals', so re-establishing the blood flow down the arm. Further details of this illustrious leader's wound were as follows:

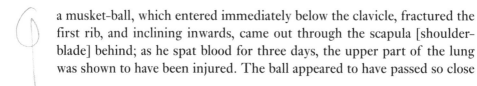

> a musket-ball, which entered immediately below the clavicle, fractured the first rib, and inclining inwards, came out through the scapula [shoulder-blade] behind; as he spat blood for three days, the upper part of the lung was shown to have been injured. The ball appeared to have passed so close

to the under part of the subclavian artery, that the greatest fears were entertained for his safety; more particularly as a marked difference in the size of the pulse was perceived in the left arm, which did not exist before. I remained three days on the field of battle, in a Portuguese officer's tent I always carried with me [this latter had been presented to him by General Turner, who had had a disarticulation of the shoulder after Badajoz]. Under repeated bleedings and the strictest antiphlogistic [anti-inflammatory] treatment, several splinters having come away, and a large piece of rib and of the scapula having exfoliated [came away, septic], he gradually recovered, so as to be able to resume the command of the Fourth Division in October in Madrid. The subclavian artery never resumed its power, and the radial [i.e. the artery at the wrist] always beat less forcibly on the left side. He perfectly recovered his health, the respiratory murmur of the lung being natural. He died suddenly in 1844, from rupture, I believe, of an aneurysm of the abdominal aorta.[13]

Whilst Guthrie was out in the scorching heat of the day, at his field dressing station, he was presented with another case, most successfully managed,

a soldier of the 27th Regiment was brought to me, who had walked to the rear, and had fallen down insensible within a few yards of the hospital station. I found a considerable fracture, with depression at the inferior part of the parietal bone before and above the ear. The end of the elevator having been introduced, a small piece of bone was first raised, then another and a third, when a thick coagulum [i.e. a collection of blood clot, an extradural haematoma] was exposed and removed. The dura mater [the thick protective membrane surrounding the brain] was not separated from the bone around to any extent, and the coagulum although thick was not large. The brain, which had been depressed, regained its level immediately; the man recovered his senses, and was cured of his wound, but remained unfit for service.[14]

Guthrie's success with severe head wounds continued. A French grenadier hit on the side of his skull by a musket ball had his wound explored, at which it was evident that the skull had fractured and the ball had been split in two by a sharp edge of the bone! The two fragments of lead were removed by gently elevating the loosened bone fragments. It having been noted that the dura was intact (a significant issue in the prevention of sepsis), the wound was closed. Infection followed, some pieces of septic bone being thrown out, but the patient survived. Another patient, a heavy dragoon, was hit on his trunk by a ball and fell from his mount. He landed on the crown of his head. When his clinical condition deteriorated, he was brought to Guthrie, who explored the wound. He found a major join of two bony plates (the sagittal suture) running along the top of the cranium violently separated by the fall and a collection of blood, oozing from the large venous sinus underneath the suture. Two crowns of the trephine saw were applied on day twelve, to facilitate the drainage of blood. Again the man survived.[15]

Of course not all such patients survived and Guthrie emphasized the risk of ever-threatening infection:

> The whole of the French wounded, who remained on the ground or were taken prisoners after the battle of Salamanca, were under my care, and among them there were several severely wounded by sword–cuts received in the charges of heavy cavalry made by Generals Le Merchant [sic] and Major general Eberhard Bock. The cerebellum [a large part of the brain lying under the cerebrum] was laid bare in two cases without any immediate bad effect. In [i.e. If] one particular part of the brain may receive such a shock at the moment of injury, as well as an external part, that no treatment can arrest the progress of the mischief, although it may be delayed; and when the patient dies, after four, five, or more weeks of alternate hope of suffering, matter may be found in some part of the brain where an injury was not expected.

Purulent matter (pus) might form beneath the dura mater in a confined spot, at a site of injury, or it may be diffused generally over the surface of the brain. The message here is that the sword cut has introduced infection by breaching the dura mater and the purulent exudates may spread under the membrane, producing meningitis and fatal encephalitis.

When he returned to Salamanca with all his charges, McGrigor was given, amongst other buildings, the convent of San Domingo, which he allocated to Guthrie along with a valuable authority, the permission to 'badger' the junta as much as he required.

Guthrie's integrity and sense of moral indignation was soon to surface over an issue that would offend any surgeon and his code of practice. Around 300 wounded Frenchmen, 'the worst of the wounded then living', were crowded in a hospital set up in the convent of San Carlos. They lay on bare ground,

> the living, the dying, and the dead, side by side, the stench was dreadful; never was humanity more outraged. They ate and drank all Mr Guthrie had to give them out of their shoes, using the same shoes and caps for all other necessary purposes of life. The Spanish authorities would not help, the junta declaring that the sooner they died the better. At last Mr Guthrie, in despair, assured them, in full junta, that he would leave a letter for the

first French general who came into the town, and there was great probability that the French army would recover it, [which they did in less than three months] stating their inhuman conduct in the strongest terms, and recommending them to hang them to a man. This made them absolutely furious. The Spanish word ahorca is an ugly one, and, when pronounced with its full guttural sound [which we can imagine that Guthrie did with feeling!], really makes one think of hanging. Mr Guthrie spoke Spanish fluently, and they did not quite like the solemn assurances that he gave them, by all the saints in the calender [sic], that he would keep his word. They at last gave in, and delivered over to him an alguazil, or police officer, to obey his orders, who he promised should never see his home again until the French wounded were decently provided for. These poor Frenchmen assured him, that although little given to praying, they had prayed for him. When he left them, in October, the officers drew up a paper, acknowledging his services, and returning their thanks in the strongest terms to him to whom they acknowledged they and their soldiers owed their lives, and the little comfort they had enjoyed. We believe this is the only instance of the kind that occurred during that war. Mr Guthrie, who never looked for thanks for doing what he thought was merely his duty, made his acknowledgements next morning, verbally; and we regret to say, being in want of a lamp in the evening, lighted it with the document they had thus gratefully bestowed; not from any disrespect to them, but simply from feeling, that the service was rendered, the thanks accepted;[16]

In this French hospital, one young wishful officer cared for by Guthrie, with a broken thigh-bone, 'who heard me cautioning the assistant surgeon who attended him of keeping it of its proper length, begged me to allow it to be an inch shorter, as that would ensure his retirement from the service to his home and friends'.[17]

There was a badly wounded French officer under Guthrie's care who recovered from his wounds and was later to be was exchanged as a prisoner of war. The French officer, long-since forgotten by our surgeon, repaid his debt to Guthrie, when, on patrol in the Pyrenean campaign of 1813, a squadron of French cavalry surrounded and captured the latter. On recognizing him, the erstwhile wounded Frenchman had Guthrie released and thanked him once more for his care.

In Guthrie's eyes, one of the great advances in the management of a wounded and infected limb was the practise of 'débridement'. This term requires clarification. Débridement most literally translated means unbridling, in other words, releasing the tension in swollen soft tissues, which might imperil the blood supply to a limb. Nowadays however, the practice of débridement has a different meaning and infers a thorough cleaning of a contaminated wound, with removal of all non-viable or dead tissues and leaving the wound open. Guthrie's 'débridement' was what we, today, would call fasciotomy. The term fasciotomy means that a long cut is made in the fascia or tough membrane holding in swollen muscle tissue. Once the fascia is divided, the tension is released and the blood flow restored. He had a case of an unidentified soldier after Salamanca who having been wounded in the leg acquired an infection through the wound. One of the bacteria must have been beta-haemolytic streptococcus (often carried on the body surface), which results in pain, tense swelling and a diffuse red colour of the skin. Septicaemia and fatality were the usual outcome. The case is briefly reported in a biography:

> The battle of Salamanca gave to Mr Guthrie the opportunity of introducing into the practice of surgery the treatment of erysipelas phlegmonodes [phlegmon is a brawny tense swelling of soft tissues], or diffuse erysipelatous inflammation of the cellular membrane, by long incisions through the skin for the relief of the tension it occasions, and the severe and often fatal constitutions which ensue. This procedure, he [once again] put in practice, in 1823 in the Westminster Hospital, with great success, contrary to the opinion of his colleagues.

The case he wrote up at the Westminster Hospital eleven years after Salamanca, had incisions in the arm, five and eight inches long. When he published this, it 'preceded by a year all others of a similar kind, and caused him to object to the claim set up by Mr Lawrence, in his paper on Erysipelas in the Medico-Chirurgical Transactions, as the inventor of that which had been publicly made known so long before, and not even then as something new. It is due to Mr Guthrie undoubtedly that this improvement in surgery is due.'[18]

Although the procedure differed from that which we perform today, the principle is important. Guthrie described how drainage of the injured parts, through the fasciotomy, would also be of benefit:

> When the inflammation, pain, and fever run high, the tension of the part being great, an incision should be made by introducing the knife [bistoury or scalpel] into the [entrance] wound, and cutting for a space of two to three inches, according to circumstances, in the course of the muscles, carefully avoiding any other parts of importance. The same should be done at the inferior or opposite opening [exit wound], if mischief be seriously impending, not so much on the principle of loosening the fascia, as of that of taking away blood from the part immediately affected, and of making a free opening for the evacuation of the fluids about to be effused.

Another serious complication, which occasionally challenged and fascinated Guthrie, afflicted a young officer who had been wounded in the action on 22 July.

Our surgeon had performed a secondary (delayed) amputation for infection and despite having removed the septic area, the patient died with chest complications. With regard to secondary operations, Guthrie wrote,

> In the most favourable state of the stump [i.e. the appearance of the wound after the second operation], the diseased parts do not extend very deep; yet inflammation is frequently communicated along the vein, which is found to contain pus, even as far as the vena cava [the main vein of the body, returning blood to the heart]. When I have met with this appearance, I have always considered the vessels as participating in [not originating] the disease, which had existed some days, and thereby more quickly destroying the patient. I further said that after secondary amputations, the febrile irritation, allayed by the operation, sometimes returns and more or less rapidly cuts off the patient by an affection of some particular internal part or viscus [organ], especially of the lungs. If it be the lungs, and they are most usually affected, the breathing becomes easy; there is little pain when the disease is compared with pneumonia or pleuritis; the cough is dry and not very troublesome; the pulse having been frequent, there is but little alteration; the attention of the surgeon is not sufficiently drawn by the symptoms to the state of the organ, and in a very short time all the symptoms are deteriorated: blisters are employed, perhaps blood letting, but generally in vain; and the patient dies in a few hours, as in the last stage of inflammation of the lungs, in which effusion or suppuration has taken place.[19]

Guthrie is describing the Adult Respiratory Distress Syndrome (ARDS, a complication affecting the lungs in serious infection) or just possibly the spread of infection along the veins to the lung tissues and the formation of multiple lung abscesses. Any serious septicaemia spreading through the venous system can carry bacteria to the lungs, liver, brain or other sites.

There was another of these cases, with a twist to the tale:

> An officer received, at the battle of Salamanca, two balls, one under the left clavicle, which was supposed to have divided the brachial plexus of nerves, as the arm dropped motionless and without sensation to the side. The other ball passed through the knee joint, which suppurated. The left side of the chest became affected; he suffered from a severe cough, followed by hectic fever, and was evidently about to sink. As a last chance, I amputated his leg above the knee, after which he slowly recovered. Fourteen years afterwards he showed me his arm in the same state, and told me that he had been indicted for a rape, but that the magistrates seeing the wooden leg and the

useless arm, while admitting the attempt, would not assent to the committal of the offence.[20]

Bleeding from combat injuries was a frequent challenge. Conservative treatment for continuing haemorrhage from a medium or larger artery would occasionally be a wiser choice and result in a successful outcome. Such a case under our surgeon's care was John Wilson of the 23rd Regiment. He was

> Wounded at the battle of Salamanca by a musket-ball, which entered immediately behind the trochanter major [i.e. in the lower buttock to the rear of the hip-joint], passed downwards, forwards, and inwards, and came out on the inside of the anterior [front] part of the thigh. The ball could not have injured the femoral artery, although it might readily have divided some branch of the profunda [second largest artery in the thigh]. Several days after the receipt of the injury, I saw this man sitting at night on his bed, which was on the floor, with his leg bent and out of it, another man holding a candle, and a third catching the blood which flowed from the wound, and which had half filled a large pewter basin. A tourniquet with a thick pad was placed as high as possible on the upper part of the thigh, and the officer on duty was requested to loosen it in the course of an hour; that was done, and the bleeding did not recommence. The next day, the patient being laid on the operating table, I removed the coagula [clots] from both openings, and tried to bring on the bleeding by pressure and by moving the limb; it would not, however, bleed.

Guthrie could not explore the thigh since there was no pointer to the bleeding vessel. A precautionary tourniquet was loosely applied to the thigh. The wound poured arterial blood again at night and pressure was successfully applied and when Guthrie reinspected the thigh the following day, no bleeding occurred. The same happened a third time. Guthrie appointed a special orderly to be in attendance on the patient, who would apply a long thick pad over the artery at the groin and below and manually compress the pad when necessary. The bleeding eventually and finally ceased. Guthrie was clearly quite moved by this case and wrote sympathetically:

> A painter could not have had a better subject for a picture illustrative of the miseries which follow a great battle, than some of the hospitals at Salamanca at one time presented. Conceive this poor man, late at night, in the midst of others, some more seriously injured than himself, calmly watching his blood – his life flowing away without hope of relief, one man holding a lighted candle in his hand, to look at it, and another a pewter

wash hand-basin to prevent its running over the floor, until life should be extinct. The unfortunate wretch next [to] him with a broken thigh, the ends lying nearly at right angles for want of a proper splint to keep them straight, is praying for amputation or for death. The miserable being on the other side has lost his thigh; it has been amputated. The stump is shaking with spasms; it has shifted itself off the wisp of straw that supported it. He is holding it with both hands in an agony of despair.[21]

Guthrie had several chest cases to deal with. The long-bladed French heavy cavalry swords produced potentially more fatal injuries in the thorax than the British sabres, slashing the torso and limbs. A heavy dragoon of the King's German Legion was wounded by such a weapon, which

penetrated the cavity of the right side of the chest, between the sixth and seventh ribs. He fell from his horse, and lost a considerable quantity of blood from the mouth and from the wound. On examining the wound next day, a black coagulum was seen filling up the orifice, the cellular membrane around being considerably ecchymosed [bruised], and little doubt existed that the oppression in breathing under which he laboured was caused by blood [and air] effused into the cavity. On separating the edges of the wound with a director [a slim grooved blunt-tipped probe], several ounces of blood, half fluid, half coagulated, by making the external opening, which was enlarged, quite dependent.

Guthrie, peering into the wound observed:

The lung was then seen in contact with the external opening of the wound, having expanded as the pressure of the blood was removed from it. The wound was closed simply, by lint, compress and by adhesive plaster, without bandage; the man was largely bled, and placed upon his wounded side on the ground, being the most comfortable position, in some degree relieved from the oppression in breathing. Two days after, the wound discharged freely a reddish-coloured watery fluid, evidently, evidently from the cavity of the chest, the exit of which was aided by keeping the wound generally dependent. This continued for several days, the fluid gradually becoming less in quantity, and purulent; under careful management he was able to go to the rear, nearly well, by the end of October.[22]

Intemperance was, rightly or wrongly, thought to be a cause of relapse in otherwise successfully recuperating patients. A dragoon of the King's German Legion was hit between the eighth and ninth ribs during the battle. The ball had penetrated the lung and the soldier's breathing was laborious. As nothing was draining out of the wound, Guthrie dilated the wound with a bistoury, removed some fragments of shattered ribs and cloth and then he evacuated a considerable amount of blood from the thorax. The fluid inevitably became septic and the patient felt something 'roll within him'. Guthrie took note of this and contemplated re-exploring his wound, but 'a sudden relapse of inflammation, from drinking some brandy, carried him off'. Guthrie, performing the dissection, found the ball rolling around free on the diaphragm.[23]

A few casualties suffering abdominal wounds were more fortunate:

A soldier of heavy cavalry, under General Le Marchant, advancing in line to charge the French infantry at Salamanca, – on which occasion the general was killed, – was struck by a musket-ball, which entered in front, between the umbilicus and the ilium [pelvic bone] of the left side, and came out behind on the opposite side, above the right haunch-bone, thus traversing the body. The bowel protruded in front, but was uninjured, and was easily restored to its place. He remained at the field hospital with me for the first three days, and was rigorous treated, as well as afterwards in the San Domingo Hospital, where he gradually recovered, and was ultimately sent to the rear.[24]

Liver wounds were usually fatal, but one of our surgeon's notable patients was fortunate and provided the doctor with an unusual mechanical problem. The patient was Sir S Barns, Lieutenant-Colonel of the Royals, who 'was wounded at the battle of Salamanca by a musket-ball, which injured the cartilages of the false ribs, a portion of the rib being removed, and passed out through the liver. A bilious discharge continued several weeks from the wound, and his life was saved with great difficulty. He returned to his duties, although suffering from a dragging pain and weight in the side, which any exertion increased.' Such was the situation until 1819 – seven years after Salamanca. He had some sort of inflammatory reaction, with abdominal pain, faintness and shock. Other episodes followed. He was treated with venesection, leeches, blistering, calomel (mercurous chloride) and opium. Was it a small episode of damage, caused by pressure of the distorted rib-cage on the liver that initiated the reaction? At any rate, Guthrie reckoned that: 'In order to prevent the bending of the body forward, and to confine the motion of the liver, which seemed liable to injury from the irregular points of bone which could be readily distinguished above it, stays, made with iron plates instead of whalebone, were adapted to his body, and from these he derived great comfort.'[25]

It seems incredible that a ball could pass across the belly cavity, wound the gut, causing extravasation of faecal material and then the patient survive peritonitis. A soldier of Guthrie's division was hit by a ball, which passed across the abdominal cavity from right to left, nearer to the back than the front of the belly. He was left for dead, but recovered slightly and was brought in to the tent on the field. 'The belly was swollen, and generally tympanitic [resonant to percussion], and some haemorrhage had taken place from the wound of entrance.' He was bled and treated with calomel, opium and antimony, thence removed to the San Domingo Hospital. On the sixth day, his bowels were 'relieved', but also a small amount of faeces were passed through the abdominal wound. He survived. In this case, the bowel and omental intra-abdominal fat had wrapped off and sealed the damaged gut. Although the abdomen was ominously swollen with a paralytic ileus (the dangerous paralysis of the bowel after a flood of septic fluid into the belly cavity), the patient had amazingly survived this localized peritonitis.[26]

A trooper of the King's German Legion was hit in the lower abdomen by small-arms fire during the battle. The ball went in on the right side and exited through the left buttock. The bladder was injured and urine flowed from both wounds for three days. Thereafter the patient was in agony and the urine would neither pass from the bladder nor the wounds. Guthrie passed a catheter, which drew off some urine. He fixed the catheter with a tape passed around the abdomen and requested the patient to unstopper the catheter every hour (it would have been better to leave the catheter on continuous drainage) and leave the stopper out at night. The catheter was rinsed through every now and again. Urine flowed through the posterior wound for a while and, as the catheter was being 'bypassed' by the flow of urine, it was removed. The wounds closed and the patient was discharged from the hospital of San Domingo.[27]

Finally, after Salamanca there was another triumph of nature over disease. A French soldier was wounded by a ball which entered him by the side of the sacrum, 'Having been rode over and bruised, he was taken prisoner and brought to me on the field of battle. From this wound he suffered comparatively little, except for a difficulty in passing urine. On the third day after his arrival at the San Carlos Hospital, or the sixth from the receipt of the injury, he passed the ball per anum. The wound quickly closed, and he aided his comrades as an orderly in the hospital afterwards.'[28]

The reverse for the French had hit hard. Having sent his wounded and heavy wagons on to Burgos, Clausel wrote to the Duke de Feltre, the Minister for War, 'It is usual to see armies discouraged after a reverse, but it is difficult to find in which the discouragement is greater than in this; and I must not conceal from you that there reigns and has reigned for some time a very bad spirit in this army; our steps in this retreat have been marked everywhere by the most revolting disorders and excesses.'[29]

George Guthrie couldn't follow his chief to Madrid. Wellington had arrived there in triumph, via Valladolid, on 12 August. Leaving a small garrison to guard the invalids and sick French, King Joseph retired from the city, abandoning 430 patients for the allies to look after. Guthrie did not finish his work for at least two months. He left the hospitals at Salamanca in September and arrived at the capital in October. The army, though triumphant, was at this time sickly and there were many casualties to be brought to the capital. Dr James McGrigor had preceded Guthrie to Madrid, and Wellington, who was sitting for a portrait by Goya, unleashed his wrath on McGrigor in no uncertain terms. This outburst was provoked by the latter utilizing some commissary vehicles for transport of the wounded, instead of seeing to the 'necessaries' of the campaign.[30] Guthrie would certainly have been appraised of this reprimand. Many medical gentlemen must have resented the constant lack of transport facilities for the sick and hurt. In mitigation, perhaps we have to understand Wellington's constant attention to combat priorities – supplies, rations, sundry equipment and ordnance. Without these he could not keep an army on the road and prosecute the war.

Guthrie was not destined to venture with Wellington to the investment and failed investment of Burgos.

Retreat, Lisbon and on to Santander

The retirement from Burgos was perhaps the most dismal part of the Iberian campaigns and left many units sick and demoralized. It was no doubt a worse withdrawal than that to Corunna. Guthrie reflected on his last combat, 'the battle of Salamanca established the surgery of the British army nearly on its present basis. Our previous battles and sieges had pointed out many faults, and had admitted of many improvements being made. They were all now tested.' When Guthrie entered Madrid with his 4th Division, there was reward to greet him. Guthrie's robust character and commitment must have impressed his chief as he comments, 'Sir James McGrigor was indefatigable, and all his officers worked well. My labours had not been in vain. I found, on my arrival in Madrid, in October that he had recommended me to the Duke of Wellington for promotion.' He was now belatedly given the brevet rank of Deputy Inspector of Hospitals. There were huge disadvantages to being young, competent and yet far from home. Others with academic qualification, good connections yet little experience could be appointed over Guthrie. His biographer commented on his problems of promotion, seniority and nepotism:

> Mr Guthrie's reward from home, for this the most brilliant service of that war, was the refusal of the Army Medical Board to confirm his appointment; he was too young! The result of it was the immediate gazetting of several other persons, who took precedence of him, and ultimately became inspectors when on half-pay. When in a similar manner, it became his turn to become an [full] inspector, the secretary-at-war changed that which had been the custom of the service, and refused Mr Guthrie that rank unless he would serve abroad [he had already twelve years overseas service to his credit!]. This had deprived him of £130 [around £7,800 today] for thirty years, which the others, who had the good fortune to be placed above him, now enjoy, if they are alive. Mr Guthrie has never complained or asked for any promotion or honours; he bides his time, and if that time should never come, he trusts judgement of posterity will decide he has not been an unworthy servant.

Guthrie's brevet rank was not made permanent until 16 September 1813. Never destined to reach dizzier heights in the service, Guthrie's immense contribution lay in his ability as an experienced army field surgeon.

Guthrie's promotion meant more responsibility. In Madrid, he saw to the establishment of general and regimental lazarettes and their proper administration and supply. He treated a man who had been involved in a fight in the city:

> A Spanish soldier was wounded in a scuffle in Madrid, in 1812, at the gate of the British hospital near the Prado, into which he was brought, with a wound on the right side of the abdomen, near and below the umbilicus, though which a portion of omentum [the fatty apron, lying in front of the bowels] protruded, about the size of a small orange. As this could not readily be returned [to the abdomen], I carefully enlarged the wound at its upper part, some three or four hours afterwards.

Guthrie needed to replace some bowel, also protruding, back into its rightful place and cut the skin a little, but this was not enough. He then divided some deeper tendinous muscle tissue with his scalpel, which did the trick. The bowel loop was released from its constriction, recovered its blood supply and returned obligingly to the peritoneal cavity. The patient was 'bled and starved', delivered to the proper authorities and recovered as the Allied army retired from the capital.[1]

Rowland Hill remained in charge of the force remaining around and in the city after Wellington had left for Burgos with the 1st, 5th, 6th and 7th Divisions, a division of Spaniards, two brigades of Portuguese and two of cavalry. The town and citadel was invested on 19 September. With inadequate siege ordnance and sappers, and an inveterate defence by the garrison and its commander Dubreton, Wellington decided to abandon Burgos and by 22 October the siege was raised. As one French officer, a prisoner of war, predicted, 'believe me, you are too far forward and will not winter on the Ebro'.[2]

Remaining behind were the 2nd, 3rd, 4th and Light Divisions, regular Spanish troops and Alten's brigade of cavalry. Guthrie had overall medical responsibility for around 40,000 of Hill's force.

After the failure at Burgos, Wellington retired across the Douro at Tudela on 29 October. He would have to join up with Rowland Hill, who now with Guthrie and his sick convoy retired from Madrid. Hill marched away from the Spanish capital, marched through the Escorial and went over the Guadarrama pass on 2 November. Ordered by Wellington, he marched west towards Alba de Tormes. The junction of the two forces being effected on 7 and 8 November, the army settled in, covering the ground between the heights of San Cristobal, north of Salamanca and down to the River Tormes at Alba. In Wellington's own words he had 'got clear in a handsome manner from the worst scrape that he ever was in'.[3] The tough part of the retreat and its miseries were yet to come. King Joseph, Soult and Marshal Jean

Baptiste Jourdan with around 90,000 effectives did not attempt an assault on the smaller Allied force.

Hill's force had to follow the Duke west. Just as at Burgos, where Dr James McGrigor had effected a timely evacuation of the sick and wounded, so did Guthrie remove most of his patients from Salamanca. Rain and hunger added to the misery of the retreating army plodding away in deep mud and forests of ilex. Discipline was often out of hand, and with rain-flooded streams to ford and grumbling aplenty, the demoralized British force staggered in to Cuidad Rodrigo, the rearguard reaching the town on 19 November. So ended a difficult episode for all, the retreat was severe and had cost around 9,000 men, killed, wounded and missing. Drunkenness, fevers, pneumonia, typhus and enteritis had taken their toll. Whilst indiscipline, hunger and the inefficiencies of the Commissariat contributed to the difficulties, on the positive side, the great border fortresses were taken, Spain south of the Tagus had been cleared and 20,000 French had been sent home as prisoners of war.

We now have to consider Guthrie's new responsibilities and his movements. His problems during the aforementioned retreat, once again, lay with transport issues and discipline. We return with him to Madrid, where

> I was now chief [i.e. Principal Medical Officer] of the army under the command of Lord Hill, composed of several divisions of infantry and cavalry, with a large and increasing general hospital in that town. The force under my charge was larger than that under his [The Duke's] immediate superintendence, but he knew it was impossible at Burgos to regulate in detail for those to the southward of Madrid, and he left me to my own resources, desiring only that I should send 500 sets of bedding from thence to Salamanca.
>
> As the Duke of Wellington's situation before Burgos became desperate, our's at Madrid became critical; we could easily have beaten Marshal Soult in open field, but that would have been of no use to us, if the Duke was forced to cross the Tormes. It would have been as bad as a defeat; we therefore retired from Madrid, the French following us closely past the Escurial [sic], and across the Guadarama [sic] mountains, into the plains of Castile.

It appears that Guthrie was a close friend and admirer of Sir Edward Packenham and shared quarters with him in the Spanish capital before the retreat. Parting momentarily from the affairs in Madrid, Guthrie reflected on Packenham's generosity to a friend's widow and children and his bravery in action. The latter attribute was recalled at the last meeting of Guthrie and his friend:

I parted with Sir E Packenham at Lord Dartmouth's door, at the corner of St James's Square, the day he started for his last command [in America]. On shaking hands I said, 'We now part for the last time; I shall never see you again.' He asked, 'Why say so; what makes you a prophet of evil?' I replied, 'I know you so well, that I feel confident you will not be able to hear the first shots fired without being in the affray; and you will be killed, I fear, foolishly.' He knew the object I had in saying this, the feeling that dictated it, and, in pressing my hand more warmly, he said, 'That I shall fall, is possible; but if I do, *you* even shall say I fell as a general commanding in chief, ought to do.' When his aide-de-camp, Colonel Wyley, returned to England, he dined with me alone, that we might talk over the last acts of the life of our departed friend. In the front of a regiment [at the action at New Orleans], which appeared to be failing in its duty, on horseback, with his hat off, he received his first wound. Feeling that he could not sit his horse, he endeavoured to dismount. In the act of lifting his right leg over the saddle, a second shot struck him a little above the groin, and it was afterwards found, had divided the great iliac artery. He fell dead, and he kept his word.[4]

Guthrie carries on with his account of the imminent crisis in Madrid, where he used much guile in procuring transport,

The order for the retreat came suddenly, but, living with Sir E Packenham, who was sick, and commanded in Madrid, it was not unexpected by those, who had shared his anxieties as to the fate of the army at Burgos. Whilst I was pressing our deputy commissary-general, and the Spanish indendant-general, to give sufficient conveyance for the removal of the sick to Salamanca; they were occupied in filling the Retiro with corn and flour, and with establishing in it a large magazine for the army.

When the order arrived, I found the deputy commissary-general on his way to the Retiro, determined to use all the means in his power to fill it with provisions. No arguments of mine would he attend to, and no more conveyance would he spare. We were now within hearing of the sentry, and I begged him to turn his horse back with me for a few yards, and then asked him if he knew that the Retiro was to be blown up at that very hour to-morrow. There never was a fellow so astonished. I trotted him back with me to Sir E Packenham, who gave him his orders, and desired him to furnish mules to move the pontoons to the army. He protested he had not a mule; that he had given me the evening before the last 40 he had. Sir E Packenham took them from me with regret, for he and I knew the pontoons would not be wanted, as a later dispatch had informed him the army had altered its march, although it did not countermand the movement of the pontoons; the bottoms of which were knocked out about a league from Madrid the next morning, – but the mules did not return.

My situation was more desperate than at Salamanca: the loss of an hospital of several hundred men would have materially injured the reputation of the army. What was to be done? I tried my old expedient of speaking Spanish, only in a more daring way. I armed all the orderlies and convalescents in the hospital, marched them into the principal market-place, and seized a dozen fine large 4-mule wagons in the name of the Spanish government. The drivers pulled out their knives at once, and swore they would not go. The mob collected around us. I showed them several doubloons, and assured them the drivers should be paid to the last farthing; and the British army was about to fight for the safety of Madrid, that the hospital must be cleared to make room for the wounded; and I appealed to the honour of the Spanish nation. It was not in vain: the mob at last cheered me; I viva'd in return and carried off the drivers with their wagons, amidst the acclamations of the surrounding populace. Two dying and two broken-legged men only were left in hospital in Madrid.

A British army can march through an enemy's country without doing almost the slightest mischief, but it cannot retreat in a similar manner. Every man that falls out becomes a marauder, and commits all sorts of mischief. The only thing to be done is to prevent them quitting their regiments on any pretext whatever, and this is to be effected by the greatest severity of regimental discipline. There are three very important personages on such occasions, the commanding officer, the doctor, and the drummer armed with his cat-o-nine tails. If they do their duty, a retreat may in general be conducted in an orderly manner; but without their best exertions the thing cannot be done, and particularly if provisions are scarce, or are not duly distributed. In the retreat from Madrid, the surgeon of each corps [unit] marched with the rear of the regiment, and reported to me every sick man and every straggler within an hour after his arrival at the bivouac. I rode with the last of the infantry and saw that no one was left behind. In this way we drove all the sick and all the lazy before us, and had descended the Guadarama [sic] pass but one day before I knew I had near 2000 of this description on the way to the rear, and who would plunder the country before them until they arrived at Cuidad Rodrigo. When we arrived within a march [fifteen to twenty miles] of Alba de Tormes, I obtained from the Deputy-Adjutant General, Colonel Rooke, since dead, one field and four other officers, who were desired to attend to my wishes; to these were added a deputy-provost-marshal, and his whippers-in. At daylight the officers were at the bridge of Alba, and the provost and I were soon occupied in clearing out the town. Before midday, all the sick were on their way to Cuidad Rodrigo, in a compact orderly manner; more than a thousand men were added to the strength of the army, not one sick man fell into the hands of the enemy, to my knowledge from Madrid to Salamanca, when my deputy duty ceased; and I know during this period the medical officers of the army did their duty in a very efficient manner.

Guthrie issued a tirade against both the parsimony of government and accusations of the historian, William Napier.

General Napier [Lieutenant General Sir William] has three times in his fifth volume commented on the officers of the medical department for negligence, and many other faults which they as individuals in Spain were not in my opinion guilty. If the country cannot give sufficient pay and allowances for good and able men, it is not the fault of the doctors. If they will not reward them when they do their duty well, who is to blame? There is no one to blame but those who have the absurdity to run human life against a paltry economy of money. If, in the defiance of all the remonstrances of all the doctors, there is no, or at best a very insufficient conveyance in the British army on service for sick and wounded men, surely the doctors are not to blame; they can only represent. It is with others to act. General Napier's third remark follows his notice of the retreat from Madrid to which I have just alluded, and would therefore appear to apply to that service. If this should be the intention of it, the military reader now has the opportunity of judging how far it is deserved or not. The Duke of Wellington's opinion was that the doctors had done their duty well; and he was shortly afterwards, in the hospital at Lisbon, pleased to express his approbation of it, and to declare before all the officers present, that he desired my conduct should be considered as worthy [of] the imitation of the whole army.

Guthrie was sensitive to criticism of a poorly paid arm of the service, working as many others, under threatening, resource-limited and frustrating circumstances! He concludes this lecture pointing out the diverse skills required on campaign, 'I trust, gentlemen, you will see the advantages to be derived from attending to other studies, besides physic and surgery.'[5]

From Salamanca, Guthrie was ordered to Lisbon, there to serve as a Deputy Inspector. He would be subservient to an Inspector and Principal Medical Officer in that city. It was quite possible that both Wellington and McGrigor required a vigorous surgeon in Lisbon to assist with difficult chronic cases and who would have little truck with malingerers. If all were to go well, the Lisbon hospitals would soon be much reduced and general hospitals opened in northeast Spain to meet the demands of the campaigns of 1813. I cannot help wondering if McGrigor, despite Guthrie's tremendous clinical skills, found Guthrie rather a tough subordinate. At any rate the reasons for the posting are not recorded. Guthrie had acquiesced and probably arrived in December 1812, to spend almost a year around Lisbon.

Probably just before Guthrie left for Lisbon, he had treated a young officer, who had been hit by a musket-ball, presumably around the time the 5th Division came into winter quarters on the Douro, after the retreat from Salamanca. Guthrie gives a detailed and interesting account of his management:

Lieutenant Edward Hooper, First battalion, 38th Regiment, was wounded by a musket-ball on the 9 December 1812. It passed through the anterior [front] edge of the liver, and glancing round the ribs [internally], was cut out about two inches from the spine.

On his being wounded, he could scarcely believe his shoulder was not the part affected [the blood and bile escaping from the wounded liver were intensely irritating his diaphragm, whose nerve supply shares common roots with the skin of the shoulder]. His pulse was intermitting; the breathing hurried and laborious, and in a short time the tunica conjunctiva became yellow [i.e. jaundiced]. He was very *largely bled*, and warm fomentations were applied to the abdomen, from which, and the bleeding, he received some temporary relief; but, in consequence of his removal that night to the rear, the symptoms were much aggravated on the morning of the 10th. He complained of acute pain over the whole abdomen, increased on pressure; vomiting; quick, hard, and wiry pulse (no pain referred to the wound). The patient had peritonitis. The bleeding was repeated ad deliqium [until syncope – fainting], warm fomentations and an enema also repeated, and a saline mixture, with a *very few* drops of tincture of opium, to allay the irritability of the stomach. On the following evening the vomiting had ceased; his pulse was less frequent and hard; pain less. On the 11th, after passing a very restless night, the pulse again rose; the abdomen became tense, but not very painful, and he made ineffectual efforts to stool. He was again bled, a large blister was applied over the abdomen, and an ounce of castor-oil was given immediately. The blister acted well, and the purgative gave him three copious stools, of dark and foetid faeces. On the 12th he complained of twitching pains, referred to the right shoulder, and was ordered one grain [0.07 gram] of calomel [mercurous chloride], with two of antimonial powder, three times a day.

On 13 January a report sent to Guthrie after his departure for Lisbon noted:

Was free from pain; pulse fuller and less frequent; urine clear; tension of abdomen subsided. The calomel and antimony were continued, and some light nourishment was allowed. From this day a gradual amendment took place. The calomel was continued until his mouth became slightly affected [probably taste and excess salivation, from the mercury]; and, as his bowels were generally torpid [constipated], from the deficient secretion of bile, a mild purgative was given every two or three days, as occasion required, and an ounce of the infusion of calumba [syn. Colomba, an aromatic root imported from Ceylon, pungent and nauseatingly bitter – prescribed as a tonic in dyspeptic and bilious cases] with quassia [an extract made of the bark and wood of an American tree, prescribed as a tonic], three or four times daily.

Such were the rigours of therapy two hundred years ago!

Lisbon's hospitals were filled with severe chronic cases of illness and battle injury, psychiatric problems, amputees and the sick and wounded French prisoners of war. Not only would Guthrie move around the hospitals but he would also be asked to consult at the two convalescent depôts at Belem and Oseiras.

There was a separate hospital for artillery and engineer patients opened in 1811, under the direction of Deputy Inspector Dr Kearsley (a surgeon to the RA in 1793, later Assistant Surgeon General to the Ordnance Medical Department). The Ordnance Medical Department, founded in 1727, was a well run and efficient service, based at Woolwich and which was absorbed into the Army Medical Department in 1853.

This posting certainly enabled Guthrie to catch up with his studies and he now wrote his second paper from the Peninsula, entitled, 'On the Facility of Performing the Operation of Amputation at the Shoulder-joint', which he sent to headquarters.

Like colleagues, he realized the dangers of prescribing mercurial preparations for the treatment of syphilis (renal failure principally). Thus he also wrote a treatise on the management of syphilis without the prescription of mercury, which was published as a memoir in *Medico-Chirurgical Transactions*. Another avenue of research was concerned with the prevailing diseases in Lisbon and its environs. He noted the low incidence of consumption and scrofula (tuberculosis affecting the lung and neck lymph nodes respectively) in Portugal and commented on the value to British patients of a sea voyage and also, the benefits of a warmer climate in patients with the disease in a 'quiescent' or convalescent state. He cautioned against sending consumptive patients to hot climates, when expectorating purulent material, i.e. when the disease was in a more advanced state.[6]

Around this time, in May 1812, Guthrie wrote some papers on the management of compound fractures. McGrigor had these circulated to all medical staff and showed them to the Duke. Wellington had sent some of these data, concerning particularly casualties of the 7th and 40th Regiments, back to the authorities at home, whereupon several 'irregularities' (in therapy) were corrected.[7]

Guthrie also had time to treat some of the more chronic and awkward Allied and French cases convalescing in Lisbon. One such case was a man who had been struck on the head by a sabre, the wound causing the patient post-traumatic epilepsy:

> I removed, in Lisbon, in the hospital appropriated to the wounded French prisoners in 1812, a portion of bone by the trephine, which had been fractured by a sword some months before: the wound had not healed, and some pieces of bone were depressed. One piece, in particular, of the inner table [inner thin layer of skull bone], was driven in and irritating the tough membrane covering the brain, the dura mater, and was the cause of the fits from which the patient had been suffering. The man recovered.[8]

One of Guthrie's French patients caused confusion with his diagnosis. He had been shot through the chest at Badajoz in April and died eight months later in Lisbon. The musket ball had exited the chest and the wound at the back had healed. Through the entrance wound on the front of the soldier's thorax, small amounts of pus exuded. The patient coughed up large volumes of this before he died. Guthrie thought the man had died from tuberculosis, since he found, at postmortem, many small abscesses throughout the lung. Whilst this was more likely, it still remained a possibility that that, over the months, the bullet had infected the lung tissue in several places, and one of these abscesses had ruptured into a bronchus (a major airway tube).[9]

Guthrie frequently recorded his failures, one of these a chest injury. When a missile, clothing fragments or splinters of rib were driven in to the chest cavity, the space between the lungs and chest wall and the diaphragm fill with blood and serum and this soon becomes infected. What is crucial to survival is that this pus can be freely drained. In this case, the musket ball was lodged in the chest and surrounded by an enormous abscess, lined by a thickened membrane, which had compressed the lung. This condition is called a chronic empyema. The patient died. Had Guthrie seen the case earlier, he could have cut into the abscess, through the chest wall, and put in a tube drain or a tent (splint) to keep open the wound. The patient would then have been nursed in a position such that the wound opening would have been dependent to encourage adhesion and drainage.[10]

Some of his patients were civilians, many of whom would have been involved in alcoholic scuffles and fights, involving insult, theft and women. Such a problem presented to Guthrie, late one evening in the city. The case involved a tricky surgical issue – that of extruded intestine. The abdominal cavity was inevitably a 'no-go' area, since there was no general anaesthesia, no muscle relaxant and few other ways of supporting both the patient and intestinal function, during and after surgery.

Guthrie examined the patient and related:

> A soldier of the Artillery was stabbed in two places, in 1812, with a long knife, by a townsman, late in the evening, and was carried into the hospital for the sick and wounded French prisoners in Lisbon. The wound in the belly was situated somewhat more than an inch to the right of the umbilicus, and was about an inch in length from above downwards; though it a considerable protrusion of small intestine, without any omentum [the fatty apron lying over the bowel], had taken place.

Guthrie explains a common method of dealing with this problem:

> This [the protruding bowel] was distended by flatus [bowel gas], and of a dark brown colour [ie its blood supply was in jeopardy] when I first saw it. The bowel being constricted by the tendinous expansion of the of the muscular fibres, the latter was carefully divided by a blunt-pointed curved bistoury [long-bladed scalpel] passed under its upper edge, and resting on the nail of the back of the forefinger, by which the intestine was guarded; the flatus having been pressed [i.e. milked] out of the intestine which was gently washed with warm water [oil or milk could be used], it was restored to the cavity of the abdomen.

Guthrie noted a slight tearing of the outer coats of the bowel, not requiring any repair. Having replaced the gut successfully – not always easy in the awake patient – Guthrie then proceeded to finish, 'The skin was then sewn up by a fine continuous suture [silk or linen] and adhesive plaster and a compress duly applied.'

The patient was frightened and faint. There was another knife wound on his back near the right shoulder-blade. This wound crackled around the entry site – indicating that the lung had been punctured and air from the lung had escaped into the tissues. The man had coughed blood and the breathing was painful and difficult. The gunner was placed on his back, with his legs slightly raised (to relax the abdominal muscles). He suffered from symptoms of infection and paralytic ileus and was duly bled to 40 ounces (1200mls) and thereafter 18 ounces daily for the next three days (around 540mls of blood per diem). Sensibly no food and very little drink were allowed. The stitches were removed on day six and in five weeks the patient was weak but well.

Inevitably, there were a few non-combat trauma cases – falls from horseback, drunken head injuries, etc. One such incident involved a deputy-purveyor, who 'received a blow on the side of the fore-part of the belly from the end of a spanker-boom, which knocked him down, and gave rise for some time to much inconvenience. He showed the part to me in Lisbon, in 1813, in consequence of the formation of a bulging ventral hernia to the extent of the spot originally injured.' Guthrie was surprised at the protrusion, which had arisen as a result of damage to the muscle fibres, or their blood supply from the impact of the ship's spar. He commented: 'the extent of the absorbtion [shrinking and disappearance] was greater than the apparent injury would seem to have warranted'. Clearly there had been much bruising and damage to the muscles. Such a problem had afflicted Commodore Horatio Nelson at the battle off Cape Vincent on 14 February 1797. Some of his abdominal muscle fibres had been badly torn by fragments from a shattered wooden block fragment, which left him with a permanent, tender but reducible hernia.

One French casualty impressed Guthrie:

A French soldier was wounded by a musket-ball on the back part of the right hip, at Alamaraz, on the Tagus, was taken prisoner, and sent to Lisbon in the autumn of 1813. The ball had lodged but gave him little inconvenience at the time, beyond some pain in the course of the sciatic nerve, subsequently followed by defect of motion on the right side. Four months after the injury, pain came on about the region of the bladder, with great desire to pass urine, which he could not do when standing, but which dribbled away when lying down. When quiet little, but great pain followed any attempt at continued motion. A catheter could be introduced, but with great difficulty when it reached the prostate gland [near the exit of the bladder], which was exceedingly tender to the touch. After a time the instrument could not be passed and the man was in great agony until something appeared to give way, and a discharge of matter took place, when the urine followed, and he was relieved. An abscess had formed, in all probability from the proximity of the ball, which still could not be felt. The man recovered, retaining however his former state of lameness and defect of power, although relieved from the vexatious irritation of the bladder.[11]

I believe Guthrie was right. The ball had damaged the sciatic nerve to a degree and lodged near the base of the bladder. Carrying in a fragment of clothing, sepsis was inevitable. An abscess had formed at the base of the bladder, near the prostate and obstructed urine flow. When the abscess burst, discharging its contents into the bladder, the urinary obstruction was relieved.

McGrigor had now set up a network of hospitals at Miranda de Douro, Zamora, Toro, Placentia, Salamanca, Valladolid, Vittori, Vera and along the coast at Corunna, St Andero, Bilbao, Passages and St Jean de Luz.[12] He also strongly promoted, as did Guthrie, a local system of care for the wounded and sick soldiers, to keep them with their battalions, where possible. McGrigor's report on the management of the sick and wounded at this time reads: 'But above all things, care was taken, that the large body of sick which now oppressed the army, should not be crowded into the general hospitals, where there was already much contagious disease.'

Every regiment fitted up a hospital for itself, where not only all the sick that occurred were treated by their own medical officers, but some chronic cases were sent from the general hospitals. Strict orders were given that few patients should be sent to the general hospital. The consequence of this measure was that, in November, although typhus and hospital gangrene were as prevalent as they had been in the retreat to Corunna in 1809, these destructive diseases soon disappeared in most regiments, the Guards and a few others excepted; and in four months' time, the army was effective and in perfect condition to take the field again.[13] During 1813, McGrigor published new Hospital Regulations and Standing Orders running to 150 pages, including a comprehensive formulary, the format of various reports to be submitted and sensible advice on the segregation of various diseases.

Having surgical governance of several hospitals in Lisbon, Guthrie had an opportunity to show the supreme commander in the Peninsula round them. Wellington had come down from Freneida, between December 1812 and January 1813 to visit the base seaport. Whilst visiting one of the city's hospitals, 'the Duke of Wellington was pleased publicly to express his approbation of Mr Guthrie's services, and to say, that if he had not attained the rank of an Inspector, he should have made him Surgeon to Head Quarters, but that as Mr Gunning had been removed on succeeding to that rank, he could not appoint him to the office with it.' This was an impressive compliment to Guthrie and we have to wonder if the appointment as the Duke's Surgeon would have been a wise career move. Guthrie's experience, expertise and research would have been wasted. His biographer mused: 'If he had gone to Head Quarters, he would not have been Professor of Anatomy and Surgery to the Royal College of Surgeons of England, not twice [actually thrice] its President.'

John Gunning, nephew of a Surgeon General, had served in the Low Countries, and had been promoted Staff Surgeon in 1799, was appointed a DIH in September 1812, after which he served with Head Quarters. Having served through the Peninsular campaigns, he was at Waterloo, as PMO of the First Corps. He also amputated Lord Raglan's arm. Moving to Paris, he served as Inspector of Hospitals (Continent of Europe). He lived on in Paris and died there aged 90 years old.

Wellington's dispatch from Freneida, on the 31 January, after the visit to Lisbon commented on Guthrie's promotion, 'What interest can I have in these concerns, – till I saw Mr Guthrie in the hospital at Belem, I do not believe I ever saw Mr.

Guthrie; although, from his reputation in the army ever since it came here, I intended to have him made surgeon to head quarters when Mr. Gunning was promoted, if he had not been recommended for promotion in another manner.' With regard to Guthrie's promotion, he wrote, 'that he considered his conduct as deserving the imitation of the whole army, and that he might rely on his promotion being confirmed'. (Guthrie was not gazetted until he was in Santander and the promotion was not antedated back to his earlier brevet rank.[14])

While Guthrie was in Lisbon, serious charges of fraud against officers of the Purveyor's Department were presented to him. Almost every sum of money entered was incorrect and the contractors were signing blank receipts! When later transferred to Santander, demonstrating his excellent administrative skills, he simplified the accounting process for the hospitals by having the accounts kept regimentally and requested these to be submitted to him weekly. These might then be compared with the Purveyor's figures for the three months that Guthrie had been at that station. Although the accounts could not be submitted to the Treasury in Guthrie's way, the Purveyor General said of the surgeon, 'that he was known to be the best physician, the best surgeon, the best officer, the best linguist in the army, and that he had now shown himself to be accountant, in doing that which no other inspectional officer could have done'.

In January 1813, Wellington learnt of the disastrous retreat of the French army from Russia. Clearly, to bolster up the Grande Armée again, Bonaparte would at worst not be able to offer much support for his 'Spanish Ulcer'. There were still around a quarter of a million French troops in Iberia. Despite the ghastly winter, Wellington with the help of the Army Medical Department and a reinvigorated army of around 80,000 effectives was to launch his final push to get the French army out of the Peninsula.

On the 22 May, he launched the campaign, faced by forces under Gazan, D'Erlon and Reille, with Clausel to the north. With Hill's corps and General Pablo Morillo's Spaniards reported moving south, were the French expecting the Allies to move in from the west up the valley of the Tagus? Wellington had concentrated his 80,000 sabres and bayonets north of the River Douro and by moving northwards, was rolling up the surprised and out-manœuvred French forces. The French evacuated Madrid and King Joseph and Marshal Jean Baptiste Jourdan fled from Valladolid. Wellington called up supplies of food, ammunition and ordnance from Corunna, ordering them on to Santander. The retiring French blew up the castle of Burgos and with a large amount of baggage retired towards the town of Vittoria. On 21 June 1813, Wellington defeated Jourdan and King Joseph near that city and drove the French towards the Pyrenees.

Following the successful but costly campaigns at Vittoria, San Sebastian and Pamplona, the northern Spanish hospitals were flooded with wounded troops and there were outbreaks of hospital gangrene (severe infection of wounds involving destruction of tissue by anaerobic and aerobic organisms) and also more than usual cases of tetanus (lockjaw).

These engagements were a great distance from Lisbon (around 300 miles) and on 24 August 1813, the great base hospital at Lisbon closed. Guthrie's work was done, just as the need for his expertise increased in the north. Overjoyed at the return to more active duties, he was posted to the large general hospital at Santander (4,000 beds), as Principal Medical Officer, where the summer campaigns furnished him with plenty of cases, as would the advance over the Pyrenees. McGrigor had had additional bedding (for 750 patients) at Santander, in the form of mobile wooden huts, sent out from England. Further east, John Hennen became PMO at the Cordelaria Hospital in Bilbao, which could accommodate 2,500 patients. The overwhelming outbreak of hospital gangrene here caused around 500 deaths overall. Hennen described the unfortunate and remarkable case of a soldier, just out from Britain, who was undergoing mercurial therapy for venereal disease. Admitted to the Cordelaria, the man was dead in forty-eight hours. The hospital gangrene had infected an open syphilitic lesion in his groin (a bubo). The patient's groin blood vessels and much of his abdominal wall were eaten away by the sepsis. The subsequent haemorrhage proved fatal.[15] Surgeon John Hennen was a capable and noted British military surgeon.

Dr McGrigor reported the army generally in a healthy state, but commented on the severity of the weather and frequently poor shelter available for the men. He wrote: 'whether it rained or snowed, the situation of the soldier was extremely unpleasant; even the Scotch Highlander felt the rigour of this alpine situation'.[16]

Guthrie probably arrived at Santander in late September 1813 and his hospital held between 1,200 and 1,400 patients. In October, he received he received 800 casualties from Vera and Le Saca. On one occasion at Santander, Guthrie was asked to see a soldier with a head wound which was not healing. The man had received the injury at San Sebastian at the end of August 1813. He had lingered on in hospital and Guthrie made the point that wounds require careful exploration as, deformed missiles could be elusive:

A soldier was wounded at the storming of San Sebastian by a ball on the side of the head, which was supposed not to have lodged. The wound did not heal, a small opening remaining, although no exfoliation [exuding of fragments of dead infected bone – sequestra] took place and the bone did not seem to be bare [i.e. exposed]. On dividing the scalp to ascertain the cause of the delay in healing, a small ball, quite flat, was found; it had sunk down a little below the hole left for the discharge to which by its irritation it had given rise.[17]

A soldier of the Light Division was wounded on the right side of his skull on the heights of Vera, some weeks before Guthrie took over his care. The ball had depressed a fragment of skull bone and was 'irritating' the dura membrane. Guthrie trephined the patient, removed the piece of depressed bone and noted damage to the dura. Post-operatively,

> The operation gave relief, but a tumour soon sprang up, evidently composed of [infected] brain. The patient was again bled, purged and starved; calomel and opium were given in moderate doses, and the protrusion ceased to increase; about the same time it changed colour, became yellow, foetid, softer, and soon wasted away, pieces of dead matter separating at each dressing, until it sunk within the level of the skull; after which healthy granulations [excessive fragile healing tissue] sprung up, and the wound healed.

This is a remarkable story of survival after an infected brain protrusion. This, often fatal complication was unpleasantly known as 'fungus cerebri' (there was no fungal infection) but was in fact a brain herniation. The usual management was as above, but often, in addition a gentle protective compress or hair ring was placed around the protrusion.

Chest complaints were common during this winter, as were dysentery and typhus. Guthrie was presented with a difficult conundrum previously alluded to. A soldier had previously undergone an amputation at a lower level on the limb and the operation site had become badly infected. The case was referred by Dr Irwin, a former cavalry surgeon, then working as a physician in Santander. Guthrie had to re-amputate the thigh of the soldier, who subsequently died of 'a sudden and fatal affectation of the lungs'. Another two similar cases had been referred by Mr Boutflower, an experienced staff surgeon at Fuenterrabia. Clearly no one understood why this complication had occurred and were uncertain of its aetiology. Guthrie had met such problems previously and he dissected some of these cases and found purulent material in the chests of the deceased. This was likely to be a consequence of infection spreading along the veins (pyaemia) from the infected site into distant organs. More cases would present in France and Guthrie published data on this problem in 1815.[18]

Not infrequently, clothing or articles worn on campaign have saved life. Such a case referred to Guthrie was

> Lieutenant Cooke Tylden Patterson, of the Light Division, [who] was struck on the left breast by a musket-ball, on the morning of the 15 July, 1813, in front of the village of Vera, in the Pyrenees. He had fallen on his back breathless, as if dead. While waiting the order to advance he had been reading *Gil Blas* in Spanish, and on receiving it, had hastily put the book in the breast-pocket of his coat. The ball had struck this, but unable to

penetrate it, had fallen on the ground at his feet, completely flattened on one side, and marked with the impression of the braid of his coat. A piece of the cover of the book, about the size of a half-a-crown, was driven in, and the leaves throughout were indented by the ball. It was some days before the effects of the blow entirely subsided.[19]

Guthrie continued his practice of conservative upper limb surgery. Whilst this was a significant step forward in surgery, Guthrie's efforts sometimes foundered for other reasons, 'Major C——— was wounded in one of the battles in the Pyrenees in 1813, by a musket-ball, which injured the head of the left humerus [upper arm bone] from side to side. Thirty years afterwards the wounds still discharged, and gave him great uneasiness. A probe discovered much diseased [chronically infected] bone. I advised excision of the head of the bone, to which he would not assent. His courage had been broken by continued suffering.'[20]

A notable casualty came Guthrie's way shortly after 10 November. General Sir Andrew Barnard, commanding the Rifle Brigade, had been wounded by a musket ball, which had entered between the second and third ribs on the right side of the chest. The ball passed through the lung and the shoulder-blade and was easily extracted under the skin nearby. Guthrie described his wounding:

> He not only felt but heard the sound of the ball as it struck him, and he fell from his horse. Blood gushed from his mouth, and continued to do so until after he was completely exhausted by bleeding from the arm to the amount of two quarts [over two litres] He was again bled at night, and the subsequent morning, which relieved all the material symptoms. During six weeks he suffered from difficulty of breathing and cough and from night-sweats. Some pieces of bone and cloth came away from the wounds, with a free discharge in the first instance, which gradually diminished until the wound closed. In eight weeks he was able to resume his command.

This is a remarkable story of endurance and recovery, bearing in mind the excessive amount of blood taken by venesection. Barnard must have been so weak and faint that he would hardly have noticed other symptoms!

Our surgeon was presented with a soldier of the ('Bloody') 11th Foot, William Downes, aged 33 years, who was shot by a firelock in the Pyrenees on 31 August 1813. The ball entered the left chest, fracturing the left fourth rib, and came out through the shoulder-blade. Spitting up blood, but not apparently breathless, he was bled, dressed, placed on a low diet and sent to Passages. From here he was shipped out to Santander, arriving on 14 September. The front chest wound discharged blood-stained pus, which he also coughed up. Towards the end of September the expectoration ceased. After this, an unusual complication of a chest wound followed. In October, the soft tissues around the entry wound were affected by hospital gangrene, which almost killed Downes. There was so much muscle destruction by the infection that he had trouble moving his left arm. He was discharged on 14 December, much weakened and with a flattened deformed left chest.[21]

Survival after penetrating injuries of the liver was rare, since the patient would succumb from bile peritonitis and bleeding. An officer was brought in to Guthrie from the Pyrenees. He had been shot just at the border of the right ribs, through the upper abdomen, and the ball was retained. Guthrie noted, 'Blood and bile flowed in considerable quantity; the skin became yellow [jaundice], the pain and swelling of the abdomen were considerable, and he was given over as lost.' Clearly, bile and blood had leaked into the officer's abdomen, caused intense irritation and paralysis of the bowel – hence the swelling. Amazingly, 'Under vigorous treatment [bleeding, purgation, emetics, food and fluid restrictions] he gradually recovered, so as to be sent to England, with a fistulous opening at the orifice of the entrance.' Guthrie saw the patient in 1817, at which time he passed a long probe five inches into the deep wound in the liver. Guthrie describes the patient's condition, 'Purulent and bilious matters were constantly discharged from the wound; his countenance was sallow, his digestion bad; he suffered from constant uneasiness, if not pain, and was altogether out of health.' Guthrie saw him annually for several more years, sometimes being able to 'feel' the clink of his probe on the ball. Occasionally the patient passed purulent matter per rectum, so there was clearly an abscess in the upper right part of his abdomen, which would occasionally discharge into the colon (large bowel). Then the wounded officer came to Guthrie no more – he may have died. Guthrie comments: 'I have never had an opportunity of extracting a ball from the liver during life, although I have seen persons live many weeks into whose livers balls had penetrated; and I have been acquainted with three persons who had been wounded through the liver, to whom little subsequent inconvenience was occasioned.'[22]

Most wounds of the kidney, ureter (the tube leading from kidney and taking the urine to the bladder) and bladder were at great risk of bleeding and sepsis from leakage of urine into the tissues. A lucky survivor was a soldier of the Light Division, wounded on the heights of Vera, in the Pyrenees. Guthrie related:

> A musket-ball had entered behind the sacrum [the tail-bone], and lodged. He was bled twice in consequence of suffering pain in the part, but was otherwise not much disturbed[!]. There was at first a difficulty in passing urine, but this gradually subsided, although he always suffered pain in micturition [passing urine], which was frequent and distressing. He remained in this state until December, when he passed with considerable effort, and after much difficulty, a hard piece of his jacket about half an

inch in length, larger than the orifice of the urethra through which it was forced.

Since the piece of cloth was not encased by proteinaceous or calcific material, Guthrie surmised that it could not have come from inside the bladder. It had ulcerated from outside into the cavity of the organ. The ball did not extrude but the patient markedly improved by the time Guthrie discharged him back to England.[23]

8

Toulouse

In July, Wellington pushed Soult back after offensive actions at Roncesvalles, Maya and Souraren. On 7 October, the Allies crossed the Bidassoa and contested the Nivelle and the Nive with the French. San Sebastian had finally fallen on 8 October and Pamplona had surrendered on 31 October. Moving into France, life became easier for the troops, with improving weather, spring pasture and better food. There were fowls to roast at campfires, wine at 15 sous a bottle, and riflemen slicing slabs of bacon onto their bread. The hospitals continued to move east.

After battling over the Pyrenees, Wellington now had a tough bastion to consider: Bayonne, a French garrison town, commanded by General Thouvenot and held by around 9,000, rising to 14,000 men. After Hill's desperate contest at St Pierre had been fought and the Adour River crossed, Bayonne, having been invested on the 31 December, was surrounded by 26 February. The Bayonne garrison, after mounting a devastating sortie on 14 April, did not finally surrender until 27 April. After the action at Orthez on 27 February, Soult was forced to retire, fighting a rearguard action at Tarbes.

Guthrie left Santander, now running down its work, in December and we find him at Aire. The hospitals then under pressure were St Jean de Luz (taking around 1,600 cases), Passages, Fuenterrabia and Orthez, each of which received around 2,000 cases between December 1813 and March 1814. During the combat at Orthez, there were two eminent minor casualties. Wellington was bruised after his sword hilt had been driven into his upper leg by a ball and his Spanish liaison officer, General Alava, was also bruised on the hip.

But Guthrie had two more serious casualties to consider. The first was Major-General Broke, who told his own story:

> Towards the close of the battle of Orthez, on the 27th Feb., 1814, a musket-shot struck me between the second and third ribs on the right side, near the breast-bone. I was then on horse-back, being aide-de-camp to Lieutenant-General Sir Henry Clinton, commanding the Sixth Division. The sensation was precisely as if I had been struck a violent blow with the point of a cane, but it did not unhorse me. I was attended in a very short time by the surgeon of the 61st Regiment, when, on removing my clothes, the air and blood bubbled out from the wound as I drew my breath. The

surgeon turning me on my face, discovered the ball to be lodged between the ribs and the blade-bone [shoulder-blade]. This he cut through, and extracted the ball, and with it pieces of my coat, waistcoat, and shirt, which were lodged between the ribs and the blade-bone. This occurred about four P.M. I was then removed to the town of Orthez, a distance of about three miles, and in the course of the afternoon, the veins of both arms were opened in at least seven different places, but scarcely any blood came away [he was shocked and cold, so his veins were collapsed]; breathing became extremely painful in a day or two, and I felt nearly suffocated [his lung had collapsed with air and blood in the chest], when, in the evening, my brother Sir Charles Broke Vere, arrived with my friend, Mr Guthrie, who examined me carefully. The agony of drawing breath was such that I could scarcely endure it. He opened one of the temporal arteries [since venotomy had been unsuccessful], and desired that it might be allowed to bleed without interruption. He afterwards left me, to visit some other wounded men, and returned in about three hours, when I told him that I felt relieved, and had much less of the suffocating pain in breathing He then opened the other temporal artery, directing as before that its bleeding should not be checked. I shortly after that dropped asleep, and on waking, could breathe freely; my recovery was progressive from that time, the wound in front, where the ball entered, being the first closed; but both were healed at the end of about eight weeks, and in about ten I was able to rejoin the army at Bordeaux.[1]

The next patient had a similar injury. It was the Earl of March, the future 5th Duke of Richmond. Whilst leading his company of the 52nd Foot at Orthez, he turned to his left to see his men and was shot in the right chest about the level of the fourth and fifth ribs. He felt as though he'd been cut in two and fell to the ground violently, speechless. There was no exit wound and the ball was retained (with bits of clothing). The wound was bound and the patient was carried on a door to Orthez. His breathing was laboured and he was in much pain. The three-mile journey was decidedly awkward and painful for March and he was faint on arrival with haemorrhagic shock and pain. There was brisk bleeding from the wound. Guthrie visited him at the outset and advised no attempt at exploration for the ball. True to form, he was bled to 8 ounces (240mls)], which relieved him a little. The following day, he had deteriorated a while and was bled again. At 9pm he was visited by Deputy Inspector Thomas Thomson (originally a cavalry surgeon, appointed DIH 21 January 1813, after serving as a staff surgeon since 1808) and Staff Surgeon John Maling (formerly of the Horse Guards and 52nd, appointed to the staff in September 1812 and later served at Waterloo – his sabre is on display at the Royal College of Surgeons of England). After Maling had passed his finger into the wound, Thomson explored the wound with a long probe. This reached across the chest without interruption. The ball was at the back of the thorax.

The next day, the sheets and dressing were soaked with blood and there was a pool of blood on the floor. He was bled seven times in all (around 2,000mls) and despite this he survived.[2] A great friend of Wellington, he was visited one night by the Duke quietly and sorrowfully. The clandestine visit was witnessed by Maling as he dozed in a chair by the patient. March recovered and would accompany Wellington on the plains of Waterloo.

At Aire, Guthrie managed not only the British wounded, but also Portuguese and French. Amongst the latter, there were many problems which had arisen through 'faulty surgery and neglect', unhealed or sloughing wounds and infected amputation stumps, many of which required re-amputation.

After Soult's rearguard action at Tarbes, Wellington finally stood before the city of Toulouse on 26 March 1814. The battle would not be properly joined until 10 April, when the Allied army of 49,000–50,000 men would have to face Soult's penultimate great effort of the war. The Marshal had a force of around 42,000 effectives, ready to defend their homeland with vigour. In early December, Wellington had learnt of the defeat of the French at Leipzig, but he did not receive news of the abdication of Bonaparte on 6 April until 12 April, two days after the carnage at Toulouse.

When Wellington, reached the city, he had to contend with three waterways around the city, the Rivers Garonne, through and to the west, Hers to the east and the Canal Royal du Midi running to the east and north of Toulouse. After some difficulties, he had a pontoon bridge laid over the Garonne, to the north of the city and on 5 April the army, around 20,000 men, save Hill's division, crossed to the east to mostly complete the investment. Hill was to face and pin down the western St Cyprien district of Toulouse. To the east, there lay the Calvinet Ridge, which was heavily defended with redoubts and artillery, as was the city perimeter. General Picton's 3rd and Baron Alten's Light Divisions were to concentrate on the northern side of the city, astride the Paris road. On their left flank, to the east, were General Manuel Freire's two Spanish Divisions, some Portuguese and a force of Sir Henry Clinton's 6th and Sir Lowry Cole's 4th Divisions, these latter would assault the Calvinet mound and redoubts under command of Beresford. Freire ordered a premature assault on the northern end of the Calvinet, but his two brigades were pushed back by murderous fire. Wellington ordered Beresford's force to abort a southern movement to attack the far end of the ridge and wheel to their right and mount an immediate assault up the Calvinet Ridge.

Guthrie had been out on the field during the assault. He was asked to see an officer who, along with two others, had been struck by a round shot, which had almost torn off the right thighs of each of three men. The officer's right femoral artery was torn across just below the groin. A colleague asked Guthrie to consider disarticulation at the hip joint. Guthrie recounted:

> The bleeding had ceased, the pulse was feeble; the countenance ghastly, bedewed with a cold sweat, and with every indication of approaching dissolution [profound pre-mortem shock]. The house being at an advanced point, and close to one of the French redoubts, the fire of round shot and musketry was so severe upon and around it as to induce me to remain, until the battery should be taken by the troops then advancing upon our flank.

Guthrie, the senior surgeon in the front line, was pinned down. He had the calmness, inquisitiveness and sang-froid to carry out the following research, during the action, 'In order to occupy my time usefully, I returned to the officer, and found that he had just expired. Desirous of seeing by what means the haemorrhage had been arrested, I cut down on the artery, took it carefully out,' He found a clot tenuously situated in the upper end of the torn artery. The man had expired from hypovolaemia (low blood volume from bleeding) and would never have been fit enough for capital surgery.[3] Someone on the ridge had witnessed the many scarlet-coated bodies of Picton's division lying in the green water meadows and wistfully called them, the 'Flowers of Toulouse'.[4]

Beresford now moved a distance south, as the Spaniards had now been pushed back anyway, he finally turned northwest and mounted an oblique attack up the ridge. In the late afternoon, the main Augustin redoubt fell. The Highlanders of the 42nd and 79th had lost half their complement in the attack. Further assaults were made from the north by the Spanish troops and the 3rd Division. Soult's force was retiring towards the canal and the city. As the dusk came on, and the fighting was on the wane, the wounded began to receive attention and they continued to trickle in on 11 April, when they began to bury the dead. Soult had fled south on the night of 11 April, taking what he could with him, except his sick and severely wounded. Casualties were less for the French, 3,200, whilst the Allies had sustained around 4,500. Excluding the lightly wounded and dead, Guthrie, now in charge of the general hospitals, had around 1,500 wounded to care for. He and other surgeons had set up field hospitals and aid posts in surrounding buildings, convents, byres, etc., through which casualties would be soon passed into the city, some on to coastal hospitals.

After the fall of Toulouse, more general hospitals were opened in the city and the evacuation route home would then be via Bordeaux. Assisted by a British resident doctor in Toulouse, many buildings were used for the injured as well as the main hospitals, such as the Hôpital des Minimes, another the Caserne de Calvet also the Dept de Mendicité. Private houses, religious establishments and an encampment outside the walls were commandeered. In these places Guthrie was given the lead role as a DIH and Principal Medical Officer in the city. Another group of casualties was given to Mr (later Dr) John Murray, an experienced surgeon, but junior to Guthrie.

Like Dr McGrigor, Guthrie assembled and published interesting statistics and the results from this battlefront, which would contrast with the somewhat dismal data following the action at Vittoria, San Sebastian and the investment of Pamplona. The latter inferior results reflected the lack of resources and delay in therapy for many badly injured men.

This was a time when Guthrie was at his zenith and he treated and reported many cases during and after the siege – a few more notable and interesting of his cases will be described. Although he worked primarily in the city, we know he travelled sometimes some miles out of town to smaller hospitals to consult with colleagues.[5]

One case exhibited a trick used by experienced war surgeons of the time. This was to place the soldier in the position he was in when he received the bullet wound in order to work out the missile's track:

> My attention was directed after the battle of Toulouse, to a soldier, whose foot was gangrenous without an apparent cause, he having received merely a flesh wound in the thigh, not in the exact course of the main artery, which, nevertheless, I said was injured. On placing the man in the same position with regard to us, that he supposed himself to have been in towards the enemy when wounded, the possibility of such an injury was seen; and dissection after death proved the correctness of the opinion.[6]

Guthrie relates the odd tale of a soldier undergoing a delayed (secondary) amputation of the thigh, which had been shattered five weeks previously at Toulouse. The patient was emaciated with a severe septicaemia and on the

> third day after the operation, from which he scarcely rallied, he complained of difficulty in swallowing, and pain in the situation of the thyroid gland [in the front of the neck, below the Adam's apple], which was found next morning to be inflamed. In spite of the means employed he died on the fourth day of this attack, or the seventh after the amputation, in a state of great emaciation. On dissection, the whole substance of the thyroid gland was destroyed, a deposit of good pus was occupying its place, which descended by the sides of the trachea [windpipe] and the oesophagus [gullet] to the sternum [i.e. into the upper chest], and had all but found its way into the larynx, between the cricoid and thyroid cartilages [supporting structures of the voice box] on the right side.[7]

This tale exhibits a very unusual case of infection in the thyroid. I have only twice heard of this in forty years of practice. It also tells us of the catastrophic spread of sepsis before the advent of antimicrobial agents.

Another of Guthrie's patients was to provide a different management problem. Private A Monro, serving with the 42nd, was hit on the left side of his skull by a musket ball. The ball, after breaking the skin, broke the cranial bone at the side, called the parietal bone. Although this was a compound fracture, no missile was retained and no bony fragments were driven in (depressed fracture). After receiving standard therapy, bed rest and low diet, he was well until 23 April, thirteen days after wounding. 'On the evening of that day he became feverish, and hasty and odd in manner.' The patient declared himself quite well and resented venesection and further therapy. The next day, despite some pain, he again resisted treatment. He remained coherent enough to deny his illness. Guthrie knew that there was intracranial infection and advised a trephining to be carried out, to release any infected matter from the skull. Guthrie left and on his return encountered a dilemma. The man's condition had deteriorated and he had again refused surgery. Guthrie thought his only chance was with the operation, so he 'directed it to be done by force, three of his own regiment with others attending to assist the surgeons. He called upon these men by name not to allow him to be murdered in cold blood, declared he was getting well, and would get well if left alone, and prayed them to avenge his death on the doctors if they meddled with him.' The attending surgeons were distressed by this dilemma and requested Guthrie to help. Presumably, under force, the trephine was applied to Monro's cranium and after the tell-tale bulging up of the dura (the brain was infected), Guthrie desisted, since he knew this man was going to die. At post-mortem, Guthrie's opinion was proved accurate, he incised the membrane, so revealing the purulent material and soft, discoloured and infected brain beneath.[8] On 29 April Guthrie trephined two more soldiers, Absolom Lorimer again of the 42nd and an anonymous soldier. He failed to save either by releasing the pus.

Not all men with septic head injuries succumbed. If the patient survived, he frequently suffered from the infected cerebral hernia following the application of the trephine. Guthrie explained that, in his combat experience, he had met with two types of cerebral hernia – one appearing within a day or two of the strike and usually fatal. This was mainly composed of blood clot and damaged swollen brain, the other, appearing three or four days after wounding, consisting mainly of septic brain. Bernard Duffy aged 24, of the 40th, was admitted to the Calvet Hospital with a depressed fracture of the frontal bone. He was bled and purged 'largely' and loose bone fragments were removed. Duffy deteriorated on 14 April and was trephined. More bony pieces were removed – one had punctured the dura. Over the next few days, he acquired a cerebral hernia. This was touched with lunar caustic (silver nitrate), which was applied daily. Thankfully, in May, less than a month after injury, Duffy was sent home via Bordeaux.[9]

Guthrie rarely employed drains or tubes to remove fluid from the thorax. One such was a soldier of the 5th Division who had received a through and through musket-ball wound at the level of ribs four and five. Some rib splinters were removed. He seemed to make fair progression until 16 April, when he became breathless and could not lie down. Guthrie inserted a gum–elastic catheter into the rear wound and removed about three pints of blood-stained serum. The patient was sent home cured two months later.[10]

There was general disbelief by the end of the war in injury from the 'wind of the ball', but tangential, glancing wounds were different. Almost as the battle was over, Guthrie was brought a Spanish soldier who had been struck obliquely by a round shot on the right side and back, an injury reminiscent of that suffered by Sir Howard de Lancey at Waterloo. The skin of the soldier was unbroken, but he was severely bruised. He passed blood-stained urine, had lost the use of his legs and he died that night. Guthrie described the findings at dissection, 'On making an incision through the skin, which was then quite a blue-black, although not torn, all the soft parts were found reduced to a state approaching to the appearance of jelly; the spine was injured, the right kidney ruptured, and the cavity of the abdomen full of blood.'[11]

A story of remarkable fortitude and survival following an abdominal wound was related by Surgeon John Murray (promoted to the staff in September 1813), who had involved Guthrie by consultation, 'Ensign Wright, 61st Regiment, was wounded by a musket-ball, on the morning of the 10 April, at Toulouse. The ball passed through the abdominal parietes [skin, fat and muscles] on the right of the linea alba [marking the edge of the central abdominal muscles], nearly half way between the umbilicus and pubes, and lodged. Sense of debility, tremor, nausea, small feeble pulse, and pain in the lower part of the abdomen, were the immediate symptoms.' Fomentations, blisters, fluid and food restriction, small doses of castor oil and the antiphlogistic regimen were prescribed and the patient was bled to fainting two or three times daily. His pulse was between 100–120 beats per minute, for which he was prescribed digitalis. The signs of infection and peritonitis continued: vomiting, swollen abdomen and small foetid 'evacuations'. An officer's diet was a little more appetizing than that for a ranker, toast, water, tea, boiled milk and water, with a little soft bread soaked in it, and small helpings of chicken or mutton broth. On the eighth day after injury, Wright passed the musket ball per rectum. We can infer that the ball passed through the colon, which resulted in a large abscess, containing the ball, which then ulcerated into the colon and was then passed on. On the fourteenth day, Wright had severe chest pain, cough and breathlessness – probably a pulmonary embolism (a clot of blood in his lung following deep vein thrombosis after prolonged immobility). He survived this and was shipped out for England in June.[12]

Three cases of men wounded at Toulouse exhibited Guthrie's trend towards conservative limb surgery. The first was Sir Hussey Vivian, referred to previously. The second was Private Robert Masters of the 40th, wounded on 12 April by a musket ball, which had lodged in his right shoulder, and the missile was embedded in the head of the humerus (arm) bone. Guthrie relates that he was

> Shown to me a few days afterwards as a case for amputation at the shoulder-joint, I directed the excision of the head of the bone as soon as the parts became more quiescent. Under venesection, purgatives, leeches, the constant application of cold [compresses], and low diet [tea, rice, bread, panada, etc.], the high inflammatory symptoms which had supervened, subsided, and six weeks after the accident the ball, and part of the head of the humerus, were removed, after an incision had been made through the external parts for the purpose. Three months after the receipt of the injury, the man was sent to England, with no other inconvenience than that resulting from the loss of motion in the shoulder, which was stiff. Any loss of movement was compensated for by movement of the shoulder blade on the chest wall.[13]

By contrast was Private Oxley of the 23rd Regiment, who had a ball pass right through his shoulder joint, injuring the head of the humerus. The referring surgeon suggested that Guthrie might wish to remove just the smashed head. The man seemed little upset by this wound and complained of 'the restraint put upon him, and the lowness of the diet'. Guthrie decided to leave well alone and after some pieces of dead, infected bone came away, the man was discharged to Britain in July with a permanently stiff shoulder. Good judgement was shown in the decision not to interfere.[14]

Compound fractures of the lower limb were a different kettle of fish. Guthrie kept records of his work and he discussed a group of the 'most favourable' (i.e. the fittest and least damaged) of fractures of the thigh-bone under his immediate care, forty-three in number. This type of wound was one of the most dangerous and he critically audited the outcome of these cases, which he elected to treat without surgery in the first instance (see Table 1).

The data are interesting. I have classified the patients into three groups by outcome. Guthrie is performing a small retrospective review. Group 1 just might have survived initial surgery had they had it but they all died, mainly because of the site of their wound or sudden unexpected deterioration. Group 2 demonstrates that, even if the men had survived, the retained leg was only worth keeping in five of eighteen cases (28 per cent) and those patients in Group 3 survived long enough for delayed surgery and had the usual high mortality associated with secondary operation. Guthrie also made the valid point that the five men who fared best by retaining their legs, all had injuries at or below the middle of the thigh-bone. The

Table 1. Results of initially conservative management of compound fractures of the femur (thigh-bone)

Group 1	13 soldiers died without surgery (30%)
Group 2	18 soldiers retained their limbs (42%) 5 well and using their limb (3 months after the battle) 2 thought the limb no better than an artificial limb 11 wished they had been initially amputated
Group 3	12 soldiers had secondary [delayed] amputation (28%) 7 died (58%)

upper end of the thigh was a far more dangerous part in which to receive a wound, being nearer the bacterial contamination of the groin or perineum.

Had all these men been amputated initially (primary amputation), one could speculate that the overall mortality would have been around 40–50 per cent, which is to say between seventeen and twenty-one men would not have survived. In this instructional review, twenty died and thirteen remained unhappy with their retained limb and thirteen never had the chance of surgery. The message is that only five of thirty of those patients who survived initially (17 per cent) profited by this conservatism. Skilful and early intervention by a surgeon such as Guthrie would have likely saved several more lives and limbs.

Guthrie's linguistic skills were again required for the management of his Spanish casualties. One of these was a 30-year-old captain in the regiment of Laredo, Don Bernardino Garcia Alvarez. He was hit in the upper part of the thigh by a musket ball, which passed through.

> The wound was not considered dangerous until the 30th, twenty days after the injury, when a considerable bleeding took place; and as the vessel from which it came seemed to be very deeply seated, the Spanish surgeon in charge tied the common femoral artery [at the groin]. I saw the gentleman in consequence of this having been done. The haemorrhage was suppressed by the operation, and the limb recovered its natural temperature, but gangrene made its appearance on the great toe on the third day afterwards. It [the gangrene] did not seem to increase, but the limb swelled as if nature was endeavouring to set up sufficient action to maintain its life; and this continued until the tenth day after the operation, when he died completely exhausted.

When Guthrie dissected the dead man's leg, he found the tied artery intact – it had been a branch of a subsidiary vessel which was damaged. Guthrie commented that it was this that should have been cut down upon and directly ligated. He succinctly ends by saying 'the ligature of the femoral artery destroyed the patient and the practice pursued must be condemned'.[15]

An infantryman with the same type of problem was managed more successfully later. Corporal W Robinson of the 48th Foot was hit in the leg by a shell fragment and was immediately amputated. He was struck by another fragment in the arm, which required disarticulation at the shoulder, eighteen days later. His progress continued.

At the end of month the ligatures had separated, and the wound was nearly healed, although a small abscess had formed on the inside, near where the upper part of the tendon of the pectoralis major had been separated from the bone [during surgery]. Sent to Plymouth [there was a military hospital here], this little abscess had formed again, and was opened on the 2nd of August, three months after the amputation. The next day blood flowed so impetuously from it [infection deep in the wound had eroded an artery], as to induce the surgeon to make an incision, and seek for the bleeding vessel, which could not be found. The late staff-surgeon Dease, [assistant staff surgeon since March 1813] warned by the case of Sergeant Lillie, strongly objected to the subclavian artery being tied above the clavicle [collar-bone] and true to the principle inculcated at Toulouse, advised the application of a ligature below the clavicle on a sound part of the artery, but as near as possible to that which was diseased. This operation was performed by the senior officer, Mr Dowling [2nd assistant surgeon, the Ordnance Medical Department], who carried an incision from the clavicle downwards through the integuments [skin and fat] and great pectoral muscle, until the pectoralis minor [lying beneath the pectoralis major] was exposed. This [muscle] was then divided, and a ligature placed beneath it on the artery where it was sound, at a short distance from the face of the stump, where it was diseased. The man recovered without further inconvenience.[16]

Staff Surgeon Dease, referred to above, had learnt from his previous error. He had directly ligated the femoral artery in the thigh of Sergeant Lillie, of the 62nd Foot, but only above the injured vessel. The sergeant bled to death from the lower half of the artery.

Guthrie mentions just one interesting case following the sortie from Bayonne by Thouvenot's men on April 1814. The Allies sustained around 500–600 casualties in the French assault. Our surgeon was probably not involved in the case and relates the problem as a dire caution to trainees. An officer, possibly of the Foot Guards or KGL,

> was wounded near Bayonne by a musket-ball on the left side; it passed through the ilium [a pelvic bone] across the pubes, and made its exit through the gluteus maximus [the largest buttock muscle] of the opposite side, but lower down. Urine flowed through both wounds at first very readily [the easiest way out], but none of any moment came by the urethra [i.e. the normal way], from which some blood occasionally oozed. The attempt to pass a catheter failed although the desire to make water was urgent and painful. After a few days the passage of urine by the external wounds became obstructed, apparently by the sloughs [and by the swollen and inflamed tissues]; great pain and misery were experienced; fever ran high; rigors and delirium followed [the] extravasation of urine, and death closed the scene. The mischief here arose from the catheter not having been passed into the bladder, which could not be effected, from the prostatic [part] of the urethra or the neck of the bladder having been injured.

Guthrie then emphasizes, 'A free opening in the bladder offers the only hope of safety.' If, as in this case, the stiff silver or pewter catheter became snagged on a fold, a large prostate gland or disrupted and traumatized tissue, then Guthrie advised heroically cutting down on the catheter as a guide and then entering into the bladder, as in a perineal lithotomy (removal of bladder stone from below).[17]

General Thouvenot gave up Bayonne on 27 April and on 30 April the Treaty of Paris was signed and the war was over. Not until June 1814 were the general hospitals shut down and the final casualties moved on to Bordeaux. Surplus hospital and surgical equipment was shipped out to America, where the War of 1812 continued. Despite the trauma of the war, the health of the army was commendable. Between January and June 1814, there had been around 5,000 admissions including malaria, dysentery, typhoid and typhus.

Before closing this productive period of Guthrie's surgical endeavours, it is apposite to present a few casualty figures he had collated. These reflect the achievements and challenges to the AMD at the end of a long and committed war.

First, there are the results in Tables 2 and 3 of surgery from 21 June to 24 December 1813, comparing wounds and the procedures carried out in field (i.e. regimental and brigade) hospitals, with those performed in the major hospital stations (i.e. general hospitals). These were results from all the major actions at Vittoria, San Sebastian, the Pyrenees and the entrance into France. The hospitals were at sited at Vittoria, Santander, Bilbao, Passages and Vera.

There are some simple conclusions that can be drawn from these data. The results are poor, particularly after surgery on the shoulder and arm, with an overall mortality of almost 50 per cent!

Table 2. Results of surgery at base hospitals

Site of surgery	No. operated	Died	Discharged/cured	Under treatment
Shoulder joint	19	15	2	2
Upper limb	299	116 (39%)	105	78
Lower limb	258	149 (58%)	65	44
Trepan	6	5	1	–
Aneurysm	2	2	–	–
	584	287 (49%)	173	124

Now, if we compare these outcomes with surgery carried out in the field there is a striking difference. One of the factors influencing these data is that the cases remaining back with their divisions etc. were less seriously wounded and the severe outbreaks of illness or wound sepsis (e.g. the scourge of hospital gangrene in Bilbao) did not involve the smaller hospitals.

Table 3. Results of surgery by divisions (Cavalry, 1st–7th and Light Divisions)

Site of surgery	No. operated	Died	Discharged/cured	Under therapy	Sent GH
Shoulder joint	19	1	11	3	4
Upper limb	163	5 (3%)	64	29	65
Lower limb	128	19 (15%)	43	22	44
Trepan	6	2	–	–	4
Aneurysm	1	–	–	1	–
TOTAL	317	27 (9%)	118	55	117*

The important data in Table 3 reflect the average performance of regimental and staff surgeons, rather than those of masters such as Guthrie. Clearly the results in smaller units are remarkably good and much improved on the previous figures. The overall mortality of 9 per cent is commendable. Sadly these data are skewed, since 117* men were transferred to a larger hospital and we have no knowledge of their fate. Interestingly, if all of these latter died, the mortality jumps to 42 per cent – still an improvement on the general hospital results. If only, say, fifty men transferred died then the mortality would have been 24 per cent. But still, these differences are still significantly influenced by case selection. Taking together the larger and smaller units, the overall surgical mortality in the campaigns leading up to Toulouse was 35 per cent, perhaps rising to 40 per cent if the transfers (with a 50 per cent mortality) had not been omitted.[18]

To get some idea of hospital mortality, the results over the winter of 1812 may be reviewed. Over the period 24 December 1811 to 20 December 1812 there were 95,075 and 81,105 admissions to general and regimental hospitals respectively – 176,180 in all. Of this group, 119,798 (68 per cent) were discharged fit and 7,193 died (4 per cent, a low average proportion). Thus, at very best, surgical mortality was between five to eight times greater than that of the rate of those dying from disease in a general hospital. Only 15 to 20 per cent of deaths in all types of hospital over the years 1812, 1813 and 1814 occurred in surgical admissions.

So, in this final campaign of the war, we must peruse the success of those under Guthrie's care in his general hospital in the city. Table 4 gives a breakdown, by injury of mortalities of those who had been lucky enough to get to hospital.

Table 4. Mortality rates, broken down by category of injury, in Guthrie's general hospital, 10 April–28 June 1814.

head injury	17%
chest wounds	33%
abdominal wounds	23%
upper limb	1%
lower limb	4%
compound fractures	36%
wounds of spine	100%
wounds of joints	25%
slight wounds	0%
amputations overall	21%

The mortality of ORs and NCOs was 12 per cent, which is four times the mortality of the officer group at 3 per cent! This survival difference is no doubt explained by the officers' better diet, earlier triage and treatment, cleaner clothes and superior state of health. All the cases of lockjaw (thirteen cases) died, a few would survive at Waterloo a year later. If we are generous and include all ranks there were 149 deaths in 1,359 patients, which is an 11 per cent mortality rate! Surely there is no better accolade for Guthrie and his colleagues. This was achieved without anaesthesia, antiseptic practice, antibiotic therapy, intravenous support, an efficient nursing cadre or blood transfusion. The results not only reflect stoic soldiers inured to hardship, deprivation and suffering, but also surgeons committed to succeed, within their limited repertoire.

Dr James McGrigor's own laudatory words crowned a vast effort on the part of surgeons like Guthrie, 'After none of the previous battles were more operations performed than after that of Toulouse and on no former occasion was more skilful surgery displayed. Great experience and reflection had at this time created among us a body of operators such as never were excelled, if ever before equalled, in the British army.'[19]

Guthrie had made notes and collected a few samples of bones damaged by gunfire at Toulouse, from amputation cases and cadavers, two of which were presented to the Westminster Hospital medical museum.[20]

Finally, he embarked for Britain via Bordeaux and must have reached home shores around July or August and was placed on half-pay in September 1814. He contemplated what had changed in civilian practice and what opportunities there were for an experienced military man, who had lost contact with surgery in England. Apart from one period of convalescence, he had been away for six years in the Peninsula, in reality much longer, taking the North American service into consideration. Little did he know that he would be back, in nine months or so, treating war casualties once again.

Peace and War – Waterloo

Guthrie was 29 years old when he returned to London. We can only wonder how out of circulation he must have felt. He had no private practice, no appointment as a consultant to a London teaching hospital and there would be little charity to the surgical war hero.

His biographer records:

> Placed on half-pay in Sept. [25th] 1814, it became necessary to work in private life. Mr Guthrie believed he had seen much, had altered his opinions on many of the most important points in surgery, and entertained the hope that the surgeons of London had not been less fortunate in their pursuits during the fourteen years he had been absent from England. It struck him that the best mode of ascertaining in what these opinions differed from his own, and thus improving his knowledge, would be, by attending as many of their lectures, and by following as much of their practice, as he could without inconvenience. He renewed, therefore, his attendance at his old school of Windmill Street, where Mr. Wilson, Sir C[harles] Bell, and Mr., now Sir B[enjamin] Brodie, lectured; the Westminster Hospital, the Lock [venereal] Hospital; the Charter-House Square Infirmary for Diseases of the Eye, and the lectures of Mr. Abernethy at St Bartholomew's Hospital. They led him to become an author and a teacher, that he might relate in what he differed from all the gentlemen he had heard, whom he found far behind on all those points on which he had had great opportunities of acquiring information, whilst he felt grateful for the communication of what they knew on those in which he had not had the same opportunities. He thus brought himself up to the level of the knowledge of the day; and it is a part of his character deserving of our approbation, that he has never failed to do so on all points connected with his profession. The manner in which he has availed himself of the stethoscope [introduced by Dr Läennec of Quimper in 1819], in his work on Injuries of the Chest, in aid of the diagnoses of the different changes which may have taken place, enhances the value of the work; and we have lately seen him making himself acquainted with the use and abuse of the speculum [a short metal, wooden or ivory bevelled tube to inspect internal

organs] of the diseases of the uterus, not that he practices in these diseases, but because, in his opinion, a surgeon of character and an examiner of the College of Surgeons should have a reasonable practical knowledge of everything connected with physic and surgery.[1]

For an indeterminate time, Guthrie took a well-deserved furlough, no doubt delighted to be reunited with his family and also now settling for a period of tranquil practice, blessed before long by more of a family. He had been 'placed on half-pay, with a month's notice to quit, somewhat like a turned-off footman, and was obliged to seek other employment'.[2] In service, Guthrie's yearly salary had been £456 (£26,200 in today's values).[3] For the moment there would have been little supplement to his reduced salary on half-pay. Deputy Inspectors with twenty years' service would qualify for 12 shillings and 6 pence each day, rising to 30 shillings after thirty years in the army. Despite having been in the service less than twenty years, he would probably still have received 12 shillings and 6 pence per diem, so halving his income. This was equivalent to £228 per annum (£14,600 today). Private practice would come through word of mouth and the non-surgical contacts and friends of Guthrie. Despite being consulted by many ex-officers or their friends, and even considering his reputation, there was much competition in the metropolis for private patients. He next spent much time finalizing and collating his case histories from the Peninsula War. In 1815 he published his treatise on gunshot injuries of the extremities.[4]

He had purchased a property for his family in Jermyn Street. Apparently, by 1815, he had acquired only two private patients. Whatever the truth of this, he clearly was struggling to establish himself in a competitive market. After all there were hundreds of surgeons returning from the wars trying to set up in Britain. Also we might surmise that a robust, tough military surgeon might not attract the 'genteel' clientele of London! In a society that appointed its surgeons in an inevitably nepotistic manner, Guthrie's supporters would have been few and his outspoken manner, coupled with his surgical zeal and ability, might have had a negative influence on his ability to progress. We can only assume that for ten months or so before the Battle of Waterloo, he studied and enjoyed the comforts of home leave, the company of his wife Margaret and 2-year-old daughter Anne, who was to become his favourite child, conceived on his sick-leave home in 1810.

Napoleon Bonaparte landed between Fréjus and Antibes on 1 March 1815 and reached Paris on 21 March after a difficult journey up through Grasse, Grenoble and Auxerre. Despite facing enormous political and logistic challenges and having bled France white, he raised a new army of around 125,000 men, the Armée du Nord and bolstered other smaller forces and garrisons. Disturbing the vastly expensive Congress of Vienna, he rapidly moved towards the now-closed border with the Low Countries, accompanied by five corps and the Imperial Guard.

Guthrie's great surgical opponent, Baron Jean Dominique Larrey, accompanied his Emperor. To meet the final French force of about 108,000 men, an Anglo–Dutch force of around 73,000 was assembled as rapidly as feasible, with men pouring in from Britain, Ireland and America. This force of two army corps was commanded by the Duke of Wellington; the first army corps under the Prince of Orange, the second by Lieutenant-General Lord Hill. Another army of 100,000 men (three corps) under the eccentric Prince Marshal Gebracht von Blücher was the nearest to Brussels. Even if these forces had been overcome by the French, Bonaparte's army would still have had to face 400,000–500,000 men of the Austrian and Russian armies, yet some way off.

There were significant problems for the Army Medical Department. First, that the new Director General, Sir James McGrigor, had only been appointed on 14 June. There could be little of his experienced governance and organizational skills brought in by this fresh threat at such short notice. Secondly, many of the well-honed and experienced Peninsular surgeons had been discharged on half-pay or had left the army and so would be absent from the momentous ensuing struggle on the Brabant plains. Guthrie was entreated by Rowland Hill, Thomas Picton and Lowry Cole to serve on the staff of their corps or divisions. The offer was made to serve as an officer on the general staff with no expense to himself. He declined these offers. Sir James McGrigor also approached him to serve for six months and Guthrie offered three. McGrigor thought this time was 'too short for the interest of the public'.[5] In 1814, Guthrie had mused that he 'had not another battle in the south of France to decide two or three points in surgery which were doubtful. I was called an enthusiast and laughed at accordingly. The battle of Waterloo afforded the desired opportunity.'[6] On further reflection, he decided to travel over to Belgium to assist and to satisfy his curiosity on these few undecided issues. He was appointed as a consultant without administrative duties.

On 15 June, in the early hours of the morning, Napoleon moved his force, crossed the River Sambre and then split the army. Marshal Emanuel Grouchy and the Emperor, with the reserve, moving off to Ligny and Sombreffe, where a desperate and bloody conflict followed over 16 June. Bloodied but not totally bowed, Marshal Blücher and Lieutenant-General Graf von Gneisnau, his strategist and second in command, moved towards Wavre, seven miles or so to the east of Waterloo. Emanuel Grouchy was detached with the 3rd and 4th French Corps, to prevent the union of the Prussian forces with the Anglo–Dutch–Belgic forces.

After the holding conflict at Quatre Bras, the Allies facing the troops under the command of Marshal Michel Ney, battalion surgeons and some surgeons on the staff moved as many of their casualties away from local field hospitals to Brussels, somewhat congesting the road northwards. As the Allied army trudged back along the same road between Brussels and Charleroi on the 17 June, heavy rainfall and fatigue must have dampened the most anxious ardour to engage with the French the following day.

Field hospitals and dressing stations were set up in the three defended farms of Hougoumont, La Haie Sainte and Papelotte. The gentle undulating terrain was ideal for infantry, cavalry and artillery, and any battalion dressing posts behind bushes, trees or in byres would be somewhat exposed. The casualties, in the main, were eventually placed in farm buildings to the rear, principally the large farm at Mont St Jean, which ultimately contained around 6,000 wounded men.

The first phase of Napoleon's attack was made by the French second corps on Hougoumont farm around 1130hours and this complex of buildings and surrounding terrain were contested all day. The light companies of the Coldstreams and 3rd Foot Guards, along with Nassau troops, defended the farm and woods, the Allied casualties being collected in the Chateau. This was set on fire by the French artillery and the injured were carried out to the farm's byres, outhouses and small chapel. Surgeon Samuel Goode of the 3rd Foot Guards performed well and was presented with the damaged battalion colours for his efforts.

For the rest of the day there was scouting, artillery fire and skirmishing but the next severe test for the Duke was an assault by 17,000 infantry of the yet to be engaged first corps of the Count Drouet D'Erlon. Preceding this massive infantry assault was a battering from the Emperor's eighty-four-gun battery on Wellington's left and centre. Commencing at 1300hours, this continued for around half an hour. Although about 2,700 discharges of round shot (8, 9 and 12 pounds ordnance) and 900 shells were fired at the Allied line, it was thought that only about 500 casualties were inflicted, on account of overshooting and soft ground obviating grazing of the missiles.[7] Aside from some ghastly mutilations and fatalities, there then followed a musketry duel between D'Erlon's men and, amongst others, Picton's troops, followed by retaliation from the British heavy cavalry. As the French approached and crushed in on Wellington's men, the Household and Union brigades moved through the infantry and hedgerows, inflicting thousands of sabre wounds, mainly on the head, neck and upper limbs of D'Erlon's men. Sadly, many of these fine horsemen, anxious to cripple Napoleon's artillery, were soon decimated themselves by French lancers and cuirassiers. The British cavalry did not employ lances, which could be remarkably lethal, like the French heavy cavalry sabre, both inflicting fatal penetrative injuries.

As Marshal Ney mounted repeated assaults on La Haie Sante farm, at Wellington's centre, a retrograde movement of the Allies was perceived and this indicated an opportunity to mount a series of French attacks by the magnificent French heavy and Guard cavalry. There were around 5,000–6,000 sabres in large trotting waves, besides other smaller regimental forays. What the French horsemen faced was a series of staggered infantry squares, quite impenetrable to even the most robust cavalry. It was a relief for the squares to face cavalry, since the French batteries fell silent. Ordnance fire would resume after the swathes of horsemen had retired. Inside the squares, the surgeons or their assistants dressed wounds and staunched haemorrhage. The dead were turned outside. Retrograding casualties was a serious problem here, since the French cavalry were omnipresent and frustrated. Whilst first aid and temporary therapy was feasible, an hour or two would pass before the injured could be cleared. The 4th Army Corps under Count von Bülow was by now engaged on Napoleon's right flank around the village of Plançenoit. The French and Prussian victims took shelter in the buildings, not always a secure environment. Even today, villagers can show visitors where casualties were mercilessly shot as they lay wounded in their houses.

Napoleon's next directive against the farm of La Haie Sainte was followed by its capture. Many wounded lying in the farm building were executed by shot or bayonet. With General Hans von Ziethen's 1st Corps now approaching and engaging on Wellington's left flank, the Emperor had few reserves and sent in the Imperial Guard, who advanced up the slope towards Maitland's Foot Guards. Close volley fire and Colonel Colborne's brigade assault from the flank and front pushed the 'Grumblers' down the hill and Wellington raised his hat for the general advance.

The whole campaign resulted in more than 60,000 wounded men, about 50,000 dead and injured soldiers and around 3,500 horses on Waterloo battlefield lying or writhing upon an area of about two to three square miles – a massive density of wounded, greater than at the Battle of the Somme in 1916. British casualties after Quatre Bras or on the retreat from there were 2,512 and at Waterloo 7,016: 9,528 in all. There were also 3,046 sick in general hospitals on 18 June.

After the battle, there were several civilian surgical visitors anxious to see, advise and assist with the surgical problems to be associated with this greatest of victories. Professor John Thomson, who held the Regius Chair of Military Surgery in Edinburgh, went to Brussels with Dr Somerville, a senior medical officer in Scotland. Having gained approval for their visit from Sir James McGrigor, the two civilian doctors set off on 4 July and arrived four days later.

There they met Deputy Inspector John Gunning (who amputated Lord Raglan's arm) and Dr Donald McNeil of the Staff. They visited the various hospitals in the city, six principal units: the Jesuits, the Elizabeth, the Annonciate, Orpheline and the Notre Dame, which housed around 2,500 British NCOs and privates; the Gendarmerie, built on lower ground, housed many of the French casualties. This latter hospital was less healthy and many of the wounded prisoners suffered with bilious remittent and intermittent fevers, mainly typhoid and malaria. The two visitors spent twelve days touring these hospitals and then travelled to Termonde to view the 250 wounded French soldiers there. They toured on to Antwerp, where around 2,500 casualties were distributed in five hospitals, the Minimes, the Facon, Augustin, Hotel du Nord and the Corderie. The latter, a rope-works to the naval arsenal, around a quarter of a mile long, and so ideal for rows of hospital cots, housed around 1,000 patients.[8] Interestingly, the care of the French casualties there was placed in the hands of a Dr Vranken and other Belgian practitioners of the town.

Thomson was clearly impressed with, and most laudatory about, the efforts of the surgeons after Waterloo. He wistfully ruminated:

> But the duties of the medical man, to whom the charge of those wounded in battle is committed, though less brilliant in the eyes of the world, are often no less dangerous to himself than the exertions of the warrior, nor less deserving of public esteem and reward. The fatigue, anxiety, and disappointments to which he is subjected, can be conceived only by those who have experienced them. The gratitude of his patients is the fruit of his success, and sometimes the reward of his labours; but in meeting with neglect, or ignorant censure, how often is this useful servant of the public obliged to be satisfied with the silent approbation of his own heart, as his only recompense for the utmost endeavours of his skill and humanity.[9]

He later wrote an excellent and illuminating account of the casualties of Waterloo, especially many fascinating post-mortem findings.[10]

Sir Charles Bell, consulting surgeon to the Middlesex Hospital and co-founder of its medical school, heard of the victory and exclaimed to a favourite pupil, John Shaw his brother in law, 'Johnnie! How can we let this pass?' Their surgical instruments being their passports, they set off on 26 June. They arrived on the 29th, eleven days after the battle and perceiving the lot of the French casualties to be inadequate, Bell undertook the care of around 300 wounded Frenchmen and operated tirelessly for five days, working twelve to thirteen hours each day. He helped with other casualties for a further three days.[11] After all this, Bell made copious notes and forty-five charcoal sketches, which enabled him later to construct seventeen evocative and unique colour images of some of the casualties of the campaign, which haunt us today with the real face of battle.[12]

John Hennen, the notable Peninsular staff surgeon, had been recalled to full-pay on 25 March 1815 and was required to take charge of the Jesuits' Hospital in Brussels. He also worked at the Gendarmerie Hospital, helping with the French casualties. Among the latter were 1,400 compound fracture cases, most much delayed in their evacuation, many lying out between eight to thirteen days. Following sterling service here, he was promoted to Deputy Inspector of Hospitals by McGrigor in September 1815. His textbook of military surgery, *Observations on Military Surgery*, is a classic account of practice in service.[13] He sadly succumbed prematurely in a yellow fever epidemic in Gibraltar, in 1828.

George Guthrie arrived after Bell and Shaw, but preceded Thomson and Somerville by five days, arriving on 3 July, just over a fortnight since the battle. He remained in Brussels for a week, departing on 10 July. His main role was clearly as an experienced surgeon and he consulted on only the most serious problems. He operated on only two patients in Brussels, sending a third home for major surgery in the York Hospital in Chelsea, on his return. He visited, but did not operate, in Antwerp. The visit, in the end an unpaid trip, had cost our surgeon in the region of £40.[14]

Clearly, he was not impressed by what he experienced after Waterloo:

> The army was not the Peninsular army, neither were all its doctors. Few, if any, of the medical staff officers had seen a field of battle. I found the assistant surgeons doing everything they should not have done. The greatest efforts were made to obviate this state of things. Amateur surgeons flocked over from London. They rectified these evils as far as they could, but nothing could recall the past or the irretrievable mischief the insufficient medical care had occasioned in the first few days.[15]

Dealing initially with the two patients Guthrie operated on in Brussels, and one he sent home for surgery, a few other cases are worthy of recall. Guthrie was always concerned at the issue of safely controlling haemorrhage from a limb with arterial damage. Recalling his condemnation of solely ligating a wounded artery 'upstream' of the injury, he soundly preached that to cut down and directly tie off the wounded artery above and below the breach in the vessel was the only reliable option.

The first man he personally treated after Waterloo was a case referred to him at one of the Brussels hospitals, Private Henry Vigarelie serving in the King's German Legion. He had been shot through in the right calf, behind the two leg bones, the missile entering the inside of the calf and exiting further down on the outside. There was no initial concern or haemorrhage, but after a few days, after some minor warning bleeds, there was a considerable loss of blood. This and subsequent bleeds were controlled by a screw tourniquet. The leg was now hot, swollen and painful. Guthrie passed his finger into the wound and through the injured tissues, where he felt a soft swelling around where the peroneal artery (one of the three branches of the main artery of the leg) was situated. Pressing on this, he controlled the bleeding. A call for amputation was made, but Guthrie thought otherwise.

What followed demonstrated his skill and Vigarelie's stoicism. Turning the injured man on his face, Guthrie made a seven-inch incision in the back of the calf. Boldly cutting down through the bruised and swollen calf muscles, he could not identify the exact location of the injured artery. The wound was deep and the tissue much disrupted and in the poor light he could not see well enough. He then cut outwards, at right angles to the longer vertical incision and having created a T-shaped wound, turned back two small flaps and saw a spot from where the blood was issuing. Passing a tenaculum (sharp hook on a handle) under this area, he lifted the vessel then carried a needle double-threaded with linen, above the spot, which controlled the haemorrhage, and passed another below the wound in the vessel. The incision was loosely closed with adhesive strips and the patient rested and given a milk diet. A week after surgery the wound 'suppurated kindly' (i.e. became infected) and the next day the sutures were pulled off. The patient recovered satisfactorily and mobilized well after his ordeal.

Guthrie's second Waterloo patient was the most memorable of his wartime career. The soldier was M. François de Gay, a wounded infantryman of the 45th Ligne, taken prisoner during the battle. He had lain out four days and nights on his back, only able to turn his head to lap water from a puddle. He had been struck from behind in the lower part of the right buttock by a large or small case round, which exited at the right groin, so shattering the neck (upper end) of the right femur (thigh-bone) and separating it from the main shaft of the bone.

With so much shattered tissue, the only surgical chance in this man, Guthrie felt, was to remove the whole leg at the hip joint. Whilst Baron Dominique Larrey had performed this seven times (one in Europe, two in Egypt, two after Wagram and twice during the Russian campaign) with possibly one survivor, Surgeon Brownrigg (a staff surgeon serving through the Peninsular and Waterloo campaigns) had one successful but undocumented case near Merida in the winter of 1812. Guthrie had had one death after this procedure, after the siege of Cuidad Rodrigo, so De Gay's case was the first properly recorded success in the British Army. There was little contemporary literature on this formidable procedure to guide Guthrie.[16]

Guthrie felt that the operation would rarely be required for musket-ball injury and damage sufficient to mandate disarticulation at the hip would arise from case, round shot or shell bursts.[17] He emphasized that this monumental procedure would have specific anatomical determinants and should only be performed under the threat of certain death, or suicide, at an early stage and with the explicit consent of the patient.

Admitted on the 5 July, De Gay was brought along for surgery on the 7th at the Elizabeth Hospital. He was exhausted with infection and his wounds were sloughing and he had a large sacral pressure sore, from enforced bed rest. The operation was carried out in good light at 2pm. We know that George Guthrie had two distinguished assistants, John Hennen and Staff Surgeon Collier. The latter surgeon had served six years in the infantry, two years as staff surgeon in the Peninsula and went onto full-pay again in April 1815.[18] Guthrie directed one to press on the femoral artery at the groin and the other to place his fingers on several bleeding vessels in the large area of exposed muscle. Surgeon James Alexander Campbell was probably in attendance and Guthrie later left De Gay in his charge, requesting almost daily reports. Campbell had previously served in the line for sixteen years, was promoted staff surgeon in March 1812 and promoted brevet DIH two years after Waterloo.

The patient was brought along for surgery, made to lie semi-recumbent on a table, or pair of panniers, and restrained. Then the operation commenced. Guthrie stood between the patient's legs, with his assistants opposite, ready to digitally compress the femoral and other vessels. A junior surgeon was ordered to hold the limb steady and rotate and move it as needed. Unlike Baron Larrey, Guthrie had not ligated the femoral artery prior to surgery (known by the French as the *ligature d'attente*) and he did not employ a transfixion of the upper thigh with a straight capital knife to cut outwards and fashion side flaps.

First Guthrie made the skin incisions, using a semi-curved or straight capital, medium-sized, pointed knife, to form two side flaps of skin, fat and muscle – the inner one longer, in order to provide adequate soft tissue cover for the other articulating surface of the hip joint (the acetabulum). Guthrie had to ligate the femoral artery and then proceed to divide twenty muscles, four sets of blood vessels (femoral, obturator, sciatic and gluteal) and several nerves, including the sciatic. When the hip joint was exposed by dissection, the limb was moved to stress the joint and the capsule of the joint opened.

All connections with the head and neck of the thigh-bone were severed and the rest of the muscles etc. divided. While all this dissection was being rapidly carried out, the assistants, with their hands compressed the flaps to control haemorrhage. If bleeding from the femoral vein was to prove troublesome, it could be ligated with a single thread, but Guthrie felt it was best avoided. After limb removal De Gay's arteries were tied off in turn, using a sharp hook (tenaculum) to tease them out, or a forceps to pinch them prior to ligation. The vessels were single or doubly ligated with silk or linen threads. The nerves were cut well short, to avoid entrapment in the scarring of the stump end. The cartilage was pared off the acetabulum and then the raw surfaces were sponged down and the integuments (soft tissues) brought together, so closing the wound with three or four stitches and some adhesive tapes.

Guthrie left the entry wound open, probably keeping it from closing down with a piece of lint. This would serve as a drainage port, for inevitable sepsis. The operation site was dressed with lint compresses and linen and then a calico roller bandage was wound round the stump, having been started around the waist. Cordials, lemonade, opiates and a simple diet, coupled with any anti-inflammatory measures, were administered.[19] Remarkably, the patient had born the operation in good spirits. He had lost merely 24 ounces of blood (about 720cc). Thomson and Somerville reviewed this case in Brussels, after Guthrie had left for home on 10

July. They reported the inevitable sepsis, which fortunately De Gay survived. Dr Campbell sent daily details to Guthrie. Of interest was a visit by Baron Larrey on 19 July. Despite the sepsis, De Gay's bedsore and wound progressed slowly but well, he remained nourished by broths, mutton chops, jellies and wine.[20] By 19 November, five months after wounding, he was ready for transfer to the York Hospital, remaining under the personal supervision of Mr Campbell. Another hip disarticulation was attempted after Waterloo, by a Mr Blicke at Antwerp (William Flamanck Blicke had served in the 86th and 10th Foot, joining the Staff in 1813). His patient was given little hope of surviving surgery, but having consented, only lived eight days.[21]

There was another patient who required this procedure during Guthrie's stay in Brussels. Our surgeon 'urged it on the man, a French soldier, for several days, but he refused until finding himself sinking, when he consented. It was too late; when I gently stated this to him, he thanked me, a tear for a moment glistened in his eye, he waved his hand once more over his head, and cried out, "*Vive l'Empereur*". He died a few hours afterwards.'[22]

In the *Clinical Lectures on Compound Fractures of the Extremities*, published in 1838, Guthrie recommended a less mutilating operation of merely removing the head and neck of the thigh-bone.[23]

The third patient was also a private in the King's German Legion. Guthrie preferred to send him home for surgery. He was hit by a musket ball, which passed through the lower abdominal wall, just above the pubic bone and lodged. Guthrie surmised that the man required time to recover and his wounds to heal, before an attempt to extract the missile. His symptoms apparently were not severe, he passed a little blood-stained urine and his wound closed. He had strangury (an uncomfortable desire to void urine) and symptoms resembling a bladder stone. Guthrie passed a metal sound into the bladder and felt the ball clink against the instrument, confirming its presence in the bladder cavity. Guthrie sent him home to the York Hospital, where François de Gay and Vigarelie were raising much interest. It is timely to recount his surgery here.

Guthrie, in the presence of, 'a large concourse of military and medical persons' removed the stone by perineal lithotomy. The man's diet had been lowered and bowels emptied by glyster (enema). Strapped up, ankles to wrists and restrained, Guthrie cut down on a bougie (sound) resting and steadied in the urethra (the penile tube leading from the bladder along the penis), with a stout scalpel or he may have cut straight through the perineum (the region between the scrotum and anus). Having opened the base of the bladder the wound into the bladder was forcibly dilated, strong forceps were insinuated into the organ, the stone was then grasped and removed. The lead ball was by now encrusted with chemical debris and this fragmented and the ball fell out of the forceps' grip. Guthrie tells the tale, 'It was done in less than two minutes; but the calculus [ball and encrustations], composed of the triple phosphates which had formed around the ball, yielded and broke under the forceps. The pieces were removed separately. The ball being heavy fell below the neck of the bladder, which, being healthy [supple], yielded to the pressure and allowed it to sink [backwards] on to the rectum.' Guthrie inserted his finger into the anus and pushed the ball upwards, so permitting removal. After the lithotomy, Guthrie would almost certainly have left a gum elastic or metal catheter in situ for a while, to prevent leakage of urine through the surgical wound. How any patient could tolerate this dangerous procedure and not be left incontinent, impotent or bleed to death beggars belief. The soldier recovered in a straightforward manner.

Meanwhile, back in Flanders, the problem of infection spreading from any serious septic focus obviously continued to puzzle and concern Guthrie. He erroneously wrote that some such cases must have been 'instances of endemic fever after secondary amputation'[24] This was clearly a not infrequent occurrence and was a source of great disappointment to many surgeons performing otherwise decent surgery. He mistakenly ascribed the death of four cases after Waterloo to an incidental attack of malaria or typhoid, when in fact, the patients died from complications of their infected wounds. These septicaemic cases all had a common theme with a fatal termination, three infantrymen and a cavalry trooper. All had wounds of the arm, wrist or hand. After their wounds had become septic, they underwent secondary amputation (between two and five weeks from wounding). Following operation, all four surgical wounds became infected and the patients died. Common findings at dissection (post-mortem) were inflamed lungs with effusion of fluid into the chest, enlarged liver with or without an abscess, and an effusion of fluid into the sac around the heart. These findings strongly suggest multi-organ failure (liver, lungs, heart and kidneys) as the agonal event, rather than unrelated intercurrent illness.

There was an abundance of injured heads after Waterloo and many of the wounds were as previously described. Another consequence of bleeding inside the skull was that of contralateral paralysis. Private Charles Murray of Lieutenant-Colonel Cooke's company, 2nd battalion 1st Foot Guards, was struck by a fragment of common shell on the left side of his skull. He remained unconscious for thirty minutes. On awakening, he was nauseated and started bleeding from his left ear, indicating a fracture in the base (bottom) of his cranium. Guthrie describes his problem. The patient 'found himself unable to move his right arm and right leg, which hung as if they were dead, and had lost their feeling'. He was admitted to the Minimes Hospital in Antwerp on 29 June and was repeatedly bled. His headache and paralysis persisted and Guthrie advised on surgery. On 3 July, some bone fragments were removed after two applications of the circular trephine saw.[25] Guthrie and his colleagues were delighted with the result, 'Immediately after removal of the bone he recovered the use of his right arm and leg, so far as to be able to move them, and to be sensible of their being touched.' He was sent to the general hospital at Yarmouth and by mid-September, his wound was healing well and his only disability was a weakness of his right-hand grip.[26] This particular case illustrates a fact as yet unknown to Guthrie and other surgeons; cross-representation of the cerebral hemispheres. Thus the right side of the brain represents the opposite side of the body, both in motor function and sensation and vice versa.

Interestingly, Guthrie quotes a very similar case treated by a Samuel Cooper in Brussels. The latter surgeon, a future President of the Royal College of Surgeons, was on the staff at Waterloo and compiled an anthology of surgery that is of immense importance to researchers of the surgery of this period.[27]

Major-General Sir Colin Halkett was wounded in front of his 5th British Brigade, which was formed in squares, ready to receive cavalry. Apparently a senior French cuirassier officer discharged his pistol at Halkett. The ball struck his neck, causing him severe pain, but no lasting damage. A second shot wounded him in the thigh, but he did not leave the field until towards the end of the day, when a third shot struck him on the side of his face. The ball entered the left cheek-bone, shattered some teeth in the upper jaw, breaking his hard palate. The ball was deflected upwards, broke up some upper jaw teeth of the opposite side and, exiting from the cheek-bone, it lay under the skin. The pain was somewhat relieved by the ball's extraction, but the general remained deaf in the left ear with tinnitus. The wound was infected and threw out fragments of dead facial bone, healing only after three years. We may only speculate on the unpleasant and long-term *sequelae* from Halkett's injuries.

Chest injuries at Waterloo continued to fuel Guthrie's interest. In non-exiting thoracic cases the ball was rarely recovered. Such a case was Lieutenant-Colonel Dumaresq, aide-de-camp to Lord Strafford. The patient related his story to Guthrie:

> While turning round, after a successful charge of infantry, at Hougomont [sic], on the 18th of June, 1815, I was wounded by a musket-ball, which passed through the right scapula, penetrated the chest, and lodged in the middle of the rib of the axilla [armpit], which was supposed to be broken. When desired to cough by the medical officer who first saw me, almost immediately after receiving the wound, some blood was intermixed with the saliva. I became extremely faint and remained so about an hour and a half, after which I rode four or five miles to the village of Waterloo, where I was bled, which relieved me from the difficulty I had in breathing; this difficulty was accompanied by severe pain down my neck, chest, and right side. I was much easier until the evening of the 19th; but in the course of the night the difficulty in breathing becoming much greater; and the

spasmodic affection having very much increased, I was bled seven times, until the middle of the next day 20th. I continued better, but was then seized with the most violent spasms in my neck, chest and stomach imaginable. I could scarcely breathe at all, and was in the greatest possible pain; I was again bled twice very largely, and my stomach and chest fomented for a length of time with warm water and flannels. I passed a very tolerable night, and continued pretty well until two o'clock the following day, when I was again very largely bled, by which I was very much relieved. I continued pretty well, and free from much pain; but my pulse having very much increased, and having a good deal of fever, on the 23rd I was bled again; after this I continued free from much pain or difficulty of respiration, and on the 26th was removed into Bruxelles [sic], when I came under your [i.e. Guthrie's] care. I forgot to mention that when I was so violently attacked I had two lavements [poultices] most vigorously applied; salts, &c., proving of no avail, took digitalis, commencing ten drops every four hours, increasing to fifteen from the second day.

N.B. – Up to this period, the 2nd of July, the devil a bit have I eaten.
[Dumaresq constructed a little ditty, complaining about his low diet!]

> Whilst with fat mutton-chops, and nice loins of veal,
> You stuff your d—d guts, your hearts are all steel,
> Oh! ye doctors and potecaries [sic], you'll all go to hell,
> For cheating our poor tripes of their daily meal.

The ball in this case was lodged in the rib, which ultimately became thickened around it. He recovered with good health, but with occasional spasms in the chest; and died of apoplexy [a stroke] in Australia, twenty-five years afterwards. His doggrel [sic] lines [and behaviour!] show the buoyant and unconquerable spirit of a soldier, who knew that his chance of recovery was small. It was a most gallant, a most friendly spirit. Peace to his manes [shades of a dead person].[28]

Guthrie quoted another case, a Corporal Dunleary of the 69th Foot, wounded on 16 June at Quatre Bras, with an identical wound and problem. The missile, not retrieved, never bothered the patient.

A grim reminder of the delay in treatment often shown to enemy casualties was the wounded French infantryman treated by Guthrie, unsuccessfully, for a through and through wound of the chest. The man died of sepsis of the lung four weeks after receiving his wound, but had lain out on the battlefield for five days.[29]

Staff Surgeon Collier related a remarkable success story to Guthrie after Waterloo. Trooper William Barrett of the Life Guards had his arm and chest injured by a musket shot, after breaking the arm, the ball passed into the chest, high on the left side and was not retrieved. The wound healed and the patient made progress until six weeks after the injury, when he became severely septic. Collier made a deep incision into the region of the chest entry wound. After removing some shattered portions of rib, he felt a bag-like structure and boldly cut into it. Two pints of thick fœtid pus were released and a tent (cloth plug) inserted to prevent the wound closing. The wound, however, did close prematurely and a second incision was required, after which a gum-elastic catheter was inserted to assist drainage.

Occasionally, a wound in the chest wall, as in the abdomen, allowed prolapse (hanging out) of the lung, which plugged the wound. Guthrie saw three such patients after Waterloo and correctly (for those days) advised dressings only, it being unwise to disturb the status quo.[30] When missiles entered the abdomen or chest a defect was produced and Guthrie was informed of a post-mortem at the Gendarmerie hospital, carried out on a French soldier who had died after a musket ball had penetrated the lower chest and damaged the lung and diaphragm (the thin sheet of muscle between the chest and belly). He expired five and a half months later, worn out by copious infected discharge from his chest. The ball had damaged the diaphragm and allowed the man's stomach to pass up into his chest. The missile could not be found, possibly having been passed out through the gut.[31] James Wilkie a 34-year-old trooper of the 12th Light Dragoons received a similar injury, but from a French heavy cavalry sabre. This time the stomach was in the chest and so severely compressed by the hole in the diaphragm that the blood supply was cut off and the stomach was black and 'dead'. Once again the man did not survive, succumbing from sepsis.[32]

Not a few abdominal wounds were seen after the battle. Sir John Elley, a Lieutenant-Colonel of the Royal Regiment of Horse Guards, was injured by a sword in one of the final manœuvres of the remnants of the Heavy Brigade. The point of the sword entered his stomach, from which he recovered, a fortunate outcome from such a potentially serious wound. This wound left him with a hernia of his abdominal wall, for which he had to wear a circumferential bandage to retain the bulge.[33]

A most incredible story of survival after a gun-shot wound of the abdomen was that of Rifleman Owen M'Caffery, a 33-year-old soldier of the first battalion of the 95th. He was shot through the lower right abdominal wall. On admission to the Minimes Hospital on 21 June, 'he was in the most deplorable state; the whole abdomen was tense and exquisitely tender [there was peritonitis from the leakage of gut contents, issuing from the damaged bowel]; the pulse small and wiry; vomiting incessant; with hiccough [as his bowels were paralysed – a consequence of the peritonitis] and ghastly visage [dehydration and sepsis]'. For three days he was bled largely, fomentations were placed on his abdomen and he was purged and made to vomit with emetics. He was given enemata and opium. A week after the battle faeces discharged from the bullet hole. He was allowed milk, rice, some potato and sugar on 26 June and he managed half a fowl by 1 July. The wounded gut had sealed off from the rest of the abdomen and over the next few weeks the fistula (a communication between gut and skin) gradually reduced and the patient recovered.

Guthrie's attention was drawn to a strange case in Brussels, Sergeant Matthews of the 28th Foot. He had a penetrating non-exiting abdominal wound by a musket shot. He walked to a village in the rear where he remained for three days. He was bled and dressed, then transferred to Brussels. Guthrie was asked to see him as he had passed the lead ball per rectum, six days after wounding. His damaged gut must also have been successfully sealed off from the abdominal cavity and his wound was healed in two months. He became very drunk in convalescence and some local abdominal pain recurred. He was treated and one day whilst attempting to open his bowels, 'he found, after many efforts, that something blocked up the anus, and on taking hold of and drawing it out, he found it was a portion of waistband of his breeches, including a part of the button-hole'.[34] What is hard to understand is that this amount of material could have been passed into the gut, with relatively so little disturbance to the patient!

To reinforce the problem of errant and deflected missiles, Guthrie related the story of Major (later Major-General) John Ross of the 95th, wounded at Waterloo. He was hit by a musket ball,

which entered at the upper part of the arm and injured the bone. More than one surgeon had pointed out the way by which it had passed under the scapula [shoulder-blade] and lodged itself in some of the muscles of the back. About a year afterwards I extracted it close to the elbow, the ball lying at the bottom of an abscess, which was only brought near the surface by time, by the use of flannel [warm poultice], and desisting from all emollient applications.[35]

Another interest of Guthrie's was that of tissue damage (without breaching the skin) caused by tangential ordnance strikes. He could find but a single case after the battle. He commented, 'the man stated that he had received a blow on the back part of the leg, he believed from a cannon-shot, which brought him to the ground, and stunned him considerably. On endeavouring to move, he found himself incapable of stirring, and the sensibility and power of motion in the limb were lost.' The soldier's leg was cold and soon turned black colour as far as the knee. The leg was amputated just above the knee and afterwards, Guthrie dissected the leg. There was a cavity, full of blood clot, below the calf muscles. The main artery to the leg (the popliteal) was occluded by clot and the two principal divisions below it had been ruptured by the tremendous force of the leg strike. Guthrie reflected on Baron Larrey's sage counsel to make an incision in the flesh should there ever be a doubt as to whether there is early mortification (gangrene), where there would be no bleeding, or the tissues might just be severely bruised.

Guthrie had amassed a great deal of data in his notes and memories. He knew he now had much to teach. The short sojourn in the Belgian capital marked the finale of his military service. He had to get home and find employment and build up his civilian career.

10

Guthrie's Combat Legacy and Post-War Efforts

On Guthrie's return from war the family moved out of Jermyn Street and bought another house, 2 Berkeley Street, from which he was now to endeavour to set up practice in the city.

James McGrigor procured Guthrie a consulting post in the York Hospital at Chelsea. He would be in charge of two of the two principal surgical wards, which would give him sufficient clinical material to teach on, alongside his lectures and demonstrations. With no emoluments, this was an honorary position, Guthrie remaining, however, on half-pay. The posting at Chelsea lasted until the hospital closed two years later, when the hospital was moved to Fort Pitt in Chatham. Guthrie gradually picked up private patients.

There were of course, the three patients from Waterloo to be managed, and they were visited by military and medical dignitaries. De Gay proved of intense and particular interest. This illustrious patient even drew the attention of royalty. Guthrie's biographer wrote:

> His Royal Highness the Duke of York went to the hospital on purpose to see these three men; and the [patient who had undergone] amputation of the hip-joint having been done on a Frenchman, His Royal Highness wrote himself to Marshal Soult, to interest him in his favour, and the man was placed, in consequence, in the Hôtel des Invalides, for years the only instance of this kind in France. The Baron Larrey had performed this operation before Mr Guthrie, but he never had the good fortune to succeed in bringing one to France. This case was therefore one of great attraction, and excited so much emulation in Paris and in London, that all who had before declared it to be impracticable and must fail, now wished to do it if they could find an opportunity; and Mr Guthrie felt himself obliged to repress this rising ardour, by pointing out their errors. In the published life of the Baron Larrey, it is stated that he advised, in consultation with Guthrie, that this operation should be done. This is, however a mistake. The Baron and Mr Guthrie did not meet in Brussels [probably at no other time did the two greatest military surgeons come together], and the operation

was performed, and the man in safety, before M. Larrey saw him.[1]

De Gay after being admitted to Les Invalides was soon capable of walking three miles on his wooden limb, which at each step was thrown forward by the muscles of his trunk. Guthrie wrote, 'He is in very good health, not quite so fat as when in England, talks of getting married, and is not, as the French express it "sage."' Presumably the latter remark refers to any difficulties he might anticipate in a marital status![2]

With regard to Guthrie's doctrine of conservative surgery, his biographer stated, 'Mr Guthrie, in his Miscellaneous Lectures, and on Compound Fractures, published in 1838, has shown the way in which the head and neck of the thigh-bone should be removed, and the amputation of the limb avoided – an operation which has not yet been done [i.e. by 1850], but which we hope, if another war should take place in Europe, Mr Guthrie may live to see succeed.'[3] Writing in 1855, in the sixth edition of his *Commentaries on the Surgery of the War*, he advised:

The great advance which operative surgery has made within the last forty years, and the success which has followed the removal of the head of the humerus, the whole of the elbow, the ancle [sic], and even the knee joint, render it imperative on surgeons of ability to endeavour to save life without the performance of so formidable an operation as that of the removal of the whole limb, more particularly when the health is good and the parts sound, with the exception of those immediately injured.[4]

Vigarelie, who had undergone what had been nicknamed, 'Guthrie's Bloody Operation', recovered uneventfully, under the watchful eye of surgeons James Alexander Campbell and Samuel Hill (assistant surgeon to the 71st Foot, later staff surgeon and elected FRS, FLS), then would return to Germany.[5] He suffered a degree of pain in the ball of his foot after walking a distance – a result of having a reduced blood supply to the leg. He remained a tribute to one of Guthrie's great contributions to vascular surgery. Interestingly, in 1828, the surgical management of this type of problem was belatedly directed by no less than the great Baron Guillaume Dupuytren, surgeon in chief at the Hôtel Dieu Hospital in Paris. Guthrie had had the intense satisfaction of correctly managing this problem sixteen years before this great French civilian surgeon's misplaced advice on the subject!

Lastly, at the York, there was the soldier of the King's German Legion who had received a musket ball into his bladder. This major operation has been described in the previous chapter and we now pick up the story. The soldier, having made a smooth recovery, Guthrie described his subsequent progress:

The symptoms of irritation did not, however, entirely pass away, as could have been wished, and I began to fear that some small piece of calculus [phosphatic debris] had been overlooked: when one morning, after considerable effort, he passed a ring of sandy calcareous matter, which had formed around the orifice [exit] of the bladder, and which being dislodged, had fortunately entered the urethra, along which it was forced by the urine. It was obviously formed by the phosphates in minute portions, which had become agglutinated together around the meatus [exit orifice] of the bladder. This he took with him to Hanover, where it, himself, and the cicatrices [scars] of his wound and of his operation attracted great notice. The ball, which was flattened on one side, I kept in a small box, together with the pieces of calculus, which were extracted, and showed them annually at my lecture on this subject for many years. One evening however, I left my little box on the table after lecture; and when I recollected, and returned for it, I found that some gentleman had borrowed, and has not yet returned it.[6]

After the war, Guthrie had taken an interest in the management of bladder stones. It was rumoured that the first crushing instrument, introduced via the urethra, to break up stones (called a lithotrite) was made for Guthrie by Mr Weiss, a well-known surgical instrument manufacturer. Apparently Guthrie, in the York Hospital, had a soldier who had a bladder stone. The procedure was quoted as being the first time lithotrity had been tried in Britain. The long instrument, curved at its tip, was passed into the bladder and a wheel control was turned outside the patient (the 'business' end was inside the bladder), to open three prongs, which were intended to catch and then grip the calculus. When the wheel was tightened to approximate the crushing jaws, the stone would fragment, after which the bladder would then be washed out, to remove the fragments. Guthrie ran into trouble with the operation, in front of a notable medical audience. His biographer records, 'The three-pronged instrument was introduced, and the stone caught; it slipped, and on attempting to catch it again, the instrument was found to be wide open, and immovable! Every one was struck with horror. Mr Weiss, senior, since dead, sat down in a faint: he thought he had been accessory to killing a man. The late Captain Kater, FRS, who was present, with a great many others, held up their hands in great alarm.' It was here that Guthrie's great calmness under pressure showed itself:

Mr Guthrie alone preserved that coolness, that presence of mind, for which he has always been remarkable. He had previously considered and calculated upon all the difficulties he might encounter, of which this was one. It was evident that the instrument was fixed [jammed] and could not be closed nor withdrawn: something was in the joint or sheath, and how to disentangle it? The calculation had been made: Mr Guthrie forced the instrument open to its utmost extent, apparently increasing the obstacle to its withdrawal, but thereby relieving it from a fold [of the lining, or mucosa] of the neck of the bladder, which it had caught, when it closed, and was withdrawn. The unanaesthetised patient, who saw the alarm of everybody at the occurrence, said – 'You may cut out the stone, Sir whenever you please, but you shall never put that three-pronged thing into me again.' The operation, by incision, [described previously] a fortnight after, was successful, and the Duke of York, on seeing the man, was pleased to grant his discharge, as an especial favour. He, however, a few days afterwards, enlisted again, for the sake of the bounty, the examining surgeon [during routine examination of his recruit] never thinking of looking at his perineum, to see whether he had been cut for the stone.[7]

During his sojourn at the York, Guthrie frequently demonstrated the importance of many of his principles to military surgeons. Soon, however, his life would start entering a new phase of teaching and he looked around for further contribution to the craft. He was significantly short of funds, which was to influence his decision when offered reward for his service. The biographer recorded:

His Royal Highness the Duke of York was pleased to have it signified to him, through Sir Herbert Taylor, his secretary, that if the honour of knighthood was an object, his Royal Highness would receive favourably, and support, an application for it. The intimation was very gratifying under such circumstances, but Mr Guthrie was at that time as poor as need be. He had married Margaret, a daughter of the late Mr Patterson, Lieutenant-Governor of Prince Edward's Island, and had reason to believe that he should have a large family, and feared, if anything should happen to him, before he was able to save some money for them, that 'my lady' might be an inconvenient title for a poor woman, he therefore gratefully declined to accept the offer so kindly made.

This was, despite his reasoning, a strange response from a man, first, struggling to establish his professional reputation and, secondly, when he had seemed to take so much pride in the very real contributions he had made to the service.

Another episode deprived Guthrie of honourable recognition on a subsequent occasion,

when the late Lord Canterbury, then Sir C Manners Sutton, was Speaker of the House of Commons, and from some political negotiation then on foot believed himself for twenty-four hours to be Minister, he offered to ask his Majesty King William to make Mr Guthrie a Commander of the Guelph. This Mr Guthrie declined, saying, 'I will wait, if you please, until tomorrow, when, after you have kissed hands, and are Minister, you can write me a letter, saying you have given it as a reward for services. It would now be only a private favour.' The reply was, 'I will then give you anything in my power, for you have deserved it from the state.' The views of the leaders of the Tory party had changed the night before; Sir C M Sutton did not return from Court, Minister, as he had expected, and Mr. Guthrie did not become a Guelph.[8]

Just over a year after Waterloo, in October 1816, Guthrie gave his first course of lectures. These were given gratis to officers in the medical service of the Royal Navy, British Army and the Honourable East India Company. This was an incredibly generous gesture and such effort reflected Guthrie's views on the lack of proper training and a chair of military surgery in England. After the 1816–17 course of lectures was completed, the grateful members presented him with a beautiful inscribed fifty guineas silver cup. T J Pettigrew related his style of lecturing, 'In his character as a lecturer, he is distinguished by peculiar earnestness, precision, and vivacity. He has great command of language, and mixes, in most agreeable manner, personal anecdotes and descriptions with the relation of his cases, so that they cannot fail to make a strong and durable impression on the minds of his hearers.'[9] He was fluent, colourful and confident in his style of delivery.

Other types of campaign were soon to challenge Guthrie over the rest of his career as he jostled for position and to acquire the power to influence post-war reforms, injustices and inequalities in the world of surgery.

In December 1816, he achieved his first great ambition. With the support of Graham, Lord Lynedoch and under the auspices of the Dukes of Wellington and York and also contributing financially to the project himself, he founded an infirmary for the treatment of diseases and injuries of the eye. This became known as the Westminster Ophthalmic Hospital in the Strand, near the Charing Cross Hospital. This hospital moved to Bloomsbury in 1928 and has since closed.[10] Perhaps this robust military surgeon surprises us by choosing such a delicate speciality as ophthalmic surgery. Soon after his appointment at the Eye Hospital, in 1823, he amalgamated several works and published, *Lectures on the Operative Surgery of the Eye; or, an Historical and Critical Enquiry into the Methods recommended for the cure of Cataract, &*.

A certain Dr Forbes was the physician and Guthrie the surgeon to the hospital. Unfortunately there was ill feeling about this appointment and the running of the hospital. His biographer wrote:

The institution of this infirmary excited some ill will and much jealousy amongst two or three evil-disposed persons, and it and its founders were rather roughly handled by these gentlemen in THE LANCET [then a journal with a highly political content]. Mr Guthrie's military spirit was chafed, and he, in an intemperate moment, threatened the Editor [Thomas Wakley] with a prosecution. He found, a little too late, that it would be better to submit than to run the risk of a trial, in which, although obtain some damages in money, he saw, from the information he had received, he could not fail to be injured in reputation, perhaps materially and permanently, from the erroneous testimony which he feared, and had reason to believe, might be given against him. The Editor of THE LANCET, as one of the Committee of the House of Commons on Medical Reform, had the opportunity afforded him of ascertaining the errors into which he had been led in regard to Mr Guthrie, and expressed his regret, the first opportunity he had of making his acquaintance, that he should have allowed advantage to be taken of the confidence he reposed in the gentlemen he then knew, by permitting then to abuse him in a manner which he was now aware was totally undeserved. This expression of proper feeling, so honourable on his part, was met by Mr. Guthrie as it deserved; and the writer of this article [was this Mr Wakley?] believes that there is no one at this moment can have a higher value for the public and private character of Mr. Guthrie, for his ability as a surgeon, or for his honour and integrity as a man, than the Editor of THE LANCET himself.[11]

Wakley introduced the *Lancet* in the 1820s and later was to be elected an MP. He proved to be a powerful influence in the medical world and became a firm friend of Guthrie.

There were heated exchanges over clinical issues between Guthrie and Dr Forbes, at the Ophthalmic Hospital, which culminated in a duel between Forbes and a proxy surgeon colleague of Guthrie's. Fortunately, neither man was hit. When Dr Forbes resigned in 1827, Guthrie was alone, but his son was appointed eleven years later to assist his father.

In 1823, Guthrie was made assistant-surgeon to the Westminster Hospital. He invited criticism, for 'he brought such a wind of change to the hospital that he practically disrupted the whole edifice, for he had two faults – he was tactless and somewhat of an opportunist', also, 'shrewd, quick, active, robust and voluble to a fault'.[12] He was appointed full surgeon to the hospital in 1827. In this same year, he was elected a Fellow of the Royal Society, an accolade that must have thrilled him more than those national awards that had passed him by.

Guthrie had, not without attempts to block his election, became a member of

College Council in 1824, at the unusually young age of 39 years. He had of course been a member of the college for twenty-two years, qualifying at the subsequently illegal age of 16.

Many reforms of the Royal College of Surgeons of London (later of England) were brought about and modified by Guthrie. Members of the College Council were allowed access to their college by the front door, but Guthrie, before being elected to the Council, as a member, and being unknown to many senior members of that body, was obliged to enter the building by the back door and was restricted to certain areas of the building. He thus with many others had to suffer

> such other little indignities as were at that time supposed to be necessary to inflict on the many, to do honour to the few. All these he felt his duty to undergo once, that he might be quite sure they existed. On becoming one of the Council, he applied himself to the study of all their papers and records, ancient and modern; and when he had made himself thoroughly well acquainted with the affairs of the College, he addressed the Council on the inconvenience occasioned by their restrictions, which caused so much dissatisfaction to their members and urged their abrogation.

In due course, members were admitted via the front of the college on the giving of a name or showing of a card.

At these times, a recently appointed member of Council was not encouraged to be so forward with their opinions and comments were made,

> That a councillor of one year's standing should so to presume surprise every one. Mr. Guthrie, who had seen the fronts and the rears of many formidable persons, under somewhat more difficult circumstances, was not in the slightest degree disconcerted by what was intended to be a most dignified rebuff; and he took the earliest opportunity of representing to them that they had been altogether acting illegally, from misreading their charter, and had rendered themselves liable even to censure in the Court of King's Bench, as well as forfeit the charter itself; in proof of which he begged that the matter might be referred to the standing counsel of the College, who decided that Mr. Guthrie was right. From that moment every measure was submitted to Council for the discussion and approval, the obnoxious restrictions were removed, and the confidence which Mr. Guthrie had declared might be placed in the good manners and honour of the members was shown to be their due.[13]

Guthrie was clearly a man for justice, openness and was also a champion of the members, features which along with his gratis lectures would bode well for his reputation, despite finding himself less popular with some dissenters and iconoclasts within Council. He was duly warned of the potential for disaster, by his former master at the York Hospital, Mr Carpue. Guthrie remained undeterred.

Not heeding these barriers and, along with Mr Robert Keate and Mr John Vincent (two senior and influential men on Council), also with the support of many other colleagues and members, Guthrie worked on to reform the college.

He was given the Chair of Anatomy and Surgery at the Royal College in July 1828, an office he held over a five-year period. Over this time he covered several topics, the anatomy and physiology of the arterial system and injuries and diseases of the arteries; the anatomy and diseases of the urinary system; the anatomy and treatment of hernia; the anatomy, human and comparative, and disorders of the eye and finally, the anatomy of the brain and head injuries. His series of lectures, often highly anecdotal and many based on his Peninsular experience, were well received and attendance was high. He contributed significantly to the anatomical debates surrounding such subjects as inguinal and femoral groin hernia and the musculature of the bladder. His series of thirteen lectures on wounds and injuries of the chest received an encouraging review in the *Lancet* of 3 June 1848.[14] These, his *Commentaries on the Surgery of the War*, which ran to six editions, along with the *Treatise on Gun-shot Wounds* (three editions) and publications on abdominal and head wounds, provided cogent advice and insight into the management of battle injuries in the Crimean War. Two of his military works were recommended to the Russian Emperor Alexander, for use by the Russian forces, by Sir James Wylie, and Guthrie was subsequently rewarded with a gift of two diamond rings by the Emperor. Guthrie's influence, through an American edition of his *Commentaries* would spread over the Atlantic and assist the practice of surgery in the ensuing and sanguinary American Civil War (1861–5).

In 1829 he wrote a memorial on the *Report of the Select Committee to the House of Commons on Anatomy*. This preceded the publication of the much-needed Anatomy Bill in 1832. He also sent some recommendations to the House to secure avenues of retrieval of cadaveric material for the instruction of anatomy and surgery.[15] He thus was instrumental, in his position holding the Chairs of Anatomy and Surgery, in shaping this Bill, which legalized cadaveric supply for anatomical dissection.

In 1831–2 Guthrie accepted an appointment as Vice President at the London College (which he held on four further occasions) and in 1833 was elected President, for the first of three terms, at the age of 48, a testimony to his skill, persuasion and integrity. In the same year, when a Committee of Enquiry was held into the 'improper conduct' of the college and Council, indeed threatening its very existence, chaired by a certain Mr Warburton, those gentlemen who had previously been critical of Guthrie, calling him a Radical and not to be trusted, now admitted, 'You are our President, no one knows the history and the affairs of the College better than you do; you have the ability to defend us if you please and we place the honour and character of this College and of ourselves in your hands alone – we rely on you.' Thwarting each challenge of the investigating committee, Guthrie was extremely well prepared for every searching question. Whatever accusative darts were shot at Guthrie, he had prepared every answer and brought the backing evidence with him into the meeting. Fortunately he had been persuading the Council that transparency, 'equity and justice' had to govern the affairs of the college. He and others deemed that while any number of Council meetings could be called and held, any matter 'affecting the public should take place at a meeting which should be open to the members, who might thus hear the speeches, and mark the votes of the different councillors, present on the occasion'.[16]

In 1834, Guthrie, six years after his appointment to the Westminster along with three other clinicians, opened a medical school in Dean Street. Through poor attendances and struggling financing, the school petered out in 1846. In 1849, however, a new building and the recruitment of more staff enabled the school to be resurrected. In 1834, the staff of the Westminster Hospital consisted of four physicians, four surgeons and an assistant surgeon. The four surgeons, remarkably, were all to serve as Presidents of the Royal College (Lynn in 1825; Carlisle in 1828/1837; White in 1834/1841; Guthrie in 1833/1842/1854).

In 1835, Guthrie and his family moved out of 2 Berkeley Street into the two properties heretofore used by the Army Medical Board, numbers 4 and 5, in the same street.

In 1839 and not without opposition, he proposed that the minimum period of hospital study for the diploma (membership of the college) should be increased from two to three years and the age at which a candidate might sit the diploma reduced from 22 years to 21. Whilst the latter proposition seemed to be successfully implemented, the former was not and Guthrie took full responsibility for that failure. Increasing the time interval before a candidate might sit the membership diploma to three years (of the four years of hospital study) might, it was felt by some, have led to idleness in the second year, no improvement in the knowledge of surgery and was hard on parental purses! Guthrie acknowledged the dissent and it was agreed to give the trainee the choice of sitting the exam at either the second or the third year of the four-year hospital course. The gradual expansion of the courses of hospital study was the start of the demise of the traditional five-year apprentice system of training. There was naturally opposition to this latter decline, but the matter was clearly an objective of the Council. We now can see opportunities for some structured hospital training for the surgeon.

Guthrie served on the Court of Examiners of the college from 1828 to 1856. He was considered a tough examiner, much feared by many candidates. Such was the fear of many candidates that they would pay the fees to attend his lectures at the Westminster to avoid being examined by him! Should candidates attend a certain surgeon's course of lectures, that surgeon was prohibited from examining the candidate.[17] Although we have little evidence of standards in the examinations, they were regarded as having become increasingly 'severe', but Guthrie fairly insisted that no candidate should be rejected, should questions exceed in difficulty the course work undertaken. Since all examinations were by viva voce only, Guthrie's brusque and dogmatic questioning would deter and terrify many candidates, but one gets the feeling he would have been fair.

In 1842–3, when Guthrie was elected President for a second term, further revisions occurred and one such was to reorganize the museum of the college, much of it the legacy of John Hunter, then a pivotal part of the educational system for surgeons. All offensive or effete artefacts were destroyed and the public were admitted for four instead of only three days a week, the other two days being reserved for students. He also made improvements to the library, and was instrumental in establishing prizes of £100 for three years in comparative and human anatomy and natural history.

In 1843, he resigned his post as surgeon to the Westminster to create a vacancy for his son, Mr C W Gardiner Guthrie, who would be appointed an assistant surgeon.

With regard to educational activities of the college, one of Guthrie's great contributions was generally to assist the training of general practitioners, then a new breed of clinicians. These men required qualification in surgery, medicine and midwifery. The Council, under his guidance, agreed to form a court of examiners for midwifery and it was on his motion that the study of the practice of physic became an essential point in the curriculum of education required by the college for the candidates' diploma.[18] These changes would make the college a leading institution in the training of general practitioners. At this time the qualifications of these doctors were MRCS (Membership of the College) and the LSA (Licentiate of the Society of Apothecaries).

There is little doubt that the period of 1843–58 (the latter year saw the passing of the Medical Act) was to prove an immensely confusing time for the whole profession.

At this time Guthrie was deeply involved in objections to aspects of a new charter for the college, which had not changed since 1745. In 1843, the contentious charter was drawn up, after much debate, by Sir James Graham, then Secretary of State, following grudging approval of Council.

A stipulation of the charter was that any new by-laws of the college had to be approved by Parliament. Life tenure of Council members was abolished. A further stipulation of the charter had been to the Law Offices of the Crown, and it contained an additional and sensible suggestion that the college should now be known as the Royal College of Surgeons of England, rather than London (despite being governed by London men!). The major problem was to be the creation of the Fellowship at the college.

It had become clear that the college required a method of electing Council members, examiners and teachers, such that the process of (self-)election should become equitable and democratic. One way this could be done was to have a more senior cadre of members, i.e. Fellows. This was to prove a very thorny problem. Although not acted upon, it was Guthrie who suggested extending the Fellowship to any member of twenty years' standing. The charter dictated that the Council was to create Fellows. It was proposed that 300 senior members of the college (out of the 10,000-odd members) were to be elected Fellows gratis and without examination, in the first six months and another 'batch' before the year was out. After electing these, others wishing this qualification would have to sit an examination. The armed forces were keen to maximize this opportunity and Sir James McGrigor (Army) and Sir William Burnett (Royal Navy) petitioned the Council with 200 names of worthy surgeons to be elected. This list had to be severely trimmed – only 93 were eventually allowed. The final proposed and rather nepotistic group consisted of 542 newly elected Fellows. The problem remained that the thousands of remaining members of the college were uncertain as to how some of them might become a Fellow, a rank that conferred privilege. By no means the least advantage of being elected Fellow was that the election implied meritocracy. For those unlucky not to be chosen Fellows, December 1844 saw the first examination for the Fellowship held at the English college.

Whilst Council approved the charter, Guthrie, in typical fashion, remained a stubborn dissenter and petitioned the House of Commons on 22 July 1844. In his document he prayed that the House would not confirm the charter until he had been heard.[19] Even in 1848, Guthrie was still wrestling with the 1843 charter. Always forthright, he took the unusual step of speaking outwith his Council's consensus in his robust independent manner. In February, he appeared before the Medical Registration Committee to explain his own and some Council members' intense dissatisfaction with aspects of the charter and also to express his concern at the general anxieties of members of the college. As noted above, the main problem was the limit in 1844 of the number of Fellows by election. After this rather biased and undemocratic selection of 542 new Fellows, any other member wishing Fellowship, however senior and competent, was not only to be examined, but also had to pay ten guineas (£916 in modern terms) for the process. The indignity of not being elected in the first tranche effectively disenfranchised many able surgeons, both in London, but principally in the provinces. In front of a parliamentary committee, investigating the charter for the college, Guthrie plied the case for increasing the number of Fellows, pointing out that, by limiting the number, many able men were passed over, if not known to a college councillor. Guthrie felt, as a senior member of Council at this time, that there should be an expansion of Fellows, providing they had been a member of twelve years or more standing and paid a fee of ten guineas. There were other similar proposals.

Whilst these objections were tabled, he also (unreasonably and surprisingly) pressed for the term of a councillor of the college to be for life, rather than the eight years sensibly ordered by the charter of 1843. He would eventually concede a re-election of councillors on a seven- to ten-year basis, provided the Fellows were involved in the process, rather than just council members. This would ensure that none but the most honourable motives were involved in the election. Also in front of the parliamentary committee, Guthrie had objected to a proposed College of General Practitioners. This opposition was probably based on the issue of members (rather than Fellows) of the college being changed to the role of general practitioner rather than surgeons or surgeon apothecaries. Overall, the charter had brought sensible and inevitable reforms. Not all of Guthrie's objections and petitions were supportable. One perhaps can understand his objections to the mode of election of the Fellowship and the limited recognition of the surgeons of the armed services.

In 1848, he was appointed Consulting Surgeon, an honorary and senior post, to the Westminster, on the death of a colleague, Mr White. Before this event he had declined the post. His attitude to surgery had by then been clearly modified by long years of conflict. His laudatory biographer continued: 'The magnitude of the operative surgery he had to undergo during the war rendered him perhaps careless in seeking or of doing operations, if it were not perhaps that he also considered this part of surgery as the last resort of science.' He had become very able in the selection of his cases and the often-harsh results in the Peninsula had tempered his risk/benefit judgements. The great experience 'he had obtained in the most desperate cases of injuries gave him a command of himself, a coolness, in addition to his natural presence of mind, which have never been excelled. The adage of the accomplished operator may be truly applied to him – the lion heart, the eagle eye, the lady's hand.'

That same year, other momentous constructive changes were proposed whilst Guthrie was on Council. First, a General (Medical) Council was established, consisting of a Secretary of State and twelve members (two-thirds of whom should be registered medical men), to regulate medical education and practice. Secondly a proposal that a charter of incorporation should be given to a Royal College of General Practitioners, candidates for general practice being examined by members of that faculty for medicine and materia medica, but for surgery, and Council remained adamant on this point, only by the English College of Surgeons.[20] Many of these important reforms, or variants, were eventually introduced through the Medical Act of 1858, which partially resolved many controversies and did much to unite the colleges of surgery in Britain.

Outside the business of the college, Guthrie also took his energies into fighting the corner of the sick-poor and persuaded the Council of the college to address the Minister for that purpose. Sadly, through lack of support by appointed poor law doctors and governmental changes, the package was not accepted in England. It would have cost the government a huge sum (£100,000 then, £9.7million in 2007) to fully implement the changes for these disenfranchised folk and Guthrie, serving on Lord Ashley's committee of the Secretary of State, made a strong case for it, which was widely encouraged. Guthrie's energy in the pursuit of this cause was largely sapped by a family bereavement at this time. However the Council gave him sanction to do what he could for the good of these people on an individual basis. Guthrie worked with Mr George Lewis, the chief commissioner, and brought about some improvements in the conditions of service for the medical men employed, and the sick-poor themselves.

He had lost his 65-year-old wife, Margaret in 1846 from cholera and, tragically, also his eldest son, the Reverend Lowry Guthrie, who died in 1848, from apoplexy – probably a cerebro-vascular accident – and left him a granddaughter. His daughter Anne never married. His other son by Margaret was Charles W Gardiner, a capable surgeon by all accounts, who died three years after his father in 1859 aged 42, of liver failure. Circumstantial evidence suggests that Charles was a man of erratic behaviour and since he succumbed from ascites (collection of fluid in the abdominal cavity) and liver failure, we have to entertain the possibility that he was an alcoholic. Guthrie did marry once more, a younger woman, Julia Wilkinson, just three months before he died. There was a 2- or 3-year-old son by this union.[21]

Guthrie's last Presidential term was in 1854, during the tumult of the Crimean War. General anaesthesia, using chloroform or ether, had been available for around a decade and Guthrie's *Commentaries*, in its 6th edition contains additional anecdotal surgical data from the Crimea and comments on chloroform, noting that it had been generally well received and only one death had been attributed to its use. In 1862, a special American edition of the *Commentaries* was published in Philadelphia, for use during the American Civil War. In generous spirit, Guthrie had presented a free copy of the *Commentaries* to every regiment in the British Army, each naval station and principal medical officers in the East India Company.[22]

Guthrie was dead a year after his last term of office as President and, dying in harness, he had shown himself once more, and finally, to be a robust, resolute and committed doctor. Unafraid of criticism or being proven wrong, he had emulated his behaviour on the field of combat with his civilian practice, full of the rights of clinicians and patients, also showing robust persuasion and integrity – a truly remarkable surgeon. Guthrie died of heart failure (he suffered with chronic bronchitis and emphysema) on 1 May 1856, aged 71 years, and was buried at Kensal Green cemetery.

Finally, we should consider some improvements that were introduced by Guthrie, during the Peninsular campaigns. First, in general matters;

(1) He was immensely interested in training and personal care of his patients. He

made a great effort to teach on and supervise his cases, often trying to separate his patients from larger general hospitals. The advantages were: essential continuity of care, less chance of coincidental contagion, sepsis and diarrhoeal illnesses.

(2) Guthrie, like his rival master surgeon in the Service de Santé, Baron Dominique Larrey, was opposed to John Hunter's earlier 'watch and see' conservative approach to wounds of the limbs that clearly mandated amputation. Hunter had, in his role of staff surgeon to the expedition to Belle Isle and later to Portugal, been appalled at the bungled and often fatal attempts of inexperienced military surgeons to ablate limbs. Thus he had adopted a delayed policy of surgery to allow 'recovery', demarcation of dead tissue and to allow nature to run its course. Surgeons such as Guthrie and Larrey evolved the skills to recognize those cases that just weren't going to recover, or who had so much damage to joint, soft tissue or bone that amputation at an early stage gave the optimal chance of survival.

(3) He spent his whole surgical career correcting earlier combat surgical doctrines. Two great surgeons, John Hunter and Sir Charles Bell, who wrote influentially on war wounds, were not extensively experienced in military surgery.

(4) He assisted McGrigor's enormous efforts to collect and collate surgical data.

(5) He increasingly believed in conservative attitudes to limb damage, in an effort to avoid amputations, e.g. the head of the humerus, the ankle and parts of the elbow joint. He counselled the avoidance of upper limb amputation unless essential. He advised on preservation of the thumb and one or two fingers and as much tissue as feasible in hand injuries, except with serious wrist damage, for which he generally recommended amputation.

There were many more specific issues by which he brought advantage to military surgery. First in vascular surgery:

(1) In the management of arterial injuries, Guthrie convinced his pupils that alarming bleeding at injury or surgery could usually be controlled by simple means, so encouraging calmness in the process of first aid.

(2) He discouraged the young surgeon from applying the tourniquet whenever bleeding could be managed by gentle but firm accurate pressure over the principal blood vessel, e.g. the femoral artery at the groin or axillary artery in the armpit. He emphasized the relatively small force required to place a finger on a major artery or over the mouth of a severed vessel or, alternatively to compress an amputation flap as a temporary manoeuvre.

(3) He regarded the ligation of a wounded artery both above and below the injury site as a fundamental issue.

(4) When a vessel was damaged, the very best option was to expose the vessel directly by dissection rather than tie off the major 'feeding' vessel above the damaged vessel, as proposed by John Hunter for surgical management of aneurysm.

Next in the management of fractures and soft tissue injuries:

(1) His recommendation to employ straight splints in the management of fractured long bones, most especially the femur. The principle of immobilizing the joint above and below the fracture implied that the knee and hip required to be kept still. So his long straight splints for fractured femur, whilst not providing traction for good alignment during union, at least provided a better chance of healing.

(2) He realized the value in decompressing swollen and infected tissue, when that swelling and pressure was squeezing shut the blood supply to the limb. Today the practice of fasciotomy (i.e. cutting the fascia or tough membrane that line the muscle compartments) is fundamental to the management of crushed or infected limb muscles.

(3) He used strong chemicals – dilute nitric or sulphuric acids – to burn and destroy granulation or gangrenous tissue in infected or mortifying wounds.

Finally, in the management of torso injuries:

(1) He introduced the concept of primary (i.e. early) closure of penetrating chest wounds.

(2) He taught that careful clinical examination of the chest by auscultation with the ear and percussion (after 1819 by the stethoscope) could help to locate collections of fluid or air in the chest.

(3) He was foremost in emphasizing the nature, pathogenesis (evolution) and management of subcutaneous emphysema – i.e. air collecting under the skin after penetrating lung injury.

(4) Apart from closure of thoracic wounds, Guthrie advised conservatism in therapy, apart from dependent drainage (sometimes with a tube or tent left in situ to properly drain intrathoracic septic fluid). This, he thought, might also encourage adherence of the lung to the chest wall.

(5) He emphasized that wounds of the diaphragm do not heal, with the consequence that the abdominal viscera may herniate up into the chest cavity.

(6) In the many anecdotal accounts of penetrating abdominal injuries, Guthrie cautioned against the use of cathartics (laxatives) and he restricted oral intake of liquids and solids, so giving the gut a chance to 'rest' after injury, or during sepsis.

(7) He often cautioned against replacing slightly protruding lung, bowel or omentum back inside the chest or abdomen respectively. Thus, although there were risks of bowel obstruction or hernia, the wound was 'plugged', which could prevent the onset of sepsis.

T J Pettigew, in his *Biographical Memoirs of Physicians and Surgeons*, gives his overarching view of Guthrie, 'Mr Guthrie's life has been one of unwearied activity and indefatigable research. He has laboriously studied to learn and improve the profession, of which he is an ornament.' Finally, Pettigrew mused, 'Mr Guthrie indeed appears to be as much a soldier as a surgeon.'[23] He was memorialized by the Guthrie Society, founded in 1887 by a Westminster physician, Dr Octavius Sturges, with an annual lecture at the hospital. The British Army remembers Guthrie through the Guthrie medal and lecture (instituted in 1962), awarded to the civilian consultant who has made a significant contribution to the British Army.

Whilst accepting all Guthrie's faults, this was a robust man of immense integrity, compassion and skill – a role model for all military surgeons. He played a significant role in honing the best military medical support for Wellington's army in the Peninsular War.

Notes

Introduction

1. John Bell, *Memoir on the Present State of Naval and Military Surgery. Addressed to the Right Honourable Earl Spenser, First Lord of the Admiralty.* Yarmouth, 20 Jan. 1798.
2. J Hennen, *Principles of Military Surgery; comprising Observations on the Arrangement, Police and Practice of Hospitals, and on the History, Treatment, and Anomalies of Variola and Syphilis* (1st American edn, from the 3rd London edn, Philadelphia, 1830).
3. G J Guthrie, *Clinical lectures on Compound Fractures of the Extremities, on Excision of the head of the thigh-bone, the arm-bone, and the elbow-joint: on the Diseases of the Peninsula, and on several miscellaneous subjects* (Delivered at the Westminster Hospital, London, 1838), 3rd lecture, p. 19.
4. R Hurt, *George Guthrie: Soldier and Pioneer Surgeon* (London, 2008).
5. G J Guthrie, *Commentaries on the Surgery of the War in Portugal, Spain, France, and the Netherlands from the Battle of Roliça, in 1808, to that of Waterloo, in 1815* (6th edn, London, 1855), preface, p. x.
6. N Cantlie, *A History of the Army Medical Department*, vol. 1 (Edinburgh and London, 1974), p. 372.
7. War Office, *A list of all the Officers of the Army and Royal Marines on Full and Half Pay* (Feb. 1806).
8. War Office, *A list of all the Officers of the Army and Royal Marines on Full and Half Pay* (March 1810). *A list of all the Officers of the Army and Royal Marines on Full and Half pay* (13 March 1815).
9. J Laffin, *Combat Surgeons* (Stroud, 1999), p. 54.
10. M H Kaufman, *The Regius Chair of Military Surgery in the University of Edinburgh, 1806–55* (Amsterdam and New York, 2003), p. 2.
11. Guthrie, *Commentaries*, preface, p. b.
12. Ibid., p. 59.

Chapter 1

1. T J Pettigrew, *Biographical Memoires of Physicians and Surgeons* (London, 1840), vol. 4, p. 3.
2. *A List of Those Examined and Approved Surgeons who are entitled to the Several Privileges, Franchises, and Immunities* (London, July 1797).
3. P J and R J Wallis, with the assistance of J G L Burnby and the late T D Whittet,

Eighteenth Century Medics: Subscriptions, Licences, Apprenticeships (Newcastle, 1988, 2nd edn), p. 250.

4. R Hooper, *A New Medical Dictionary containing an explanation of the terms in Anatomy, Physiology, Practice of Physic, Materia medica, Chemistry, Pharmacy, Surgery, Midwifery and the various branches of Natural Philosophy connected with Medicine* (London, 1802).

5. M Crumplin, *Men of Steel* (Shrewsbury, 2007), p. 149.

6. H Everard, *History of Thos. Farrington's Regiment subsequently designated the 29th (Worcestershire) Foot – 1694 to 1891* (Worcester, 1891), p. 252.

7. Personal communication from Miriam Walls, Information Management Specialist, Parks Canada, mainland Nova Scotia Field Unit, Halifax.

8. R Hamilton, *The Duties of a Regimental Surgeon considered with Observations on his General Qualifications and hints relative to a More Respectable Practice etc.* (1787), vol.1, pp. 14–93.

9. G J Guthrie, *Commentaries on the Surgery of the War in Portugal, Spain, France, and the Netherlands from the Battle of Roliça, in 1808, to that of Waterloo, in 1815* (6th edn, London, 1855), pp. 345–6.

10. Everard, *History of Thos. Farrington's Regiment*, p. 271.

11. J W Fortescue, *A History of the British Army*, vol. 6, *1807–9* (London, 1910), p. 185.

12. W Johnston, *Roll of Commissioned Officers in the Medical Service of the British Army* (Aberdeen, 1917), pp. 172 and 186.

13. J Hale, *The Journal of James Hale*, introduced by Peter Catley (Windsor, 1998), p. 20.

14. Horse Guards, *Instructions for the Regulation of Regimental Hospitals and the Concerns of the Sick* (Sept. 1812), pp. 30–1.

15. Everard, *History of Thos. Farrington's Regiment*, p. 274.

16. W Warre, *Letters from the Peninsula 1808–1812* (London, 1909), p. 21.

17. C Hibbert (ed.), *A Soldier of the Seventy-First* (London, 1976), p. 15.

18. C Hibbert (ed.), *The Recollections of Rifleman Harris* (Gloucester, 1996), p. 12.

19. Everard, *History of Thos. Farrington's Regiment*, p. 274.

Chapter 2

1. N Cantlie, *A History of the Army Medical Department*, vol 1 (Edinburgh and London, 1974), pp. 292–3.

2. J Hale, *The Journal of James Hale*, introduced by Peter Catley (Windsor, 1998), p. 23.

3. G J Guthrie, *Clinical Lectures on Compound Fractures of the Extremities, on excision of the head of the thigh-bone, the arm bone and the shoulder-joint: on the Diseases of the Peninsula, and on several miscellaneous subjects* (London, 1838), p. 3.

4. Ibid.

5. H Everard, *History of Thomas Farrington's Regiment subsequently designated the 29th (Worcester) Foot – 1694 to 1891 (Worcester, 1891), p. 279.*

6. G J Guthrie, *Commentaries on the Surgery of the War in Portugal, Spain, France, and the Netherlands from the Battle of Roliça, in 1808, to that of Waterloo, in 1815* (6th edn, London, 1855), p. 391.

7. P Edwards, *Talavera: Wellington's Early Victories* (Swindon, 2005), p. 49.

8. Everard, *History of Thos. Farrington's Regiment*, p. 280.

9. C Hibbert (ed.), *The Recollections of Rifleman Harris* (Gloucester, 1996), p. 20.

10. Hale, Journal, p. 25.

11. W Warre, *Letters from the Peninsula 1808–1812* (London, 1909), p. 25.

12. J Weller, *Wellington in the Peninsula* (London, 1992), p. 39.

13. Hibbert, *Rifleman Harris*, p. 18.

14. Guthrie, *Commentaries*, p. 198.

15. Ibid., p. 5.

16. M Crumplin, *Men of Steel* (Shrewsbury, 2007), pp. 82–3.

17. Guthrie, *Commentaries*, pp. 58–9.

18. Ibid., p. 453.

19. Everard, *History of Thos. Farrington's Regiment*, p. 287.

20. Guthrie, *Commentaries*, p. 595.

21. Guthrie, *Clinical Lectures*, 3rd lecture, p. 25.

22. Cantlie, *History of Army Medical Dept*, pp. 299–300.

23. Ibid.

24. Guthrie, *Clinical Lectures*, 3rd lecture, pp. 27–8.

25. Guthrie, *Commentaries*, pp. 393–4.

26. Ibid., pp. 198–9.

27. Ibid., p. 334.

28. Weller, *Wellington in the Peninsula*, p. 70.

29. W F P Napier, *History of the War in the Peninsula and in the South of France from the year 1807 to the year 1814* (6 vols, London and New York: Warne & Co., 1890), vol. 6 (book 11), p. 1.

Chapter 3

1. G J Guthrie, *Clinical Lectures on Compound Fractures of the Extremities, on excision of the head of the thigh-bone, the arm bone and the shoulder-joint: on the Diseases of the Peninsula, and on several miscellaneous subjects* (London, 1838), 6th lecture, pp. 46–7.

2. H Everard, *History of Thomas Farrington's Regiment subsequently designated the 29th (Worcester) Foot – 1694 to 1891 (Worcester, 1891), p. 296.*

3. Guthrie, *Clinical Lectures*, 3rd lecture, p. 26.

4. Everard, *History of Thos. Farrington's Regiment*, pp. 298–9.

5. Guthrie, *Clinical Lectures*, 6th lecture, p. 48.

6. G J Guthrie, *Commentaries on the Surgery of the War in Portugal, Spain, France, and the Netherlands from the Battle of Roliça, in 1808, to that of Waterloo, in 1815* (6th edn, London, 1855), p. 373.
7. P Edwards, *Talavera: Wellington's Early Victories* (Swindon, 2005), p. 175.
8. Everard, *History of Thos. Farrington's Regiment*, p. 303.
9. Edwards, *Talavera*, p. 178.
10. Ibid. p 179.
11. Ibid. p 196.
12. M Crumplin, *Men of Steel* (Shrewsbury, 2007), pp. 83–4.
13. Edwards, *Talavera*, p. 198.
14. Guthrie, *Commentaries*, pp. 334–5.
15. Ibid., p. 84.
16. Ibid., pp. 391–2.
17. Everard, *History of Thos. Farrington's Regiment*, p. 307.
18. Edwards, *Talavera*, p. 214.
19. Guthrie, *Commentaries*, pp. 465–6.
20. Edwards, *Talavera*, p. 223.
21. Guthrie, *Commentaries*, p. 500.
22. Edwards, *Talavera*, p. 233.
23. ' A Biographical Sketch of GJ Guthrie, Esq., F.R.S.', *The Lancet* (1850), vol. 1, p. 727.
24. Everard, *History of Thos. Farrington's Regiment*, pp. 312–13.
25. J Laffin, *Combat Surgeons* (Stroud, 1999), p. 51.
26. 'Biographical Sketch', pp. 729–30.
27. [reference for Hussey]
28. Everard, *History of Thos. Farrington's Regiment*, p. 313.
29. 'Biographical Sketch', p. 730.
30. Ibid.

Chapter 4.
1. I Fletcher, *Bloody Albuera: The 1811 Campaign in the Peninsula* (Oxford, 2000), p. 61.
2. 'A Biographical Sketch of GJ Guthrie, Esq., F.R.S.', *The Lancet* (1850), vol. 1, p. 731.
3. Ibid., p. 730.
4. Ibid., p. 731.
5. Fletcher, *Bloody Albuera*, p. 124.
6. Ibid., p. 95.
7. Ibid., p 100.
8. 'Biographical Sketch', p. 731.
9. Fletcher, *Bloody Albuera*, p. 101.

10. M Sherer, *Recollections of the Peninsula* (Staplehurst, 1996), p. 165.
11. Everard, *History of Thos. Farrington's Regiment*, p. 327.
12. Guthrie, *Commentaries*, p. 431.
13. Ibid., p. 445.
14. Ibid., p. 486.
15. Ibid., pp. 535–6.
16. Ibid., p. 549.
17. Ibid., p 585.
18. Ibid., pp. 593–4.
19. 'Biographical Sketch', pp. 731–2.
20. Ibid., p. 730.
21. Guthrie, *Commentaries*, p. 561.
22. Fletcher, *Bloody Albuera*, p. 112.
23. Kempthorne, *Journal RAMC*, 54, pp. 145–6.

Chapter 5
1. G J Guthrie, *On Gun-shot Wounds of the Extremities* (London, 1815), p. 138.
2. C Oman, *A History of the Peninsular War* (London, 1996), vol. 5, p. 165.
3. E Costello, *The Story of a Peninsular War Rifleman*, ed. E Hathaway (Swanage, 1997), p. 148.
4. 'A Biographical Sketch of GJ Guthrie, Esq., F.R.S.', *The Lancet* (1850), vol. 1, p. 732.
5. G T Napier, *Early Military Life of General Sir George Napier* (London, 1884), p. 182.
6. Ibid., p. 184.
7. W N Bruce, *Life of General Sir Charles Napier* (London, 1885), pp. 25–30.
8. Napier, *Early Military Life*, pp. 136–7.
9. G J Guthrie, *Commentaries on the Surgery of the War in Portugal, Spain, France, and the Netherlands from the Battle of Roliça, in 1808, to that of Waterloo, in 1815* (6th edn, London, 1855), p. 195.
10. Ibid., pp. 536–7.
11. Ibid., pp. 62–3.
12. Ibid., p. 540.
13. Ibid., pp. 571–2.
14. Ibid., p. 607.
15. Ibid., p. 62.
16. Guthrie, *On Gun-shot Wounds*, p. 143.
17. M McGrigor, *The Scalpel and the Sword* (Dalkeith, 2000), p. 178.
18. Guthrie, *Clinical Lectures on Compound Fractures of the Extremities on Excision of the head of the thigh bone, the arm-bone and the elbow-joint: on the diseases of the Peninsula and on Several Miscellaneous Subjects* (London, 1838), 7th lecture, p.63.

19. McGrigor, *Scalpel and Sword*, pp. 179–80.

20. W Napier, *English Battles and Sieges in the Peninsula* (London, 1879), p. 146.

21. McGrigor, *Scalpel and Sword*, p. 180.

22. Ibid., p. 183.

23. H P Elkington, 'Some Episodes in the Life of James Goodall Elkington, an Army Surgeon in the Peninsular days, together with Extracts from his Journal', *Journal of the Royal Army Medical Corps*, 16 (1911), p. 90.

24. Ibid., p. 92.

25. Guthrie, *Clinical Lectures*, 3rd lecture, p. 30.

26. *Commentaries*, p. 9.

27. Ibid., p. 214.

28. Ibid., p. 386.

29. Ibid., p. 28.

30. Ibid., p. 123.

31. Ibid., p. 202.

32. Ibid., p. 476.

33. Ibid., p. 519.

34. *Commentaries*, p. 598.

35. McGrigor, *Scalpel and Sword*, p. 280.

36. Ibid., pp. 185–6.

37. Ibid., p. 188.

38. J McGrigor, 'Sketch of the Medical History of the British Armies in the Peninsula of Spain and Portugal during the late Campaigns', paper read to the Medical and Chirurgical Society, 20 June 1815, p. 384.

39. McGrigor, *Scalpel and Sword*, p. 281.

Chapter 6

1. 'A Biographical Sketch of G J Guthrie, Esq., F.R.S.', *The Lancet* (1850), vol. 1, p. 730.

2. I Fletcher, *Salamanca 1812* (Osprey Military Campaign Series, 48, London, 1997), p. 29.

3. J Laffin, *Combat Surgeons* (Stroud, 1999), p. 52.

4. I Fletcher (ed.), *The Peninsular War 1812–1814: An Eyewitness Story* (London, 2007), p. 57.

5. J W Fortescue, *A History of the British Army*, vol. 8, *1811–1812* (London, 1917), p. 477.

6. 'Biographical Sketch', p. 732.

7. G J Guthrie, *Clinical Lectures on Compound Fractures of the Extremities, on Excision of the head of the thigh-bone, and the elbow-joint: on the Diseases of the Peninsula, and on several miscellaneous subjects* (London, 1838, 7th lecture), p. 60.

8. Ibid., 2nd lecture, p. 13.

9. I C Robertson, *Wellington at War in the Peninsula 1808–1814: An Overview and Guide* (Barnsley, 2000), p. 212.

10. G J Guthrie, *Commentaries on the Surgery of the War in Portugal, Spain, France, and the Netherlands from the Battle of Roliça, in 1808, to that of Waterloo, in 1815* (6th edn, London, 1855), p. 567.

11. Guthrie, *Clinical Lectures*, 7th lecture, pp. 61–2.

12. Guthrie, *Commentaries*, p. 2.

13. Ibid., pp. 467–8.

14. Ibid., p. 335.

15. Ibid., p. 373.

16. 'Biographical Sketch', p. 732.

17. Guthrie, *Clinical Lectures*, 7th lecture, p. 62.

18. 'Biographical Sketch', p. 732.

19. Guthrie, *Commentaries*, pp. 42–3.

20. Ibid., pp. 26–7.

21. Ibid., pp. 219–21.

22. Ibid., pp. 458–9.

23. Ibid., pp. 488–9.

24. Ibid., p. 567.

25. Ibid., pp. 582–3.

26. Ibid., p. 599.

27. Ibid., pp. 606–7.

28. Ibid., p. 612.

29. J W Fortescue, *A History of the British Army*, vol. 8, *1811–1812* (London, 1917), p. 551.

30. R L Blanco, *Wellington's Surgeon General: Sir James McGrigor* (Durham, NC, 1974), p. 131.

Chapter 7

1. G J Guthrie, *Commentaries on the Surgery of the War in Portugal, Spain, France, and the Netherlands from the Battle of Roliça, in 1808, to that of Waterloo, in 1815* (6th edn, London, 1855), p. 549.

2. J W Fortescue, *A History of the British Army*, vol. 8, *1811–1812* (London, 1917), p. 590.

3. Ibid., p. 608.

4. G J Guthrie, *Clinical Lectures on Compound Fractures of the Extremities, on Excision of the head of the thigh-bone, and the elbow-joint: on the Diseases of the Peninsula, and on several miscellaneous subjects* (London, 1838), 1st lecture, p. 6.

5. Ibid., 7th lecture, p. 64.

6. Ibid., pp. 57–8.

7. T J Pettigrew, *Biographical Memoires of Physicians and Surgeons* (London, 1840),

vol. 4, p. 12.

8. Guthrie, *Commentaries*, p. 347.

9. Ibid., p. 481.

10. Ibid., p. 485.

11. Ibid., pp. 605–6.

12. J McGrigor, 'Sketch of the Medical History of the British Armies in the Peninsula of Spain and Portugal during the late Campaigns', paper read to the Medical and Chirurgical Society, 20 June 1815, p. 392.

13. Ibid., p. 388.

14. Pettigrew, *Biographical Memoires, p. 5.*

15. N Cantlie, *A History of the Army Medical Department*, vol. 1 (Edinburgh and London, 1974), p. 364.

16. McGrigor, 'Sketch', p. 394.

17. Guthrie, *Commentaries*, p. 372.

18. Ibid., p. 43.

19. Ibid., p. 393.

20. Ibid., p. 124.

21. Ibid., pp. 477–8.

22. Ibid., p. 586.

23. Ibid., p. 605.

Chapter 8

1. G J Guthrie, *Commentaries on the Surgery of the War in Portugal, Spain, France, and the Netherlands from the Battle of Roliça, in 1808, to that of Waterloo, in 1815* (6th edn, London, 1855), p. 469.

2. Ibid., pp. 470–2.

3. Ibid., pp. 210–11.

4. J G Humble and P Hansell, *Westminster Hospital 1716–1966* (London, 1966), pp. 52–3.

5. Guthrie, *Commentaries*, p. 204.

6. Ibid., p. 4.

7. Ibid., p. 44.

8. Ibid., pp. 366–8.

9. Ibid., pp. 377–8.

10. Ibid., p. 474.

11. Ibid., p. 540.

12. Ibid., pp. 572–5.

13. Ibid., p. 123.

14. Ibid. p. 124.

15. Ibid., pp. 221–2.

16. Ibid. pp. 243–4.

17. Ibid., p. 611.

18. Ibid., pp. 155–6.

19. M McGrigor, *The Scalpel and the Sword* (Dalkeith, 2000), p. 232.

20. Humble and Hansell, *Westminster Hospital*, pp. 52–3.

Chapter 9

1. 'A Biographical Sketch of GJ Guthrie, Esq., F.R.S.', *The Lancet* (1850), vol. 1, p. 733.

2. G J Guthrie, *On Wounds and Injuries of the Arteries of the Human Body with the Treatment and Operations required for their care* (London, 1830), p. 60.

3. www.Bankofengland.co.uk – educational section, inflation calculator.

4. G J Guthrie, *On Gun-shot Wounds of the Extremities requiring the Different Operations of Amputations with their after-treatment* (London, 1815).

5. 'Biographical Sketch', p. 733.

6. G J Guthrie, *Commentaries on the Surgery of the War in Portugal, Spain, France, and the Netherlands from the Battle of Roliça, in 1808, to that of Waterloo, in 1815* (6th edn, London, 1855), preface to the 5th edn, p. v.

7. M Adkins, *The Waterloo Companion* (London, 2001), p. 301.

8. J Thomson, *Report of Observations made in the British Military Hospitals in Belgium after the Battle of Waterloo with some remarks upon Amputation* (Edinburgh, 1816), p. 12.

9. Ibid., pp. 3–4.

10. Ibid.

11. G Gordon-Taylor and E W Walls, *Sir Charles Bell His Life and Times* (Edinburgh and London, 1958), p. 87.

12. M K H Crumplin and P Starling, *A Surgical Artist at War* (Edinburgh, 2005).

13. J Hennen, *Principles of Military Surgery comprising Observations on the Arrangement, Police, and Practice of Hospitals (3rd London and 1st American edn, 1830)*.

14. J C Watts, 'George James Guthrie, Peninsular Surgeon', *JRSM*, 54 (1961), p. 768.

15. C A Ballance, 'Lecture: Stories from the Campaigns of Napoleon and Wellington', *JRAMC*, 29 (London, 1917), p. 360.

16. Guthrie, *On Gun-shot Wounds of the Extremities*, p. 117.

17. Ibid., p. 133.

18. Hennen, *Principles of Military Surgery*, p. 216.

19. Guthrie, *On Gun-shot Wounds of the Extremities*, pp. 181–2.

20. G J Guthrie, *A Treatise on Gun-shot Wounds, on inflammation, erysipelas, and mortification, on Injuries of the Nerves and on Wounds of the requiring the different operations of amputation* (3rd edn, London, 1827), p. 344.

21. Ibid., p. 351.

22. G J Guthrie, *Clinical Lectures on Compound Fractures of the Extremities, on Excision of the head of the thigh-bone, and the elbow-joint: on the Diseases of the Peninsula, and on several miscellaneous subjects* (London, 1838), 5th lecture, p 39.

23. Ibid.

24. Guthrie, *Commentaries*, p 50.

25. M Crumplin, *Men of Steel* (Shrewsbury, 2007), p. 254.

26. Guthrie, *Commentaries*, p. 327.

27. S Cooper, *A Dictionary of Practical Surgery comprehending all the most interesting improvements, from the earliest times down to the present period etc.* (London, 1822).

28. Guthrie, *Commentaries*, p. 478–9.

29. Guthrie, *Commentaries*, p. 482.

30. Ibid., p. 499.

31. Ibid., p. 502.

32. Ibid., pp. 503–4.

33. Ibid., p. 538.

34. Ibid., p. 575.

35. Ibid., pp. 13–14.

Chapter 10

1. 'A Biographical Sketch of GJ Guthrie, Esq., F.R.S.', *The Lancet* (1850), vol. 1, p. 733.

2. G J Guthrie, *A Treatise on Gun-shot Wounds, on inflammation, erysipelas, and mortification, on Injuries of the Nerves and on Wounds of the requiring the different operations of amputation* (3rd edn, London, 1827), pp. 350–1.

3. 'Biographical Sketch', p. 733.

4. G J Guthrie, *Commentaries on the Surgery of the War in Portugal, Spain, France, and the Netherlands from the Battle of Roliça, in 1808, to that of Waterloo, in 1815* (6th edn, London, 1855), p. 77.

5. G J Guthrie, *Medico-Chirurgical Transactions*, 7 (1816), pp. 330–7.

6. Guthrie, *Commentaries*, p. 610.

7. 'Biographical Sketch', p. 734.

8. Ibid., p. 734.

9. T J Pettigrew, *Biographical Memoires of Physicians and Surgeons* (London, 1840), vol. 4, p. 21.

10. R Hurt, 'George Guthrie (1758–1856): Surgeon to the Duke of Wellington, and a Pioneer Thoracic Surgeon', *Journal of Medical Biography*, 15/1 (Feb. 2007), p. 41.

11. 'Biographical Sketch', p. 734.

12. Hurt, 'George Guthrie', p. 43.

13. Anon., review, *The Lancet* (27 May 1848), p. 611.

14. 'Biographical Sketch', p. 735.
15. R Hurt, *George Guthrie: Soldier and Pioneer Surgeon* (London, 2008), p. 106.
16. 'Biographical Sketch', p. 735.
17. Hurt, 'George Guthrie', p. 43.
18. 'Biographical Sketch', p. 736.
19. Journal of House of Commons (London, 1844), pp. 527, 531.
20. Z. Cope, *The History of the Royal College of Surgeons of England* (London, 1959), pp. 43–4.
21. Hurt, *George Guthrie: Soldier and Pioneer Surgeon*, pp. 114–16.
22. Hurt, 'George Guthrie', p. 42.
23. Pettigrew, *Biographical Memoires*, p. 21.

Bibliography

Primary Medical Sources

Anonymous (T Wakley?) 'Biographical Sketch of GJ Guthrie Esq. FRS, Late President of the College of Surgeons', *The Lancet* (1850), vol. 1, pp. 727–36

'Guthrie, Charles W. Gardiner', entry in Plarr's *Lives of Fellows*, vol. 1 (1930), p. 482

'Guthrie George James', entry in Plarr's *Lives of Fellows*, vol. 1 (1930), pp. 482–4

Guthrie, G J *On Gunshot Wounds of the Extremities requiring the different Operations of Amputation* (London: Longman, Hurst, Rees, Orme & Brown, 1815)

Guthrie, G J 'Case of a wound of the Peroneal artery successfully treated by a ligature', *Medico-Chirurgical Transactions*, 7 (1816), pp. 330–7

Guthrie, G J *A Treatise on Gunshot-Wounds, on inflammation, erisypelas, and mortification, on injuries of Nerves, and on Wounds of the Extremities requiring the Different Operations of Amputations: in which the various methods of performing these Operations are shown, together with their after-treatment; and containing an account of the author's successful case of amputation at the Hip-Joint* (London: printed for Burgess & Hill, 1827)

Guthrie, G J *A Letter to the Right Hon. The Secretary of State for the Home Department, containing remarks on the Report of the Select Committee of the House of Commons, on anatomy, and pointing out the means by which the science may be cultivated with advantage and safety to the public* (Tracts 9/5, London: Royal College of Surgeons of London, 1828)

Guthrie, G J *Memoir on the Treatment of Venereal Diseases without Mercury, employed at the military Hospital of the Val de Grâce [translated from the French of HNJ Desruelles] To which is added, Observations of the Treatment of the Venereal Disease without Mercury by GJ Guthrie, and various Documents showing his mode of Treatment* (Philadelphia: Carey & Lea, 1830).

Guthrie, G J *Remarks on the Anatomy Bill now before Parliament: in a letter addressed the Right Hon. The Lord Althorp, and given to the members of either House on their personal or written application to the publisher* (Tracts 1370/6, London: Royal College of Surgeons of London, 1832)

Guthrie, G J *Clinical Lectures on Compound Fractures of the Extremities, on Excision of the Head of the Thigh Bone, the Arm Bone and the Shoulder-Joint: On the Diseases of the Peninsula and on Several Miscellaneous Subjects* (London: J. Churchill, 1838)

Guthrie, G J *On Injuries of the Head affecting the Brain* (London: John Churchill, 1842)

Guthrie, G J *Facts and Obsevations relating to the Administration of the medical relief to the Sick Poor, in England and Wales: addressed to the Members of the Commons House of Parliament* (Tracts 1216/12, London: Royal College of Surgeons of England, 1843)

Guthrie, G J *On Wounds and Injuries of the Arteries of the Human Body with the Treatment and Operations required for their cure* (London: J. Churchill, 1846)

Guthrie, G J *On Wounds and Injuries of the Abdomen and Pelvis* (London, 1847)

Guthrie, G J *On Wounds and injuries of the Chest* (London: H Renshaw, J Churchill, 1848)

Guthrie, G J 'Lectures on some of the more important points in surgery: [II] Gunshot Wounds', *The Lancet* (1852), vol. 1, pp. 165–8.

Guthrie, G J 'Lectures on some of the more important points in surgery: [III] Gangrene, inflammation and surgery', *The Lancet* (1852), vol. 1, pp. 233–5

Guthrie, G J 'Lectures on some of the more important points in surgery: [IV] Limb amputations', *The Lancet* (1852), vol. 1, pp. 417–21

Guthrie, G J 'Lectures on some of the more important points in surgery: [V] Amputation', *The Lancet* (1852), vol. 1, pp. 553–8.

Guthrie, G J 'Lectures on some of the more important points in surgery: [VI] Wounds of the knee and ankle joints', *The Lancet* (1852), vol. 2, pp. 47–51

Guthrie, G J 'Lectures on some of the more important points in surgery: [VII] Amputations of the arm', *The Lancet* (1852), vol. 2, pp. 117–21

Guthrie, G J 'Lectures on some of the more important points in surgery: [VIII] Secondary amputations and compound fractures', *The Lancet* (1852), vol. 2, pp. 187–90

Guthrie, G J 'Lectures on some of the more important points in surgery: [IX] Phagadena, pourriture d'hopital and sloughing ulcer', *The Lancet* (1852), vol. 2, pp. 256–9

Guthrie, G J *Commentaries on the Surgery of the War* (6th edn, London: Henry Renshaw, 1855)

Guthrie, G J *Directions to Army Surgeons on the Field of Battle* (5th edn, Washington, DC: US Sanitary Commission, 1864)

Bell, B *A System of Surgery* (6 vols, Edinburgh: Bell & Bradfute, 1796)

Bell, J *The Principle of Surgery* (New York; Collins & Perkins, 1810)

Cooper, S *A Dictionary of Practical Surgery* (London: Longman, Hurst, Rees, Orme & Brown etc., 1822)

Hennen, J *Principles of Military Surgery* (Philadelphia: Carey & Lea, 1830)

Henry, W *Events of a Military Life, being recollections after service in the Peninsular War, invasion of France, the East Indies, St Helena, Canada and elsewhere* (London: Pickering, 1843)

Yearsley, P M 'George James Guthrie, a Biographical sketch', a paper read to the Guthrie Society on 9 June 1892, published in the *Westminster Hospital Reports* (London, 1893), vol. 8, pp. 71–8

Secondary Medical Sources

Ackroyd, A, Brockliss, L, Moss, M, Retford, K and Stevenson, J *Advancing with the Army: Medicine, the Professions, and Social Mobility in the British Isles, 1790–1850* (Oxford: Oxford University Press, 2006)

Anonymous, 'George James Guthrie (1758–1856) English military Surgeon', *Journal of the American Medical Association*, 200/5 (1 May 1967), pp. 408–9

Ballance, C A 'Lecture: Stories from the Campaigns of Napoleon and Wellington', *Journal of the Royal Amy Medical Corps*, 29 (1917), pp. 357–74

Blanco, R L *Wellington's Surgeon General: Sir James McGrigor* (Durham, NC: Duke University Press, 1974)

Cope, Z *The Royal College of Surgeon of England: A History* (London: Anthony Blond, 1959)

Crumplin, Michael *Men of Steel* (Shrewsbury: Quiller Press, 2007)

Crumplin M K H 'Wellington's Combat Surgeon', *Newsletter Annals of the Royal College of Surgeons of England* (London, XXXX)

Fye, W Bruce 'George J. Guthrie', *Profiles in Cardiology in Clinical Cardiology*, 21/2 (1998), pp. 229–30

Grimsdale, H 'George James Guthrie (1758–1856) Founder of the Royal Westminster Eye Hospital', *British Journal of Ophthalmology*, 3 (1919)

Howard, M *Wellington's Doctors: The British Army Medical Services in the Napoleonic Wars* (Staplehurst: Spellmount Publishing, 2002)

Howell, H A L 'George James Guthrie', *Journal of the Royal Army Medical Corps*, 14 (1910), 577–87

Hurt, R 'George Guthrie (1785–1856): Surgeon to the Duke of Wellington, and a Pioneer Thoracic Surgeon', *Journal of Medical Biography*, 15/1 (Feb. 2007), pp. 38–44

Hurt, R *George Guthrie: Soldier and Pioneer Surgeon* (London: Royal Society of Medicine Press, 2008)

Kaufman, M H, and Wakelin, S J 'Amputation through the Hip Joint during the Pre-Anaesthetic Era', *Clinical Anatomy*, 17 (2004), pp. 36–44

Laffin, J *Combat Surgeons* (Gloucester: J M Dent & Sons, 1999)

Pettigrew, T J 'George James Guthrie FRS', *Biographical Memoirs of the Most Celebrated Physicians and Surgeons* (London, 1840), vol. 4, pp. 1–22

Wakelin, S J, Oliver, C W and Kaufman, M H 'Hip Disarticulation: The Evolution of a Surgical Technique', *Injury, International Journal of the Care of the Injured*, 35 (2004), pp. 299–308

Watts, J C 'George James Guthrie, Peninsular Surgeon', *Proceedings of the Royal Society of Medicine*, 54 (1961), pp. 764–8

Primary Military Sources

Everard, H *History of Thos. Farrington's Regiment, subsequently designated the 29th (Worcester) Foot, 1694–1891 (Worcester: Littlebury & Co., 1891)*

Johnston, W B Roll of Commissioned Officers in the Medical Service of the British Army: 20th June 1727 to June 1898 *(Aberdeen: Aberdeen University Press, 1917)*

Napier, W F P History of War in the Peninsula and in the South of France *(6 vols, London and New York: Warne & Co., 1890)*

Oman, C A History of the Peninsular War *(6 vols, London: Greenhill Books, 1996)*

Secondary Military Sources

Armit, W B 'Halifax 1749–1906: Soldiers who Founded and Garrisoned a Famous City', Research Division Halifax Defence Complex

Brett-James, A *A Life in Wellington's Army* (London: Donovan, 1994)

Cantlie, N *A History of the Army Medical Department*, vol. 1 (Edinburgh: Churchill Livingstone, 1974)

Edwards, P *Talavera: Wellington's Early Peninsular Victories 1808–9* (Swindon: Crowood Press, 2005)

Fletcher, I (gen. ed.) *The Peninsular War* (Staplehurst: Spellmount, 1998)

Fletcher, I *Badajoz 1812* (Oxford: Osprey Military, 1999)

Fletcher, I *Bloody Albuera* (Swindon: Crowood Press, 2000)

Fletcher, I (ed.) *The Peninsular War 1808–11; The Peninsular War 1812–1814; The Waterloo Campaign 1815* (London: Folio Society, 2007)

Robertson, I C *Wellington at War in the Peninsula: An Overview and Guide* (Barnsley: Leo Cooper, 2000)

Weller J *Wellington in the Peninsula* (London: Greenhill, 1992)

Index